Teachers'
Pedagogical Thinking

American University Studies

Series XIV
Education

Vol. 47

PETER LANG
New York • Washington, D.C./Baltimore • Boston • Bern
Frankfurt am Main • Berlin • Brussels • Vienna • Oxford

Pertti Kansanen, Kirsi Tirri,
Matti Meri, Leena Krokfors,
Jukka Husu, & Riitta Jyrhämä

Teachers'
Pedagogical Thinking

Theoretical Landscapes,
Practical Challenges

PETER LANG
New York • Washington, D.C./Baltimore • Boston • Bern
Frankfurt am Main • Berlin • Brussels • Vienna • Oxford

Library of Congress Cataloging-in-Publication Data

Teachers' pedagogical thinking: theoretical landscapes,
practical challenges / Pertti Kansanen... [et al.].
p. cm. — (American university studies. Series XIV, Education; vol. 47)
Includes bibliographical references and index.
1. Teachers—Psychology. 2. Teaching—Psychological aspects.
I. Kansanen, Pertti. II. Series.
LB1775.T4179   371.1'001'9—dc21   99-057716
ISBN 0-8204-4897-4
ISSN 0740-4565

Die Deutsche Bibliothek-CIP-Einheitsaufnahme

Teachers' pedagogical thinking: theoretical landscapes,
practical challenges / Pertti Kansanen...
–New York; Washington, D.C./Baltimore; Boston; Bern;
Frankfurt am Main; Berlin; Brussels; Vienna; Oxford: Lang.
(American university studies. Ser. 14, Education; Vol. 47)
ISBN 0-8204-4897-4

The paper in this book meets the guidelines for permanence and durability
of the Committee on Production Guidelines for Book Longevity
of the Council of Library Resources.

Printed in the United States of America

Contents

Introduction   Background of the Study   1

PART I   COMING TO TERMS WITH TEACHERS'
               PEDAGOGICAL THINKING   9
Chapter 1   Teaching-Studying-Learning Process   11
Chapter 2   Making Educational Decisions   17
Chapter 3   The Model of Teachers' Pedagogical Thinking   23

PART II   LINKING VARIOUS APPROACHES   33
Chapter 4   Teachers' Pedagogical Mind Set   35
Chapter 5   Moral Perspectives in Teachers' Thinking   51
Chapter 6   Rules and Recipes of 'Good' Teaching   59
Chapter 7   Processes of Supervision in Teaching Practice   71

PART III   APPROACHING THE PRACTICE
               OF TEACHING   79
Chapter 8   Teachers' Pedagogical Minds   81
Chapter 9   Teachers' Moral Dilemmas   91
Chapter 10   The Logic of Rules and Recipes   103
Chapter 11   Reflection in Counselling Situations   127

PART IV   PRACTICAL ARGUMENTS IN TEACHING   145
Chapter 12   The Nature of the Teaching-Studying-
               Learning Process   147
Chapter 13   Empirical Findings of Teachers' Argumentation
               and Justification   155

PART V	TEACHERS' PRACTICAL KNOWLEDGE LANDSCAPE	179
Chapter 14	Justification of the Knowledge Claims	181
Chapter 15	Towards Balanced Educational Decisions	187
References		195
Name Index		213

Background of the Study

The Idea of the Book

The purpose of this book is to increase the reader's understanding of teachers' pedagogical thinking. We claim to provide an original and unique view into an important educational area that has been at the center of research for some time. In order to fulfil this task we attempt to clarify what we mean by teachers' pedagogical thinking and what it entails. In addition, we try with our own empirical research to solve and demonstrate several crucial problems in the teaching-studying-learning process in general and how teachers deal with everyday problems in this process. Teachers are constantly encountering problems or situations where they must immediately do something, make a choice among realistic alternatives, reflect on their own actions, and evaluate the progress of the whole instructional process.

How Do Teachers Think and Decide?
What Do We Know of this Phenomenon?

Knowledge of teachers' thinking has almost always been of great interest in educational research. The theme of teacher thinking became, however, a special research theme only in the 1970s and gained much attention due to an article Clark & Peterson (1986) in the third Handbook of Research on Teaching. This article summarized the early results of the topic and indicated avenues for new research. Of special interest since the beginning have been practical theories, reflection, and other metacognitive points of view in teacher thinking. A vast literature has been amassed in this field, and the theme of teacher thinking is now a standard topic of discussion.

The popularity of the research on teacher thinking is naturally connected with the shift of interest from the behaviorism-based models to a more cognitive approach. Introspection or reflection that in principle had been impossible in research contexts suddenly became a new way of approaching educational problems. Professional journals became filled with articles that emphasized not only the theme of teacher thinking but all kinds of cognitive processes in a teacher's work. A special research association, the International Study Association of Teacher Thinking (ISATT), was also established, and the congresses organized by ISATT have demonstrated the popularity of the topic. The original goal of the theme has gradually shifted to more specific issues and more general viewpoints. This development is clearly illustrated by the activities of ISATT, which has recently changed its name to the International Study Association of Teachers and Teaching wile retaining the old acronym ISATT.

Most of the research on teacher thinking has been done in the area of educational psychology. This means a psychological starting-point with cognitive processes in the foreground. The content of the instructional process has not been primary; instead personal practical viewpoints have been predominant. This is understandable because thinking has been in the specific focus of research. The field has gradually diversified, and the educational focus has steadily gained ground. This viewpoint has also been our challenge; thinking in an educational context is not just any kind of thinking. It is special and has its own qualities. It is pedagogical by nature.

What Does 'Pedagogical' Mean in Teachers' Thinking?

In the European tradition educational discussion and people involved in the teaching-studying-learning process are strongly tied up with the very context to which they belong. Teachers and students are not free to do whatever they want; there are certain responsibilities and duties that come along with the educational context. The instructional process is usually carried out within an institution, and with that institution come certain aims and goals to direct the process. These are usually expressed in a document we call a curriculum. Curriculum is a concrete, mental, and symbolic context for the teaching-studying-learning process and for all activities in that institution we usually call a school. In school teachers work and students study, and this whole activity is organized according to the curriculum. To differentiate between activities and principles in school and elsewhere the term 'pedagogical' has been introduced. 'Pedagogical' takes its meaning from the curriculum, from the aims and goals stated there. In German there is a more apt term, 'didactical', but applying it in English is problematic. We prefer pedagogical in these circumstances.

In everyday life and everyday language we often use the same expressions as in research reports. In the educational context these words or concepts take on additional and special meaning. 'Interaction', for example, is a common term and is often compared with 'communication'. It may have symmetrical and democratic nuances for people living in a democracy. If we speak, however, of 'pedagogical interaction', the meaning becomes more precise. It may still have democratic nuances in such contexts, but it is unclear whether it still has symmetrical ones. The people participating in this process are not just anybody; they are teachers and students. 'Pedagogical' in this context refers to a bounded system, and it is accompanied by certain values. Teachers and students are expected to act in accordance with these values; they strive to achieve the aims and goals of the curriculum. Pedagogical thinking is thinking in these circumstances and may be evaluated only according to the criteria stated beforehand in the curriculum. In spite of the fact that not all values are made explicit, the mental boundaries of the curriculum still exist. Being pedagogical is thinking according to the aims and goals stated in the curriculum. Most pedagogical thinking takes place in connection with schools and in teachers' minds, but it also has an important place in students' thinking, the purpose being that students may also be acting pedagogically.

'Pedagogical' also means taking stands. Thinking may be descriptive reflection and the noting of facts and situations without personal standpoints. In educational contexts acting means making decisions continuously, and it also means choosing between alternatives in order to arrive at a certain result. Educational decisions require criteria, and these we find in the realm of the curriculum. Not all criteria are stated explicitly; the teacher must therefore deduce, reflect, and elaborate when coming to a decision. Pedagogical thinking is normative—thinking according to certain values. To get to know it is to ask the teacher what kinds of arguments lie behind the decisions.

Purposiveness

It may be claimed that all action is somehow or other intentional. When intentions acquire content they become more concrete and are directed to certain specified goals. Everyday activities may be said to be intentional but most often without special judgment of what the goals are. Educational activities always have goals, be they conscious or unconscious. The teacher has the task of thinking and acting in the instructional process in accordance with certain given goals. Usually these are in line with his own personal goals and the requirements of the society which employs the teacher. In the school curriculum we call the overall intentions 'purposes'. Purposes are comprised of more specific goals and even objectives that must be known to the teacher. In addition to knowing the goals a teacher must accept and act according to them. After long experience it is supposed that a teacher gradually internalizes the aims and goals of the curriculum, incorporating them into his/her own thinking. If so, commitment to the curriculum is high. However, strong commitment is not without its problems either.

Thinking and acting according to the purpose stated in the curriculum is characterized by purposiveness. This quality of thinking and working develops gradually during professional experience, and it is also a characteristic of pedagogical thinking. Making educational decisions with purposiveness in mind looks for arguments and justification in the values in and behind the curriculum. Purposiveness means normative thinking, but the quality of this thinking is determined by teachers' pedagogical expertise.

Research-Based Teacher Education as a Means to Teachers' Pedagogical Thinking

Another crucial question is how to improve the quality of teachers' pedagogical thinking. Our answer is research-based teacher education, by which we mean a system of teacher education in which research is the overlapping idea, the main organizing theme, in the whole teacher education program. A reflective teacher is one who uses the principles of research in his/her thinking in making decisions but is not a professional researcher. Acting like a practitioner researcher describes a teacher's pedagogical thinking in practice quite well. In teacher education this means studying research methodology from the very beginning to the end, research integrated into all study periods, and teaching practice supported by and integrated with theoretical studies and discussions. At the University of Helsinki, Finland, such a program has been in operation some 20 years, and the experiences have been encouraging. All teachers in Finnish schools pass a Master's degree and write a Master's thesis as well. Research-based teaching is an attitude to justify the practice with arguments like ones used in genuine research work. In teachers' pedagogical thinking this means better quality of justifying educational decisions.

The Structure of the Book

In order to better understand teachers' pedagogical thinking we have examined literature dealing with this topic. Much of what we consider important is elaborated in the first two parts of the book. Our reason for presenting the background of the research in this area is that it makes it easier for the reader to understand not only the rest of the book but also the huge problems and possibilities that knowledge of the subject opens.

Getting to know teachers' pedagogical thinking is not an easy task. It is useless to interview teachers and ask them directly how they justify their decisions. If teachers become conscious of what you are seeking, they usually start to tell you what they think you expect of them. You must question in a way that they may speak without bias. Fortunately, the theme is multifaceted and almost all practical situations may be used as starting-points for discussions. In addition, many methodological and methodical approaches are possible. Some of them have been utilized in this book. An important viewpoint is that each of the various approaches needs a theoretical justification of its own. Every method in these approaches exploits different empirical procedures. Every approach is, however, a necessary contribution to the overall understanding of the theme.

Part I
Coming to Terms with Teachers' Pedagogical Thinking

Part I consists of three chapters that aim at building a coherent picture of the circumstances in which teachers are working. What is teaching? What is learning? What is their reciprocal relation? Examining these ontological questions reveals that the teaching-learning process is conceptually insufficient: it must be expanded into a teaching-studying-learning process. Interaction is seen as the basic concept in this process.

Second, the complex area of making educational decisions is outlined. The descriptive and the normative sides are taken into consideration and various possibilities to get to know it are discussed.

Third, a suggestion for a model to help orient the reader in the diversity of teacher thinking is outlined. Pedagogical level thinking is introduced and two concepts, the aspect of purposiveness and the aspect of methodology, are also introduced as kinds of anchor concepts for the next part of the book.

Part II
Linking Various Approaches

To get a comprehensive picture of teachers' pedagogical thinking various approaches are used. They may be viewed in part as independent studies contributing to our common understanding. Each of them sheds light on a different aspect of the common problem. We deemed it necessary to introduce their theoretical starting-points to justify the empirical data that is presented later. Each of them tries also to indicate the potential behind the teacher's voice that may be discovered in teachers' everyday talk.

Teachers' pedagogical mind set and moral perspectives are popular themes in teacher thinking research. The approach here, however, is modified for our purposes using the viewpoint of practical theories and ethics of education as guiding principles to approach practice.

Receptology is an ancient motive in all teaching and teacher education. In spite of idealistic challenges, anonymous recipes, advice, and guidelines are commonly used. Apparently they are rooted so deeply in our belief systems that we use them against our better understanding. We try to find a place in a teacher's mind for these recipes and what kind of belief systems lie behind them.

The supervisory process is a special context in which supervisor and student-teacher are compelled to justify their educational decisions. It may be claimed that the process provides direct access to teachers' pedagogical thinking. Supervisory discourse offers a possibility to analyze and interpret interaction in reality through discussions that occur in the context of this process. The special roles, however, must be taken into consideration in the interpretations.

In spite of different avenues of approach to teachers' pedagogical thinking, they share the common aspect of getting to know teachers' arguments when they justify their educational decisions. What are the arguments like? Theoretically they are supposed to be intuitional or rational. Or are they mixed? This problem leads us to the next part of the book.

Part III
Approaching the Practice of Teaching

The approaches presented in part II present new knowledge based on original empirical studies. The data bearing on teachers' pedagogical mind sets derive from narrative interviews of 29 elementary school teachers. The interviews are analyzed, and a special pedagogical mind set is built.

The study of teachers' moral dilemmas is based on an interview study of 33 secondary school teachers. Moral dilemmas identified by teachers are analyzed and organized in four categories. Each of them is discussed, and some solving strategies provided by the teachers are also presented and discussed.

The approach examining recipes in practice teaching and teacher education in general is twofold, deductive and inductive. In the deductive approach a large number of teaching recipes were collected from the literature and a questionnaire of 204 recipes was filled in by 41 supervisors and 62 class teacher students. In addition to our Finnish data 42 German supervisors and 36 student teachers also filled in the questionnaire. The belief systems of both data sets were structured by factor analysis and compared. In the inductive approach 196 supervisors and 230 student teachers answered an open questionnaire in which they could report recipes they had used themselves or had observed being used. A very interesting finding was that recipes, advice, and guidelines are commonly used, although the fact is at first strongly denied.

Supervisory discourse was analyzed on the basis of a data set consisting of 40 supervisory conferences conducted by 24 supervisors. The discussion was analyzed and categorized in four levels: factual, evaluative, justificatory, and critical. Profiles based on the course of discussion were drawn. Three different profiles could be identified: descriptive, normative, and reflective.

Part IV
Practical Arguments in Teaching

In this part the core of teachers' pedagogical thinking is analyzed. In each approach presented earlier the empirical data produced material for analyzing the reasons given by teachers for making educational decisions. To start with, the arguments lying behind their decisions were supposed to be intuitional or rational. Quite soon it became clear that mixed arguments also must be taken into consideration and that oversimplifying division must be elaborated. In teachers' interviews, in somewhat longer passages, the mixed model came forth clearly.

With the help of Stephen Toulmin's analysis of arguments some intuitional and rational justifications were identified. Deanna Kuhn's framework also made it possible to identify chains of justification of various kinds. The justification behind recipes was sought using second-order factor analysis.

Part V
Teachers' Practical Knowledge Landscape

The two chapters in this part conclude the discussion and bring the results back to the beginning. The theoretical starting-points are viewed in the light of the results and experiences of the writers. The model of teachers' pedagogical thinking outlined in the beginning is compared with the moral languages presented by Robert J. Nash. Teachers' pedagogical thinking is, we think, an idea to be developed and promoted more generally. Our firm conviction is that it is possible to develop teachers' pedagogical thinking, and that research-based teacher education, among other possible methods, is a proper means to that end.

Contributors

The contributors are researchers and university teachers in the Department of Teacher Education, University of Helsinki, Finland. The research project on teachers' pedagogical thinking is one of the main focuses of the Department's Research Center of Teaching.

Pertti Kansanen is Professor of Education, Ph.D., and the senior member of the team. His special research interests include research on teaching in general, ethics of education, and comparison of German didactics with American research on teaching.

Kirsi Tirri, Ph.D., is Professor of Education. Her special interests are research on moral education and teacher education.

Matti Meri, Ph.D., is Researcher and University Lecturer. His special interests are research on hidden curriculum and recipes for teaching.

Leena Krokfors, Ph.D., is Researcher and University Lecturer. Her special interests are research on teacher education and early childhood education.

Jukka Husu, M.A., is Researcher and doctoral student. His special interests are research on teachers' practical knowledge and issues of virtual pedagogy.

Riitta Jyrhämä, M.A., is Researcher and doctoral student. Her special interests are research on teaching recipes and supervision.

PART I

COMING TO TERMS
WITH TEACHERS'
PEDAGOGICAL THINKING

Chapter 1

Teaching-Studying-Learning Process

Interaction as a basic concept of teaching is introduced. The whole process is expanded from a teaching-learning process to teaching-studying-learning process that may be called an instructional process. Along with studying, the active role of the student is emphasized. Interaction is seen as a totality containing the whole instructional process, and may also be indirect.

Interaction

The most basic feature in the teaching-studying-learning process is action, but not the action of some individual *per se* but the interaction of all the persons who participate in the process. The teacher and her/his students build a net of interaction that is situated in a certain context. This context is the school. Interaction is taking place all the time, and the nature of this interaction may vary and have various characteristics. The teaching-studying-learning process, when started, is a continuous flow of activities. It is cyclical by nature, with the same phases always following each other with a new content and towards the aims, goals and objectives stated in some way in the curriculum.

In an early article, Philip W. Jackson (1966) divided teaching into two phases: preactive teaching and interactive teaching. This same division is also used in some other articles, e.g. in the review of teachers' thinking by Clark and Peterson (1986). Jackson's notion, however, can be logically extended where interaction is used as a base for the whole process. The first of Jackson's phases refers to the planning section of the teaching-studying-learning process and other activities that precede the teaching itself. If we accordingly consider interaction as a basic starting point and notice that reflection is also taking place after the interactive phase, we can divide the interaction into three phases: the preinteractive phase, the interaction proper, and the postinteractive phase.

The flow of situations builds a continuous cycle where the postinteractive phase always starts a new preinteractive phase integrating into a permanent process of planning, teaching, and evaluation. Gage and Berliner (1984) have also come to this same conclusion in their book *Educational Psychology*. The conception of the teaching-studying-learning process as a continuous flow of episodes and situations is in itself quite a common way to understand the nature of this process. The terminology, however, often does not express this essential feature.

In addition to the interaction that takes place face to face in the classroom, there is also indirect interaction between the teacher and the students. The teacher is preparing her/his lessons and s/he must always take the previous history of the class into consideration along with the characteristics of the students and the contextual factors that build the frames for her/his planning. The students, on the other hand, do their homework and ponder their tactics to prepare for the next instructional situation.

Defining interaction in such a way, with its extension to indirect interaction, facilitates a general concept of the teaching-studying-learning process. With the concept of interaction one can understand all the activities of the teacher and the students using one basic concept. It is the curriculum with its aims and goals that binds all the participants into a totality of interaction. In practice, it is the content of the teaching-studying-learning process that keeps their minds on joint activities.

With the modern technology, indirect interaction becomes more central and more important, too. In distance education instruction is no longer face-to-face interaction, even though we may call it direct instruction. Through much technological equipment, on-line contact makes the interaction direct, even though the teacher and her/his pupils may be situated in different places. The distance in itself no longer plays a hindering role in organizing teaching-studying-learning processes. The early results seem to indicate that the interaction in the classroom, where instruction is mediated from another classroom follows the same pattern as in normal instruction (cf. Husu, 1996). In self-guiding studies, teaching material has always been a link between a specific teacher and the student; and with modern technology, this possibility becomes more usual than before. A library consisting of all kinds of teaching material may in the future emphasize the indirect side of interaction more than before.

The nature of interaction in itself is a complex expression. An essential question regarding its nature is whether it is possible for the relationship in a teacher-student interaction to be symmetrical. This is the question especially posed by the representatives of the critical school. In the teaching-studying-learning process, however, it is the teacher who always has the responsibility, through legislation, to steer the process. That is why there is also power and authority in the teacher's actions that are not to be neglected. Interaction in the teaching-studying-learning process can accordingly never be symmetrical. However, it can be as democratic as possible within these conditions.

The teaching-studying-learning process cannot take place in a vacuum. In the school context, instruction is always directed by the curriculum with its theoretical and political foundations. The societal frame of reference brings its ideological ideas into the teaching-studying-learning process to be followed by teachers in their practice.

Teaching and Instruction

It is not possible to define teaching or instruction with one word or one brief concept without considering the background of the whole educational system and the specific curriculum in which the very educational process is taking place. Furthermore, these concepts have different nuances in different languages that perhaps also mirror different kinds of thinking. We turn here to the terminology of Anderson and Burns (1989, 3–15). They define teaching as:

> ". . . an interpersonal, interactive, typically involving verbal communication, which is undertaken for the purpose of helping one or more students learn or change the ways in which they can or will behave." (1989, 8).

Instruction, on the other hand, is conceptualized as a broader concept

> ". . . as inclusive of teaching (that is, teaching is one aspect or component of instruction)" and "Knowing something about instruction helps us gain a more complete understanding of teaching." (1989, 9).

The instructional process is, thus, a wide concept consisting of all the important components taking place in classroom instruction, as well as of the steering factors defined in the curriculum. The teacher's task in this process is to develop the best possible ways to promote learning in her/his students.

The Place of Learning in the Instructional Process

The instructional process within a school always has two sides participating in the process: the teacher and the students. There are several students at the same time and it is the teacher's responsibility to guide their development along the aims and goals set in the curriculum. The activity of the teacher, teaching, is purposive, aiming at the development of the pupils' personal development. It is a well-known fact that teaching in itself does not necessarily imply learning. Teaching is rather a kind of action that is aimed at pupils' learning or other kinds of outcomes without any guarantee on the teacher's part (e.g., Smith, 1987).

Although the activities of the teacher and the activities of the students can be linked in many different ways, the problem of the nature of their reciprocal relationship remains. According to Ryle (1949), in everyday language we can divide verbs into two categories, task words and achievement words; or according to Scheffler (1960) they can be divided by their intentional use and success use. With the first category, we mean the activity itself without any outcomes, the instructional process proper. In the research area of teacher effectiveness, this same class of activities were known as process criteria. In the other category, consisting of achievement words or success use of the words, there are some results implicit in the expression. In the area of the teacher effectiveness research this was stated by using product criteria.

As mentioned above, it is a widely held conception that teaching does not necessarily lead to learning or other changes as a result. In this respect, teaching interaction may differ from interaction in other fields. A very familiar situation exemplifying this difference is the act of selling and buying. This analogy, however, cannot be transferred into the instructional process as such. In the instructional process there can be teaching without learning and there can also be learning without teaching, although this point is not as clear as the first one. It depends on how we define teaching and whether it is necessary to have a person, a teacher, in order for an act to be called teaching. In self-studies, too, there always are some factors or impulses affecting and steering thinking, and eventually leading to learning or some other changes. Fenstermacher (1986, 38–39) uses another analogy with the terms "racing" and "winning", and although there is no interaction between these terms in the same meaning as in the instructional process, his "ontological dependence" describing this relationship is also very accurate in regard to teaching and learning. Pearson (1989, 78–83) presents the same criticism, pointing out at the same time, however, that in this way it is possible to avoid characterizing the relation between teaching and learning as causal.

The actions of the two agents, the teacher and the students, in the instructional process become very complex if we take into consideration that there can be numerous students participating in this interaction at the same time. Quite soon it becomes impossible to think of the net of possible interactive relations. The position of learning in this process is of the utmost complexity. We are used to thinking of learning as some kind of change, but we can also pose the question in the opposite way: Is all kind of change learning? It is very easy to notice that the aims and goals in the curriculum consider changes from a larger perspective than what we are used to when we call something learning (cf. Uljens, 1992).

A further important point is to notice that learning by nature is unconscious. We cannot get learning to take place by means of willpower or by means of a decision on the part of the student. The instructional interaction aims at learning, but it is only possible to steer the activities of students with the purpose of fostering learning. Or the student can wish and try to do something that s/he or the teacher thinks will probably lead to learning. But learning in itself occurs unconsciously depending on various personal and contextual factors.

If we describe the activities of the teacher as teaching, it is logical to call the activities of the students as studying. This interaction may bring about some results that we usually think of as changes, and an important part of these changes is learning. Learning occurs in the teacher's mind as well as in the student's mind, but naturally their content is of a different kind. In this way the whole instructional process can be understood as active on behalf of both sides. Studying as a concept is active by nature, and we can avoid referring to learning as something passive, which may occur through conditioning or because direct observation does not reveal what is happening in the student's mind. Studying, on the other hand, can always be understood of as active (cf. learning by doing) and perhaps as conscious, too.

Following this short analysis, the instructional process can be conceived of as the teaching-studying-learning process in which the outcomes of the process are included in the description primarily as learning. Learning always requires some activity, some form of studying. It is doing something, exercising, practicing, thinking, but in school this occurs in the realm of the curriculum. It would be better, perhaps, to speak of teaching in the school and learning in the school. The degrees of freedom of the participants are not unlimited.

Chapter 2

Making Educational Decisions

Teachers are making educational decisions all the time. When making decisions thinking is no longer descriptive, it becomes normative. In the context of education this means pedagogical thinking. Of particular interest is how teachers justify their decisions and the reasons they give for their actions. The content of teachers' pedagogical thinking may be anything but getting to know it is problematic.

During a relatively short time, research on teacher thinking has grown into one of the most common and important themes in the area of research on teaching. Since the overview made by Clark and Peterson (1986), the focus has widened and various theoretical backgrounds have been developed. This has been in line with the change of the research paradigm. According to its new ideas, research methods have concentrated on qualitative techniques. The most usual themes have dealt with such questions that focus on teachers' conceptions, meanings, intentions, goals and aims. And because the only way into the teacher's mind is by asking her/him about these things, many kinds of questioning techniques have become popular. Usually the research object is cognitive by nature, and quite often it is in some way related to the other popular area concerning knowledge. Content knowledge, pedagogical content knowledge, curricular knowledge (Shulman, 1987) and their many variations are in the focus of research. In the area of research on teaching, the old process-product paradigm has been totally rejected and replaced by a cognitive-mediative paradigm. But the basic problem remains: intentions and conceptions must be questioned. As of yet, we have no possibilities of going into the teacher's mind.

One particular point of view is to question how teachers move in their thinking from the descriptive to the normative (Kansanen, 1993). This is a very broad perspective, however, it opens a research line that is totally different from the cognitive mode of questioning. The idea is that when the teacher makes a decision, it is no more a descriptive consideration, but instead it becomes normative at the very moment the decision is made. The teacher may have a thoroughly systematic thinking-basis for her/his decision, but in practice a teacher's work is constantly making educational decisions. There s/he must take stands and evaluate all the time what s/he is doing. It may be unconscious, too, but nevertheless it is normative on some basis.

Why call making educational decisions pedagogical thinking? In any case, thinking in a pedagogical context is such an extensive area that it must be restricted in some way. It is self-evident that pedagogical thinking means teachers' thinking when working in the teaching-studying-learning process; it does not mean e.g. teachers' economic thinking. The pedagogical context is so wide that it is not possible to have all of it in focus at the same time. The particular theme in this context may vary; it may be whatever topic that is interesting from a research point of view. It is important that when the teacher is working s/he cannot avoid thinking, reflecting, pondering or contemplating her/his decisions in some way. What is happening in this process, or how the decisions are made, and especially how they are justified, is of particular interest to us. From the content point of view, this idea offers any number of research aspects. Every aspect of pedagogical content has its own features and is important in its own way, but what is common when the teacher is working with her/his questions is the background thinking or what kind of justification s/he is using.

The next question is how to get to know this kind of teacher thinking. The questioning does not differ from other research on teacher thinking, in principle. There are, however, different kinds of situations and some of these may be more suitable for questioning than others. From the beginning it was clear that there are many alternative ways to approach a teacher's thinking. Experience taught us quite soon that usual interviews or stimulated recall situations were difficult. At the same time, a very useful research finding appeared revealing that teachers very seldom spoke about justifications or went beyond the action level. They carefully described what they had done, and when asked more questions, they thoughtfully produced more details of this description. Why-questions showed that they had not thought about the things from that point of view.

It became clear that teachers do not use the same terminology as researchers, and the teachers' answers must be interpreted in the context of their own thinking and not through the language of the research and the researchers. The early results suggested that teachers do not have a theoretical side that guides their work. A closer look at this problem showed, however, that the way of explicating ideas during this interview interaction, or questioning in general, may be different than the respective language of the researchers, and it may contain much theoretical background-thinking in its own right (Kansanen, 1981).

Gary Fenstermacher (1994) analyzes thoroughly the nature of knowledge in teacher research and he takes up the many sides of knowledge as a concept and as an application in the research into teaching. What we are looking for, however, is not this kind of justification but decisions that are partly made based on this knowledge, mainly with normative premises consisting of the values, aims and goals behind the practical solutions. In this way the teacher's attention is also directed towards the curriculum, where the value basis of teaching is to be found. It is impossible for the teacher to break the boundaries of the curriculum; her/his work always takes place in the context of the curriculum. In his recent article, Fritz Oser (1994) said quite exactly what we try to stress with pedagogical thinking and with its normativity:

> ". . . I believe that any single teaching act undertaken in the classroom or in any teaching setting has a moral core. The unit of analysis is the decision a teacher makes to help students learn, communicate, share, reflect, evaluate, and so forth. Teaching responsibility is a moral motivation concerning any concrete teaching act." (Oser, 1994, 59)

It is our conception that the very point of decision-making turns the descriptive thinking towards the normative side; and in addition to the knowledge basis, many other factors have an influence on this process. Richard Shavelson emphasized this same point, asking in his article (1973): "What is *the* basic teaching skill?". His answer to this question was decision-making, and especially decision-making during the actual teaching process. It shows the important and central role of decision-making in the teaching process, though the moral point of view was not the essential idea in his text.

In our model of teachers' pedagogical thinking when analyzing the aspect of purposiveness, the two-sided background concerning values in the teaching-studying-learning process was brought out (Kansanen, 1993, 56-59). The deontological aspect and the teleological aspect, that is in everyday language purposes and consequences, are combined in spite of the fact that both of them have an important independent place in the model. Oser has analyzed this relationship further quite extensively and he uses the expressions "responsible" and "effective teaching" in this respect (Oser, 1994). He builds a hierarchy describing this relationship using four levels: the interpretative, additive, complementary and correlational or regulative. He also exemplifies how this hierarchy functions with increasing mutuality and better knowledge, as we proceed from the first level to the higher ones. He looks at this totality and claims that

> ". . . a theory of professional responsibility must explain why (according to the regulative model) and how effectiveness and morality influence each other and can be taken into consideration at the same time." (Oser, 1994, 64).

The basic idea in a teacher's pedagogical thinking is just this point, namely combining the deontological aspect with the teleological aspect with the intent of paying attention to the teacher's conscious understanding of the totality of the teaching-studying-learning process. However, there may be different degrees of this consciousness (Kansanen, 1993, 56–59). It seems that Oser has analyzed this aspect further and presents in his four levels of responsibility a total of 10 different conceptual forms in the context of professional morality (Oser, 1994, 69–108). They run from the positivistic view to the discourse view and, as said, in a hierarchical order.

Purposiveness in the teacher's pedagogical thinking is supposed to indicate how deeply the teacher has become acquainted with the purposes, aims and goals given in the curriculum. However, mere knowledge of these value aspects is not enough; they must be accepted and finally internalized if they are to be used as a moral background in the teacher's thinking. This means commitment and loyalty to the curriculum and to those who have power over the curriculum; and it is thus, at the same time, a threat to the autonomy in a teacher's work. This short analysis is aimed to show that the critical aspect is of utmost importance in the pedagogical thinking, so that the teacher does not loose his individuality and personal approach in the teaching-studying-learning process. Commitment brings the idea quite close to Oser's dimensions of the teacher's ethos model (Oser, 1991, 201–202), where responsibility is explained with the equilibrium between justice, care and truthfulness. The viewpoint in Oser's consideration, however, is professional morality. We try to analyze these aspects using pedagogical language wherever it is possible.

In spite of a large repertoire of possible research methods to find out what teachers think, it is difficult to determine how to explore a teacher's mind, particularly in this context. In principle, any theme can bring out how teachers justify their decisions. Our interest, however, was not to analyze the content side of this thinking, when for example punishing, grading or selecting pupils for group work would have been suitable for this purpose. It is rather the system and organization of the teacher's theoretical thinking that is of interest to us. Quite soon we noticed that teachers did not provide any justifications if not especially asked for. That created a very awkward problem because we did not want to influence or give any hints about what we were striving for with our questions. If the teachers were asked about using punishments and then were asked why they were doing what they did, they would give answers that would be relevant to the content and situation. But the answers would tell very little about their theoretical justifications concerning the value system behind their decisions.

We came to the conclusion that we must somehow ask what teachers think about teaching and about the teaching-studying-learning process in general, but in such a practical context that justification would seem to be natural. That is why the idea of using empirically-based guidelines, advice and recipes given by supervisors during the student-teaching program seemed an appropriate method to extract just this kind of making educational decisions. It was very easy to extend this method to ordinary teachers and student teachers. The starting point was a text by Hilbert Meyer (1991, 27–55) and research conducted in the context of teaching receptology—Rezeptologie (Mitzschke et al., 1984; Alfs et al., 1985).

It is interesting to note that the supervisors first said that they did not give direct advice or recipes, but our empirical studies have shown quite clearly that it is very common to give recipes and it is equally clear that the student-teachers ask for them. We must emphasize that the recipes as such are not important, but the idea that we can get into a teachers' mind with the help of recipes is important. Knowing what kinds of recipes the supervisors are using opens the way to the background of these recipes, and they offer the content basis of questions and discussion where the justification and implicit theories can take place. This idea can be transformed into the context of schoolteachers, students and pupils, and thus we hope to gain knowledge of a teacher's pedagogical thinking and of the value-basis in making educational decisions in the teaching-studying-learning process in general.

Advice and recipes are naturally not the only way to get to know how teachers think and make decisions. Calderhead & Robson (1991) applied the concept of "image" when they asked student-teachers what knowledge they had of teaching and learning at the beginning of their studies. It seems that Calderhead & Robson used the term "image" as help in their interviews, and to support its use they also mentioned the affective component with particular feelings and attitudes (1991, 3). They claimed that the concept of image was useful in describing knowledge about teaching and in ". . . synthesizing quite large amounts of knowledge about teachers, children, teaching methods and so on" (1991, 7).

Carter and Gonzalez use another method, namely the idea of well remembered events. With that they mean "an incident or episode a teacher observes or experiences in a school situation and considers, for his own reasons, especially salient or memorable" (1993, 223). The writers postulate that, through such events, it is possible to gain insight into a teacher's knowledge and to this end, they analyze how teachers interpret the events they choose as important. With the analyses of two student-teachers' interviews, the conclusion was that "well remembered events are a useful strategy for gaining access to student teacher's classroom knowledge" (1993, 231). It is easy to agree with the writers, the well remembered events are wide enough as a theme. And their content focuses on the general aspects of teaching making it quite easy to determine the questions about the justifications behind their motives.

A third example is taken from a study made by Mitchell (1994). In spite of using a seemingly narrow teaching skill, "questioning" as an interview focus, he succeeded in getting to know the more general aspects of a teacher's implicit theory. Even though the concrete results indicated that "each teacher's implicit theory in relation to questioning is a unique, idiosyncratic, dynamic, incomplete and relatively general representation of the teacher's views on this skill at a particular point of time" (1994, 82), it is very easy to notice how the questions serve as a means to obtain information about a teacher's thinking in general. The teachers' statements could have been classified as "aims, beliefs, goals, expectations, values, conceptions, images, metaphors, rules, principles, and models of practice" (1994, 71) as Mitchell comments when referring to the previous literature on teachers' implicit theories. The same may be seen in the text by Marland & Osborne (1990, 96), where they refer to such elements of teachers' theories of action as beliefs, goals, conceptions, images, metaphors, rules, principles and dilemmas. All of these have also been used in earlier reports.

Chapter 3

The Model of Teachers'
Pedagogical Thinking

To understand better teachers' pedagogical thinking, we present a frame of reference based on what we know of the theme. Essential is the personal belief system
that is supposed to constitute the background in making decisions. Personal belief
systems are described with help of level thinking. Two central concepts are high-
lighted. The teaching-studying-learning process is guided by a curriculum and by
that curriculum's aims and goals. This is supposed to lead to certain purposiveness in making decisions. A second point of view is how the teachers think, and
this relates to methodological questions. Teacher education is supposed to be the
way through which it is possible to develop teachers' pedagogical thinking.

Making educational decisions is generally selecting between different alternatives. It is continuous and unavoidable, the existence of alternatives
is, however, a necessary condition (cf. Fitzgibbons, 1981, 11–19). There
must be open alternatives from which to select. The selecting itself is
conscious, but the level of consciousness may differ from clearly motivated decisions to almost unconscious selection. It is common to present
behind this selection process some kind of personal belief system, as
Kindsvatter et al., (1992, 1–19) express it. Fitzgibbons (1981, 23–24)
calls those beliefs concerning education a person's philosophy of education. This personal belief system may also be conscious or unconscious,
or more generally partly conscious. Kindsvatter et al. divide the system
into two bases, the intuitive and the rational. Our thinking follows these
same lines. The details of this system, however, may be interpreted in
many ways. The personal belief system is thought to be behind the decisions; many times it is thought to be hierarchical by nature. The intuitive
bases and rational bases may be independent from each other; however,
some kind of interaction is more plausible. The intuitive means one's own
experiences; it may be founded on personal needs or tradition.

Rational bases include pedagogical principles, research findings, scholarly contributions and examined practice. It may quite easily be widened to a more detailed structure where there is interaction between the bases, and the reasons given consist of common elements from both the intuitive and rational bases.

Some examples show the nature of these justifications. If we take authority as a possible base for giving reasons for making educational decisions, we can easily count numerous indications of authority. If the teacher bases her/his decision on some kind of authority, it may be intuitive or rational or both. There may be many categories of authority, but it is essential that the teacher openly believes and does as her/his authority implies. This authority may be a colleague or some background group (e.g. teachers' association or teacher-parents association), some university professor or a priest. It may be some administrative department or the Board of Education. Some model or ideal may serve as an authority. Furthermore, a textbook or a school of thinking, an ideology or some other normative system may function as an authoritative basis in making educational decisions. On the other hand, the analysis of this decision-making may be based on content categories or classifications in various disciplines, such as education, psychology, sociology or epistemology. It is important to produce a system with concepts that reflect teachers' ways of looking at instructional matters in appropriate and coherent terms. What is difficult is to find an insider viewpoint into a teacher's thinking.

A popular way to describe the various aspects in a teacher's implicit theory or personal belief system is to look at it from various levels. Although it is questionable whether the different aspects or factors really build a hierarchy or are in a hierarchical relation to each other, it is in any case a clear way to analyze them.

In Figure 1, the pedagogical level thinking is presented. In describing this quite common way of looking at the relation between the various factors, the idea of König (1975, 26–31) is utilized. König speaks of object theories and metatheories. Object theories examine practice on the action level and one may build models and totalities of the phenomenon in question. In principle, it is possible to build many kinds of object theories, depending on the aspect under consideration. Important, however, is that these possible object theories may in turn be examined and a potential totality, metatheory, may be built on these. König calls an object theory a theory of educational practice, and a metatheory, a theory of education, a discipline.

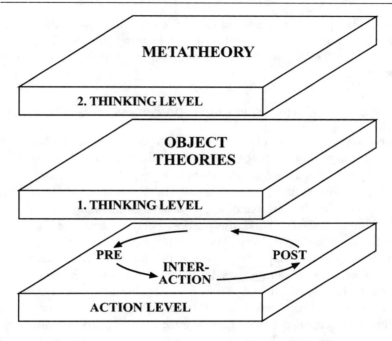

Figure 1. Pedagogical level thinking.

This idea is also applied by Guhl & Ott (1985, 25–31), and they use Heimann's didactic theory (Berliner Didaktik) as a starting point when considering the instructional content. The instructional process is the basic level that is here called the action level, according to their terminology. On the action level the instructional process proceeds in successive cycles consisting of preinteraction, interaction and postinteraction. A structural analysis is done on the first thinking level, where the concepts developed are analyzed and their mutual relationship is established. The second thinking level builds the frames for a potential metatheory, where the object theories are combined or analyzed with the intention to build a new and more abstract totality.

Working on the action level is everyday teaching. Educational decision-making is happening all the time; how it is done varies, however, from teacher to teacher. There are some hints that if attention is directed on the action itself, thinking may become confused (cf. Schön, 1983). However, when questioned, teachers are able to give reasons for their actions. The analysis of these reasons or justifications are build on two cardinal concepts of the teaching-studying-learning process. These are purposiveness and interaction as presented through the methodological thinking during interaction.

The Aspect of Purposiveness

As a prerequisite for education, a certain purpose is always prebuilt into its definition, guiding the process with all its minor parts and details. This purpose permeates the whole educational process where it becomes specified at various levels and in various areas. There is purpose all the time in this process. On the one hand, purpose gets its meaning through the curriculum; on the other hand, this purpose becomes a part of the thinking of the participating persons. They, the teacher as well as the students, have intentions that they bring into the process with all of their own experiences acquired during their former lives. Purposes come into the curriculum from somewhere, but they must also become internalized into the thinking of the participants before they can be present in the process. The crucial question becomes how to integrate the purposes of education, defined and specified in the curriculum as goals, aims and objectives, into the thinking of the teacher and of the students.

The degree of consciousness in the teacher's thinking about purposiveness can vary quite a lot along a dimension from being a total technician to being an independent decision maker. The instructional process can be steered from outside to previously specified aims and goals without the teacher's personal contribution. The instructional process is then of a quasi-teleological character (von Wright, 1971, 57–60) and it is directed, for example, by ready-made teaching material or by a very narrowly-defined curriculum. On the other hand, the teacher may be fully aware of the aims and goals of the curriculum. To be defined as purposive in the instructional process, the teaching needs to follow the principles expressed in the curriculum. This is, however, not enough. The aims and goals must be accepted into the teacher's own thinking and finally internalized into the teacher's way of living.

In the various phases and situations of the instructional process, understanding of the origin of the values behind the curriculum is postulated to have a decisive significance in contemplating what is right or wrong, invaluable or useless in the interaction. Although it is not probable that teachers consciously make up their minds in this respect and have a conscious insight into the origins of these values, they may nonetheless play an important part in the teacher's implicit theory.

The aims and goals may be thought of as being of a consensual character. In this case they can be accepted, but at the same time they are understood as relative and changeable as to their obligation. They may be criticized and discussed, there is a certain tolerance in their realization. Their origin is understood to be in the societal context, and they must be accepted in the society by the majority of its representatives. They are also political, and in this meaning democratic, too.

The more the teacher reflects on the premises of her/his teaching and the whole instructional process, the more the value questions come into her/his consciousness. The purposes of the curriculum and her/his own intentions may become integrated to build a personal conception of the instructional process. With the internalized purposes as her/his intentions, the aims and goals gradually receive the character of some kind of a deontological theory with moral responsibilities. The understanding of the nature of values behind the curriculum is then of central importance. Teachers work with different degrees of moral consciousness, depending on their commitment to the aims and goals directing their action.

Speaking according to the language of normative ethics (cf. Frankena, 1973, 12–33), we can combine the value questions with the goals and aims of the written curriculum. In this way we can also link the content of the curriculum to the teacher's purposes. If the teacher knows the curriculum, its purposes, aims, and goals, it is possible for her/him gradually to make them to become a part of her/his thinking and internalize its content as part of her/his responsibility. In the teacher's pedagogical thinking, the decisions that are made during the preinteractive phase of the instructional process derive their reasons through a certain kind of deontological thinking; that means through the content, and behind the content through the aims and goals, that reflect the value base of the curriculum. In practice, the aims and goals to a certain degree determine the freedom of the teacher's thinking. And by approving of these, they become a part of her/his own thinking. A teacher's intentions become identical with the purposes of the curriculum. The teacher follows certain rules and administrative regulations as self-evident action, but not without criticism.

Pedagogical responsibility also comes into action on the other side of the process. Although a deontological understanding of the curriculum has its obligation, the teacher's work is evaluated according to its results as consequences in her/his students' personal development. This teleological aspect of the instructional process must be in harmony with the purposiveness of the teacher's thinking. Combining the deontological aspect with the teleological aspect reflects the teacher's conscious understanding of the totality of the instructional process within the curricular frame. On the other end of this dimension there is the quasi-teleological action, where decisions are determined through technological means, such as textbooks and other teaching materials, without the teacher's personal contribution to their use. This kind of action may be substituted by any agent in the instructional process. The development of professional thinking in the instructional process follows along this dimension to the conscious thinking about the position of values in the whole process of instruction. Purposiveness may be an idealistic characteristic of the teacher's thinking and action, but in any case it is the core of a teacher's pedagogical thinking, according to this model.

There is a certain difference between purposes and intentions. In this text the term purpose is used in the context of the curriculum, where it is seen as goals, aims, and objectives. Intentions, on the other hand, are in the mind of the teacher. The students have intentions, too. It is, however, the intentions of the teacher that are defining the intentional situation (cf. Pearson, 1989, 65–71) in the instructional process. Nevertheless, as Clark and Peterson note (1986, 273) the teacher has many other kinds of intentions during her/his work besides bringing about learning. That is why it is important to try to combine the teacher's intentions with the purposes of the curriculum. If that process succeeds, the thinking can be called purposive, and the teacher has internalized the aims and goals of the curriculum into her/his thinking; hence we can call it pedagogical thinking.

The Aspect of Methodology

In addition to the factor of purposiveness, methodology in thinking is the second essential concept in understanding a teacher's thinking. In this case, research methodology is specifically emphasized. Although it is understandable how difficult it is to have the whole instructional process as the research object in one research project, the teacher must always think about how the totality is functioning. How then is it meaningful to require knowledge of research methodology in the teacher's thinking, since it means understanding different approaches and different research traditions which include every possible research method? It is naturally a question of a certain kind of attitude that in general reflects problematizing the decisions in the instructional process.

The question of what kind of research methods are necessary in pedagogical thinking is a problem in teacher education. Understanding research methodology and knowing how to use at least some research methods, it is suggested, increases the teacher's autonomy and independent pedagogical thinking. The more the teacher has expert knowledge of her/his work and understands on which premises her/his decision-making is based, the more freedom and autonomy s/he has in her/his work and the more critical s/he can be within the curricular frame.

One approach for analyzing the importance of the knowledge of research methodology is to look at the teacher's work from different levels (König, 1975, 26–31; Guhl & Ott, 1985, 88–113; Knecht-von Martial, 1986, 26–28). On the action level (Figure 1) along the interaction dimension there is planning, implementing and evaluation, with numerous contributing factors influencing the practical work. On this level, basic teaching skills are needed and practical experience, as well as practical situations, guide the teacher's work. This means thinking mostly of immediate problems and their practical solutions at a given time. This description is simplified, of course, but it emphasizes the continuous flow of problem episodes requiring the teacher's decision-making. Without readiness for pedagogical thinking, without understanding the purposive and methodological character of her/his work, the interaction only takes place on the action level.

On the first thinking level, the teacher may have an inquiring attitude directed at her/his own action. The instructional process is then the object of her/his thinking. With conceptual analysis, and by means of empirical research knowledge, it is supposed to be possible for the teacher to build theoretical models to help her/him to function in the process. The idea is moving from practice through theorizing back to practice. In this practice, s/he needs theoretical knowledge in research methods as well as in pedagogical content knowledge; both are important. One possible result of the analysis on the thinking level could be the understanding of the basic concepts and their interaction, that must always be considered in any practical situation.

A further requirement in the teacher's professional development would be achieving the second thinking level, the metatheoretical level. Acting on the first thinking level quite soon reveals that there are numerous occasions to build theoretical models and frames for a teacher's work. It is naturally possible to begin to compare them with each other and to experiment with different examples. On the second thinking level, the teacher may notice that behind the different theoretical models there are also different ontological hypotheses guiding the model building. It may not be possible to compare the models themselves, but this can be done with their background determinants. The value questions must be taken into consideration, too. All the time there is a lively interaction between the various levels.

Knowledge of research methods and the whole aspect of methodology does not mean that the teacher would act like an educational researcher in her/his classroom. Her/His inquiring attitude, however, prevents the intervention of outside authorities from confusing her/his teaching with topical novelties or with unprofessional viewpoints. Raising the teacher's thinking as high as possible towards the second thinking level is supposed to relieve her/him of thinking about authoritative boundaries and strengthens her/his autonomy in the teaching profession.

Teaching and thinking on the action level can be thought of as a continuous process of action research. The teacher, however, must continuously take the curricular frame and the school context into consideration. The different phases of the interaction process have their own methodical requirements, too. The planning phase concentrates on the purposes, aims and goals and emphasizes the analytical thinking skills. Making educational decisions in planning requires kinds of justification different than the same during the interaction proper. Making and analyzing the curriculum, in order to implement its ideas in reality, is based on a qualitative content analysis in some way. The knowledge of educational and developmental psychology requires an understanding of psychological research principles. The postinteractive phase with evaluation contains skills in assessing learning and other changes. This means knowledge of the psychometric methods. All these examples show that the aspect of methodology is extensive and many-sided. It cannot mean an expert knowledge of research methods; rather what is aimed at in a teacher's thinking is a kind of all-round mastering.

The idea of teachers' pedagogical thinking requires a solid background in teacher education. Although the model of teachers' pedagogical thinking may be universal, the context and programs of teacher education vary greatly in different countries. Research-based thinking constitutes a systematic way of reflecting on everyday problems in classrooms, without prejudices or biases, and of extracting a reliable knowledge of research literature through journals and reports. This may be an idealistic view, but there is some experience of this kind of program in teacher education (Kansanen & Uljens, 1996). The important parts in the research-based programme is personal participation in research work during teacher education studies, and writing a thesis based on one's own research. In addition to doing one's own research, readiness in reading and understanding research documents is a necessary condition to act according to the model of teachers' pedagogical thinking.

Although a research-based paradigm is here suggested as a foundation for teacher education, the programs in practice are too wide to follow only one model. Usually they are eclectic by nature and contain elements from many possible orientations. The research-based model is greatly reminiscent of what Zeichner (1983) and Tom (1985) have called an in-quiry-oriented paradigm. From Zeichner's description, many similar char-acteristics may be picked up. A very important feature is the idea of au-tonomy, in the hope it is developed through critical inquiry. The prospective teacher is expected to problematize her/his actions and institutional back-ground, that form the rationales for the studies and for the instructional process in general. Reflection requires understanding to pose appropriate questions and to find personal answers to them. Readiness to experiment with one's own teaching, and competence to justify one's own decisions characterize the work according to this model. The main hypothesis be-hind the teachers' pedagogical thinking is that competence in thinking of teaching as a research process and using research methods as guiding principles provide the teacher with freedom in developing her/his profes-sional competence as well as possible. Development of critical awareness of the rationales cannot be avoided when justification for decisions and actions are required.

Tom (1985) further analyses the inquiry-oriented paradigm and looks at it via three dimensions, and tries consequently to clarify its content. The dimensions are the arena of the problematic, the model of inquiry, and the ontological status of educational phenomena. He shows that most of the models that belong to the inquiry-oriented family are rather re-stricted, and use some narrow point of view as their starting point. The conception of the research-based teacher education means looking at the teaching-studying-learning process as a totality that consists of many kinds of thinking and action, and that needs an all-round competence in prac-tice. The starting-point in the individual teacher's reflection is usually the practical process, the teaching-studying-learning process, that is going on all the time. The whole problem area can be approached through enlarg-ing circles, in which every phase requires a knowledge of its own meth-ods and where the interaction with other phases is always present.

The model-building with its ideas and wide perspectives is what is behind the practical research project. The other side of the coin is to investigate empirically how the things are in reality. A normative purpose may be the development of teacher education according to the principles if the results of the project encourage to that kind of activity.

PART II

LINKING VARIOUS APPROACHES

Chapter 4

Teachers' Pedagogical Mind Set

The chapter traces the development towards mindful orientation with the aim of investigating and understanding teacher knowledge. Mindful orientation is framed by analyzing the development of the conceptions of teacher, students, and context. The concept of pedagogy is used in order to encompass the various encounters engaged in by teachers in their work. The stance presupposes that teacher knowledge is viewed from the perspective of phronesis, rather than knowledge as episteme. The chapter proposes a mind set approach that uses relational knowing in order to develop a fuller understanding of teachers' thinking in its social contexts. The chapter also explores more general ways in which minds are thought about in their cultural contexts, and the pedagogical practices that relate to those ways of thinking.

Teachers' Professional Landscapes

The 1990's seems to have become an era of both individual and team-based pedagogical action—at least in the Scandinavian countries. In Finland the general curricular frames have been abandoned to a great extent and now they are being replaced by local and school-centered curricular guidelines. Teachers are at the center of this educational enterprise: it is their professional task, both individually and collectively (as a school community), to shape the school-centered curricula according to their best professional understanding and capability. The duty is a challenging one because it covers the totality of the educational processes from classroom practices to general educational aims and goals and to the special characteristics the schools are aiming at.

The change taking place in the teaching profession can be viewed as a two-fold transformation. The first one means the shift of administrative power from the general and bureaucratic (macro) level to the practical and local school level. This change taking place in educational policy coincides with the second transformation in which the teacher's professional role is changing from being the implementor of general curricular guidelines to being the inventor of more personal and situation-specific approaches in teaching. Together these two transformations mean the empowerment of teachers in the sense that, from now on, teachers are more responsible for the totality of the instructional process taking place in schools.

The situation can be seen as a sort of testing ground for teachers' pedagogical capabilities to cope with professional issues on both the practical and intellectual levels at the same time, and at the same place, on the school level. Teachers are becoming active curriculum makers instead of passive curriculum users (Clandinin & Connelly, 1992).

The situation can also be described as contextual and integrated. The situation is contextual in the sense that teachers work in their schools and classroom settings where changes are taking place. Teachers' work is situated—that is, it takes place in institutions, cultural and social fields, and in response to individual and social pressures that are often unrepeatable. The prevailing situation can be regarded as integrated in the sense that teachers, both factually and now also officially, have to take care of and take into consideration the totality of the instructional process they intend to perform. As Whitehead (1995) has presented; teachers' simultaneously need both the practical capacities to engage in educational processes and the theoretical capacities to relate their educational actions to educational theories, or even produce their own living educational theories.

The restructuring of school curricula and pedagogical practices are of little value if they do not take teachers into account. Teachers do not merely deliver the curriculum. As mentioned, their professional tasks now also encompass the developing and redefining of the curriculum. It is what teachers think, what teachers believe and what teachers do at the classrooms level that ultimately shapes the kind of education young people get. According to Hargreaves (1991, vi), growing appreciation of this fact is placing work with teachers and understanding their teaching at the top of many research and improvement agendas.

Research on Teachers' Thinking— Practice and Beyond

Teaching is usually associated with practical activity—and practical problems. This is manifested by both teachers themselves and by many educational researchers. If we ask teachers to tell us about their work, they usually describe very carefully what they have done or are planning to do in their classrooms. Teachers seldom speak about, for example, justifications for their reported actions or look into their actions. Brown & McIntyre (1993) focused their study on the practical perspective of teaching and found that teachers were quite unable to report to others the mental processes involved in their classroom practices. To quote the title of the book by Brown and McIntyre, it seems difficult, even for the teachers themselves, to "make sense of teaching".

A vast amount of educational research has been conducted to study teachers' classroom behavior. In general, the studies were greatly inspired by the idea that 'effective and good teaching' can be reduced to external competencies that the teacher performs. Even in the modern cognitive-mediated paradigm now prevailing in the educational sciences, this practical connotation has survived: the practice of teaching (Jackson, 1986), practical knowledge (Elbaz, 1983), and personal practical knowledge (Clandinin, 1985; Connelly & Clandinin, 1985), just to mention a few conceptual phrases, present various examples of this keen interest in the practical activities of teaching and in teacher thinking, too.

The stable and keen interest in practice does not mean that nothing has changed. Actually, quite a lot has changed. Notably, the definitions of practice have evolved, and the concept of practice is nowadays often coupled with other concepts (e.g. teaching, knowledge, personal) which give it extra layers of meaning. Notwithstanding, the research on teachers' thinking has preserved its common ground on practice, but it has also moved beyond that.

Conceptions of Teachers

Clark (1986, 8–9) has traced the past development of teacher thinking research and has found three interconnected and partly overlapping phases in the conceptual development in research on teachers' thinking:

1. The teacher as a decision-maker, in which the teacher's task is to diagnose needs and learning problems of students and to prescribe effective and appropriate instructional treatments for them. The teacher is seen as a sort of physician who operates in a bounded rational world of education by defining problems and seeking satisfactory solutions to them.
2. The teacher as a sense-maker, in which decision-making is seen as one among several activities teachers perform in order to create meaning for themselves and their students. The teacher is seen as a

reflective professional (Schön, 1983). Clark (1986, 8) sees this as a move towards a more abstract conception of a teacher in which primarily a diagnostic-prescriptive way of thinking is accomplished by a more general view of teaching as a profession that calls for extensive knowledge of teaching and student learning. It is assumed that reflectively, a professional teacher can interpret, adapt and skillfully apply her/his knowledge to particular situations in which s/he performs.

3. The teacher as a constructivist, who continually builds and elaborates her/his personal theory of teaching and education. This third phase means the widening of teachers' problem space: no more do we believe that teachers solely can define and resolve problems they encounter in their profession. Powerful influences beyond the control of individual teachers also create problems teachers have to live by. No longer is teachers' thinking seen as a monolithic and consistent issue that leads the life of teachers. Instead, it is admitted that teachers often hold multiple and conflicting theories and explanations about teaching and, as Clark (1986, 9) emphasizes, the amazing thing is that this kind of "inconsistent, imperfect and incomplete way of thinking" works rather well in the complex and practical world of classrooms.

The reason why teachers accept merely satisfactory solutions to the problems they have to deal with is not that they are merely lazy and ignorant, but because many of the problems that they face are genuine dilemmas (Berlak & Berlak, 1981; Lampert, 1984, 1985) that have no optimal solutions. Any teaching situation simultaneously presents many conflicting issues with which teachers must find a way to live. This because pedagogical situations are in no sense linear and it is difficult in educational talk to discuss functioning in a complex setting where problems do not have single solutions towards which one moves in a linear fashion.

Bruner (1990, 4) has criticized the cognitive-constructivistic approach that its emphasis has shifted from meaning to information, from the construction of meaning to the processing of information. He argues that computing has become the model of the mind and due to this the concept of computability has replaced the concept of meaning in a broad cultural sense. According to Bruner (1990, 8), there exists a danger that there are fewer places for the mind in our cultural systems—the mind in the intentional states like believing, desiring, intending and grasping a meaning.

Perhaps we are moving towards some kind of mindful orientation (van Manen, 1991a, 149) in the research on teachers' thinking. This trend does not primarily deal with single and discernible thought traits. Instead, it presupposes that "global assessment comes first" (Jackson, 1992, 407) and more than easily distinct thought habits, this kind of thoughtfulness is concerned with relationships that can be sketched out in teachers' thinking.

During this decade teachers' minds, in the moral and ethical sense, have become of major interest (cf. e.g. Goodlad *et al.*, 1990; van Manen, 1991b; Sockett, 1993; Hansen, 1993; Oser, 1994a). The concept of virtue has reappeared both in philosophical (MacIntyre, 1985) and educational writings (Buchmann, 1990; Fenstermacher, 1990; Elbaz, 1993; Hansen, 1994; van Manen, 1994a), and it has its critics, too (e.g. Fenstermacher, 1994a). Perhaps this can be interpreted as a fourth phase of teacher conceptions in research on teachers' thinking: the teacher is seen as a meaning-maker who aims at shaping and influencing what students become as persons when living through pedagogical situations in schools and classrooms.

In sum, as Clark (1986, 9) points out, in teacher thinking research we have moved away from internally consistent and mechanical paradigms towards more inconsistent, imperfect and incomplete ways of thinking. We are moving towards an understanding that what goes on inside classroom walls (and particularly inside teachers' minds) is closely related to what goes on outside those walls (and outside teachers' minds).

Conceptions of Students

During the three phases our way of thinking about students has also evolved. In his analysis Clark (1986, 9) tends to overstate when he argues that during the last few decades students were regarded as objects to be acted upon by teachers. His argument that students were seen as passive and merely as sources of clues for the teachers' own behavior seems to be exaggerated. When looking back, the cultural image of schooling and teaching could have been like that, but it is important to note that the actual pedagogical practices that took place in the past perhaps were not so different from the present ones. The context of interpretation (cf. Seddon, 1994) has changed. And this change has caused students to gradually come more to the forefront in educational studies. They are recognized as partners in the educational process because students, like teachers, are seen as thinkers, planners, and decision makers themselves (Wittrock, 1986).

Shulman and Carey (1984) have analyzed different conceptions of students as learners in various educational perspectives. According to them, rather than presenting students as objects, passive recipients of teaching, gradually they are considered as individuals that actively make use of their own cognitive strategies and their previous knowledge base. In this view, students are seen as active, inventive, knowledge bearing, and self-conscious. This is in accordance with our critical remarks concerning the role of the student learner, who has been transformed from being passive recipient of teaching in to an active meaning-maker, This means that students as learners not only find out what is sensible in teaching, they actively make sense of their own studying. They have their own perspective on teaching, a studying perspective, which can be different from the one the teacher is intended to communicate. In short, students are constructivists, too.

Gradually, the view of individual student learning is giving way to a more dynamic and social view of students who also learn from each other. This kind of constructivistic view of student activities is consistent with the ideas of social education, which largely have been absent from the scene of educational thinking—but not from pedagogical practices. Shulman and Carey (1984, 517) have suggested that we should view students more as collectively rational. That is, how students exercise their abilities in groups and how they pursue their multiple and perhaps mutually-shared goals. Studying in groups calls for students who are capable of coordinating their individual work with their peers and to understand how different individuals can contribute to the group's efforts.

Student learning, as collectively rational, emphasizes that the ability to work/study as a member of a community is a contingent part of student learning. The view emphasizes that students are no longer viewed as individual and isolated objects of teaching, but rather as active members of the instructional process In sum, students' studying efforts are seen as multidimensional and embedded in various contexts, and based on understandings between both parties involved, i.e. teachers and students.

Conceptions of Context

Side by side with this conceptual development in the research of teacher thinking, the context of teaching has also been broadened. At first the unit of teacher thinking was the school classroom where the teacher's constant decision-making was taking place in order to diagnose and help student learning.

Gradually the notion of context has become more dynamic and collectively defined. The context was not seen as totally predetermined and fixed, instead it was based on a mutually-negotiated understanding between both parties involved, i.e. teachers and students (Clark, 1986; Erickson, 1986). The school classroom, and the teacher in it as the unit of analysis, was shattered e.g. by Jackson (1966, 1968). Those complexities that are nowadays being regarded as some sort of basic knowledge in the field are eloquently presented by him: *The way teaching is* in the school context.

Clark (1986, 12) summarizes that we have moved away from a rather impoverished and fragmented notion of context as a collection of background variables, to a richer, more dynamic, and collectively defined understanding of context. Context is not a variable, or a collection of more or less mechanical components, that lies outside of the object of interest. Teachers and teaching in schools are embedded by the surrounding world and they are also affected by it.

Seddon (1995) has analyzed different conceptions of context in educational literature, covering different methodological approaches. According to him, the most common conception of context rested upon an "inside/outside" metaphor. Mainly the context was regarded as external reality, the source of "outside" influences that tended to disturb whatever was important "inside" the object of interest. This conception has lead to the stripping of context from the object or event of interest.

Constructivistic notions of student learning and action have paved the way to more extended views of context. Instead of "outside/inside" metaphors, context is seen both as actual and symbolic: it is a field for action and the medium within which individuals construct their understandings of the situations. For pedagogical practices this extended view of contextuality is worth noting. The stance emphasizes that both the actions taken and the symbolic constructs made inform each other, comprising a larger whole. Indeed, the term context comes from Latin *contextus*, which means "a joining together" (Goodwin & Duranti, 1992, 4). Albeit, teachers and students interact with their contexts in order to create multiple/mutual understandings which inform their action in and on the world.

Seddon (1994, 36–37) speaks about "practice-based" contextualism in which the relationship between the context and its objects is understood as a kind of ongoing, immensely complex cultural encounter in which:

"There is nothing essential about context or its objects. We 'chunk' up the world as a basis for research and everyday practice. But this chunking is a methodological procedure shaped by distinctive frames of explanation, both formal and informal. There is no such thing as an unproblematic phenomenon such as 'education', 'school', or 'individual' that can be simply observed and understood."(Seddon, 1995, 401)

Why is context, and the way it is used, significant today? According to Seddon (1995, 401), it is because the modern changing of schooling is greatly a contextual change. It implies that the face-to-face relationships of teachers and students are not changing that much, nor that the teaching/studying practices around those relationships are very different from that from those of the past, but that the milieu within which educational practice occurs is shifting greatly. For example, the emergence of virtual classrooms (cf. Tiffin & Rajasingham, 1995; Husu, 1997) calls for new methods in teaching and studying, as well as novel ways of thinking about the whole instructional process taking place in schools.

The context of education is no longer something that can be taken for granted, merely as a background for something else that is important. Instead, context is brought to the forefront of educators' attention. Therefore, to a great extent, it is the context that defines what is real and what is relevant from the perspectives of teachers and students, albeit researchers.

When context is understood as interpretative and discursive practice that constitutes the real and relevant, what emerges is the fluidity of context. Context appears subjective, the reality from the perspective of participants in any setting (Duranti & Goodwin, 1992). This kind of interpretative approach makes an ontological claim first. It infers that our being and acting in our contexts is interpersonal and shares our cultural manners. The perspective implies that our ways of relating to the world/ contexts are primarily not ways of thinking, but ways of being. It is a question of relating to the totality of things that shape our thinking. And this totality may not be reduced to particular units of thinking. Packer & Winne (1995, 20) see that contextuality in teachers' thinking can be seen in the thinking itself as a joint function of what is in the context and what teachers' are capable to recognize and perceive about that context.

However, these idiosyncratic features of individually-experienced contexts should not be overstated. This because, even if individual teachers are each differently positioned, they also act within commonly-experienced social and institutional settings. These settings have a long history and have relatively stable social effects that are rooted in their contemporary practices. Consequently, while there are changes and emerging challenges, there are also continuities that structure the practice.

In sum, if context is understood as practice-based, the challenge is not to identify a tiny piece of reality to study by choosing a small topic. Rather, as Seddon (1995, 403) argues, the challenge is to construct a frame for analysis and explanation that enables us to grasp significant aspects of education and to make explicit the ways of seeing and interpreting them.

Knowledge Teachers Live By

The title is borrowed from Buchmann (1987), who sees that it is unclear whether much of what teachers know is professionally-special to them. Special in the sense that the knowledge teachers employ can be considered highly different by character or degree from ordinary knowledge or common sense. This is because people acquire knowledge by taking part in various cultural patterns. Such participation allows them to become members of various groups and to perform respective social roles within them.

Education and schooling are such cultural patterns, while teaching and studying are pervasive activities that teachers and students respectively perform. Every teacher has been a student at some time. In practice, this meant a tight schedule of watching and hearing teachers and fellow students approximately five hours a day, five days a week, for twelve years. Lortie (1975) calls this "the apprenticeship of observation", which gives future teachers, as well as other fellow citizens, a close-up and extended view of what it is to be a teacher or a student.

It follows, as Buchmann (1987, 152) argues, that the knowledge base of teaching will not be considered special and that adults on both sides, teachers and parents, will be ambivalent about its real value. Teachers feel entitled, but also forced, to use their common sense in teaching. However, this does not mean to belittle professional knowledge of teachers that evidently exists and is widely discussed (e.g. Carlgren & Lindblad, 1991; Russell & Munby, 1991; Fenstermacher, 1994a; van Manen, 1994b; Sockett, 1993; Clandinin & Connelly, 1995). The point is just to suggest that the knowledge teachers use cannot be placed on either side of the divide between "specialized knowledge which particular individuals need in their occupational roles and common knowledge which all adult individuals need as members of the community" (Znaniecki, 1965, 25 in Buchmann, 1987, 152).

Relational Knowing

Teaching is embedded in practical actions. It is situated in and between teachers and students. Teachers cannot help but stand in relation to their students. Van Manen (1994a) argues that this pedagogical relation largely depends on qualities or virtues that the teacher has been able to develop and internalize as part of her/his person. The concept of pedagogy is used in order to capture that great variety of elements in teachers' thinking.

However, we humbly acknowledge that teachers' thinking consists of a very broad spectrum of issues that is too hard to handle at one time. Therefore, we have limited our interest to teachers' thinking within the context of schooling. Here we follow the thoughts of Fritzell (1996), as we intend to focus our attention on the scope of pedagogy. We also share van Manen's (1991b) view, according to which, being pedagogical means going beyond mere teaching to encompass all kinds of encounters where teachers can contribute to their students upbringing. In a sense, being pedagogical implies something like "The Call to Teach" (Hansen, 1995) which inspires teachers to search various ways to teach with courage, conviction and confidence.

We approach teachers' pedagogical minds from two perspectives: the perspective is internal when it deals directly and explicitly with pedagogical practice itself, and external if it concerns educational matters but refers to actual pedagogical practice only indirectly or implicitly. When doing this we hope to avoid pedagogical split vision (Fritzell, 1996). It means that there has been a tendency to use either the internal or external perspective exclusively, as if the other did not exist. However, the understanding of teachers' thinking requires a comprehension of pedagogical practice in terms of the concrete interrelations of individuals and their embeddedness in their contexts.

Defined this way, the pedagogical approach emphasizes that a teacher's knowing mind is interrelated and contextual. However, we must simultaneously acknowledge that pedagogical relationships between teachers and students are not symmetrical. Teachers are mainly responsible for the pedagogical relationships which occur in schools. Therefore, it is important to study them.

Interrelating Cultures

Olson (1988) has criticized the research on teachers' thinking as relying too much on the cognitive perspective. By cognitive perspective he means the idea that teachers and teaching are adequately understood in terms of a person's cognitive contents and capacities. The trouble is that this view has important limitations. What is crucial in understanding a teacher's thinking is not a teacher's personal and private affairs, but rather what is interpersonal and common in them. Teachers and their thinking are parts of a bigger picture: a culture which, according to Bruner (1986, 123), provides a "forum for negotiating meaning and for explicating action".

Thus, characterizing teachers' thinking as their personal capacities easily leaves aside the curricular frame factors in which teachers operate: schools, classrooms and the overall environment in which they and their students act. As Olson argues (1992, 17), this social context of action is not teachers' personal property. Rather, it is as an interpersonal domain that vastly constitutes both teachers' professional practice and their thinking. Consequently, what teachers tell about their practice to a great deal is a reflection of their culture, and cannot be properly understood without reference to that culture (Olson, 1988, 169). Teachers' thinking reflects the understanding of the culture which they belong to. The personal component emerges from the fact that it is the individual teacher's construction of what is regarded as essentially public.

The attempt to understand culture and its meaning in teachers' thinking is to pursue a context within which those relationships can be intelligibly described (Geertz, 1973, 14). When studying teachers' thinking, we need an understanding of various contexts teachers live by, in order to make sense of their thinking and action. Accordingly, when interpreting teachers' thinking, we need to employ wider perspectives that have the capacities to give us a more coherent and complete picture of their minds. As Ryle (1949, 32) has put it:

> " 'Intelligent' can't be defined in terms of 'intellectual'. . . . When I do something intelligently . . . my performance has a social procedure or manner, not special antecedents."

Harrison (1978, 45) echoes the same thought in his phrase: "when someone acts intelligently, he acts his mind". What does this mean? Dewey (1931) rejected any conception of the mind that regards mind as isolated from persons and things. According to him, "Mind is primarily a verb. It denotes all the ways in which we deal consciously and expressly with situations in which we find ourselves" (Dewey, 1931, 263). As Greene (1994, 435) argues, this stance leads to "viewing knowing primarily as a personal search for the meaning of things with respect to acts performed and with respect to the consequences of those acts when performed". Thus, knowing is what is obtained by acting to resolve practical situations. As such "... (knowing is not) independent of who and what one is as a person. It is, instead, an organic property of human being, of acting in thoughtful and discerning ways. ... to know is to a form of competence, an ability to navigate the puzzlements and predicaments of life with moral and intellectual surefootedness ..." (Fenstermacher & Sanger, 1998, 471).

Van Manen (1991a, 206) reminds us of the etymological connection between thought and mind. According to him (ibid.), the word mind shares roots with the term man, human, with both words standing for "the one who thinks", "who remembers". It is a question of "capabilities of the organized conscious or unconscious mental process .. that results in reasoning, thinking, and perceiving" (Webster Dictionary). It is a question of human deliberation that accommodates itself to what it finds and is responsive to complexities of all kind. Nussbaum (1986, 301) calls this the flexible quality of human reasoning, which allows the appearances to govern themselves and to be normative for the correctness of human reasoning. But how can we capture this unified procedure or manner in teachers' thinking?

The Matter of the Practical

One way to deal with the problem is to consider teachers' thinking from the different knowledge perspectives. Kessels & Korthagen (1996) argue that the dominating conception of rationality in educational sciences has seen knowledge as *episteme* instead of knowledge as *phronesis* (cf. Jonsen & Toulmin, 1988; Nussbaum, 1986). Knowledge as *episteme* is usually connected to the scientific understanding of problems and, according to Kessels & Korthagen (1996, 18), it considers knowledge as propositional, general by its nature, and it is formulated in abstract terms. *Episteme* is essentially conceptual.

When knowledge is viewed from the *phronesis* perspective it looks quite different. Kessels & Korthagen (1996, 19) stress that it is mainly concerned with the understanding of concrete cases and complex situations. It considers knowledge as variable, particular by its nature, and it is mainly formulated in concrete and context-related terms. In the case of *phronesis*, we begin with particulars of the situation. Then we start to think about this situation in the light of our own understanding.

Phronesis deals with practical complexities and lived experiences. Aristotle views this practical capacity of human thought as essentially loose or indefinite by nature. He argues that "every statement concerning matters of practice ought to be said in outline and not with precision . . ." because ". . . statements should be demanded in a way appropriate to the matter at hand" (Aristotle, Nic. Eth., Book VI, 1103b–1104a). And in practice, the matter at hand in educational situations tends to be imprecise by nature. Lampert's (1984, 1985) notion of teaching as dilemma-managing sums up the point in question here.

Regarding the research on teachers' thinking from the perspective of *phronesis*, the basic question can be formulated as "what is perceived?" To be able to choose appropriate actions, teachers above all must be able to perceive and distinguish the relevant features. These cannot be transmitted in some general and abstract form because, as Nussbaum (1986, 303) emphasizes, it is a matter of fitting one's choice to the "complex requirements of a concrete situation", taking all of its contextual features into account.

However, as Kessels & Korthagen (1996) remind us, the perception we are now talking about is not just the normal sensory perception. *Phronesis* deals with more than meets the eye. It is the sort of eye that individuals develop simultaneously, both to look at and look beyond the events and objects at hand. Eisner (1991) speaks about "*The Enlightened Eye*" that is based on the qualitative thought of human understanding. It signifies that we are not seeking to reveal reality as it really is. Instead, we must be content with a mind-mediated version of it. This is because we are ultimately stuck with our judgements and interpretations, the vehicles for our meaning-making.

Nevertheless, the problem is that to others meanings are usually hidden or veiled. Therefore, what we need are descriptions and interpretations that are adequate enough to reveal structures and levels of experiential or textual meanings (van Manen, 1990, 181). As a result, if we succeed, we will get a description or interpretation that we can nod to, recognizing it as a kind of description or interpretation that helps us to understand the thoughts and experiences of others, as well as our own. Van Manen (1990 27) speaks about a "phenomenological nod", which means that a good description or interpretation is collected by lived experience, and helps to recollect lived experience.

The standpoint of the knowledge as *phronesis* is the person. The knowledge is personal, practical and contextual. It is not a question of some general principle that is somehow related to the person, but instead, how the person is interrelated with the knowledge itself. Therefore:

"The appropriate criterion of correct choice is thoroughly human being, the person of practical wisdom. This person does not attempt to take up a stand outside of the conditions of human life, but bases his or her judgement on long and broad experience of these conditions". (Nussbaum, 1986, 290)

Teachers' Minds—Where Are They Set and What Is Their Setting?

To be able to outline this wider, perception-based type of knowledge in teachers thinking, we do not primarily need ready-made theories nor tightly defined and solid concepts. What we need is the knowledge and understanding of the concrete situations teachers perceive, the experiences they have, the plans teachers intend to execute, and how they reflect upon the consequences. Kessels & Korthagen (1996, 21) argue that without such a perceptional standpoint, hardly no knowledge of practical relevance, in the sense of *phronesis*, is formed. Teachers' pedagogical thinking seems to be linked with the type of knowledge that is mainly perceptual and subjective (e.g. Elbaz, 1983; Nias, 1988, 1989; Clandinin & Connelly, 1987, 1995, 1996; Carter & Doyle, 1987; Lampert, 1984, Powell, 1996). But on what issues are teachers' minds set? And how does this setting work? To clarify these interrelated problems we have employed the concept and method of mind set.

We see mind set as a useful conceptual tool for examining how teachers look at the events and problems that concern them in their practical affairs. It aims at better knowing about differing patterns of perceiving and reasoning. In practice, mind set helps us to conceive the way teachers define and understand issues they deal with within their profession. We have used the idea of mind set both conceptually and methodologically in two complementary ways.

First, the narrower concept of the term, the mind set refers to a quite stable mental attitude towards perceiving objects or events. It answers the question: what is perceived? What is the content in teachers' thinking? According to Fisher (1992, 23), it means simplifying the object or event perceived to a personal frame of reference, to understand it. This object or incident can be regarded as a focal event that, according to Duranti & Goodwin (1992, 3), teachers treat selectively in their thinking. The question then becomes: what do teachers treat as focal? And, what can be regarded as a contextual background in which this focal event is embedded? Goffman (1974, 2–8) speaks about factors of selective attention and personal involvement that have the capacity of making the world real to us. According to him, any event can be described in terms of a focus, a certain key to understanding the whole phenomenon.

Second, the broader concept of the term, the mind set refers to an integrative and interrelated context in teachers' thinking. It answers the question: how does teachers' thinking occur? What kind of design for perceiving and reasoning can possibly be outlined to describe teachers' thinking? It is a framework of mental constructs (e.g. beliefs, images, assumptions, and habits of reasoning) of the external world by which teachers' professional knowledge is sorted out and given meaning. In this sense mind set can be used as a kind of summary or guide, or a heuristic way to explore teachers' thinking.

Chapter 5

Moral Perspectives in Teachers' Thinking

The chapter discusses the importance of professional morality in teachers' every-day work at school. Different aspects of morality are explored within the framework of the ethos model developed by Oser. The chapter argues for practicable strategies in dealing with the moral aspects of problem-solving by adapting the discourse position. Learning goals in the moral domain are identified as important aspects in the curriculum. Different approaches in ethics teaching are presented to promote moral learning in students. These approaches include implicit and explicit moral education. Values clarification, applied Kohlberg and discourse ethics are identified as alternative approaches to ethics teaching in schools.

Introduction

In the recent decades, a growing interest in the moral domain of teaching has been witnessed among educational researchers and teacher educators. This trend to emphasize the ethical nature of teaching and the teacher profession has been reflected in the texts by Tom (1984) and Strike & Soltis (1985). In the 1990s the moral dimensions of teaching have been further conceptualized (Goodlad et al., 1990; Sockett, 1993; Oser, 1994a). All these researchers have used the term morality as a key word in describing the professional ethos of teachers. Regardless of the subject matter, grade level of the students, or the nature of interaction between a teacher and his classroom you can always interpret the moral messages in a teacher's decision-making. In fact, you can study everything that is involved in the educational process from an ethical point of view, pedagogical ethics emphasizes the ethical nature of all education.

Moral messages in schools are delivered through moral instruction and moral practices. Usually moral instruction as a formal part of the curriculum only takes place in religious schools or in specific moral education lessons. In an ethnographic study of the moral life of schools, the researchers seldom found this type of formal curriculum in the schools. More frequently, they observed moral instruction within the regular curriculum. This kind of instruction addressed altruistic and ideal moral behavior as a part of the subject matter across different subjects. In addition, the observers list rituals and ceremonies, pictures and posters with moral content and spontaneous moral comments during the activity as part of the moral instruction given by schools. Moral practices include classroom rules and regulations, classroom practices, personal qualities of teachers and the morality of the curricular substructure. This classification indicates that morality is hidden, but present in any teaching and classroom interaction (Jackson *et al.*, 1993).

The moral dimension of teaching might become more concrete when a teacher faces a conflict in his professional conduct. Many educational conflicts require decision-making on the part of the teacher. It might be assumed that teachers are good problem-solvers in moral dilemmas, based on earlier research findings. According to a Greek study, teachers ranked very high in their moral reasoning. Helkama refers to a particular study in which Kohlberg's scale was used to measure the level of the moral development of teachers. Of nearly one hundred teachers, more than a half scored the postconventional level of stage 5 in their judgments (Helkama, 1993, 65). The results of this study might indicate that teachers have a good potential for reaching just solutions in their judgments. However, according to the model of professional morality presented by Oser, responsible judgments in educational settings require more than justice-oriented solutions (Oser, 1991). In addition, the real life dilemmas a teacher encounters in his work are evidently very different from the hypothetical dilemmas formulated by Kohlberg. Teachers have indeed expressed their difficulties in the moral domain. In a recent American survey, teachers reported that they are ill prepared for dealing with ethical dilemmas in their classroom. The major conflicts experienced in teaching were judged to be ethical in nature by 70 per cent of teachers. The majority of the teachers surveyed did not see clear ways to resolve the conflicts they had faced (Lyons, 1990).

In our study, we aim at investigating the current strategies that teachers apply to moral dilemmas they encounter in their professional conduct. We adopted a case-study approach by exploring the moral dilemmas as identified by teachers from one particular school. These teachers were subject-teachers in the lower-secondary school. The school is located in a capital area, with a very diverse student population. The teachers of the school had been very active in participating in various kinds of research projects to improve teaching and learning in their school. They all acknowledged the need to be more prepared for the moral dilemmas they are challenged to face in their everyday work with a diverse student population. We found this particular school, with highly motivated teachers and a diverse student population, to be an ideal school to study teachers' moral dilemmas and their solution strategies.

Our methodological approach to teachers' thinking regarding moral dilemmas was to interview all teachers. In a personal interview, the teachers were asked to identify a difficult moral dilemma they had faced in their professional conduct. The teachers were encouraged to describe the dilemma in detail and to give as much information as possible about all those participants involved in the particular dilemma. Our goal was to get as accurate a picture of the dilemma as possible. Our approach was very close to the idea of well-remembered events, as adapted by Carter and Gonzalez (1993). After the dilemma was identified, the teachers were asked about the strategies they had used in their attempts to solve it. The teachers themselves were also asked to evaluate whether the strategies used in those problem-solving situations had been effective enough.

In the following chapters we discuss the main categories of moral dilemmas, as identified by the teachers. In particular, we concentrate on the reasoning behind teachers' solution strategies to these dilemmas. The empirical results of our study are explored in the theoretical framework of teachers' ethos model, as identified by Oser (1991).

Teachers' Professional Morality

Oser (1991) has proposed a distinction among three types of morality: normative, situational and professional. Professional morality is connected to nonmoral, functional, professional acting. As long as everything goes along without any conflicts, the teachers usually do not need to consider the ethical standards of their acts. It is only in those situations when the normal routines of instruction are interrupted that teachers need to consider the principles for solving the existing dilemma. The types of principles teachers refer to in these conflicts define their professional responsibility, which manifests itself in professional acts.

Teachers' professional morality can also be called their professional ethos. Oser has outlined a model for studying teachers' professional ethos (Oser, 1991, 202). He argues that moral conflicts in educational settings arise when three types of moral claims cannot be met at the same time.

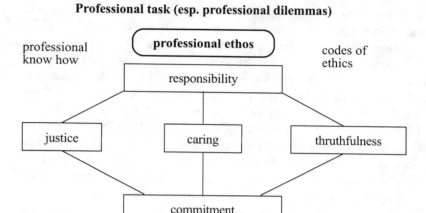

Figure 2. Dimensions of the teachers' ethos model (Oser, 1991, 202).

These claims of justice, care and truthfulness are critical issues in a teacher's professional decision-making. Professional morality emerges in strategies of coordinating these moral dimensions, in the search for an adequate solution to a problem. The differences between an individual's professional morality can be seen as differences in a teacher's strategies in coordinating these dimensions. Central to his theory of professional morality is the hypothesis of qualitatively different forms of decision-making strategies. Oser has identified five types of orientations in a teacher's attempts to solve professional moral dilemmas:

In the avoiding orientation, the teacher tries to "solve" the problem by not facing it. S/he does not want to take any responsibility for difficult questions. Somebody other than the teacher needs to find the balance between justice, care and truthfulness. In the delegating orientation, the teacher accepts the fact that s/he has some responsibility for dealing with the situation. The teacher does not want to make any decisions her/himself but delegates the decision-making to somebody else (for example, the principal or the school psychologist). In the single-handed decision-making the teacher tries to settle the problem by taking it into his own hands. The teacher views her/himself as an "expert" who has the ability to solve the problem quickly and often in an authoritarian manner. The teacher does not need to justify his decisions to the other interested parties. In the Discourse I (incomplete discourse) orientation, the teacher accepts her/his personal responsibility for settling the problem, and s/he explains how s/he has balanced justice, care and truthfulness in each new situation. The teacher also knows that the students are able to understand a well-reflected balance of justice, care and truthfulness. The final orientation is called Discourse II (complete discourse), in which the teacher acts similarly to someone with a "Discourse I" orientation. The teacher goes one step further: S/He presupposes that all students and other persons who are concerned and involved are rational human beings who are also interested in and capable of balancing justice, care and truthfulness. The teacher supports this principle even in critical or aggressive situations (Oser, 1991, 191–205).

The concepts of justice, care and truthfulness that Oser uses in defining the professional responsibility of teachers have also been widely used in other models and orientations of moral judgment (see e.g. Kohlberg, 1976; Gilligan & Attanucci, 1988; Noddings, 1992). A more detailed study of the contents of these concepts is provided in Tirri (1996a, 48). These concepts were also regularly referred to by teachers in our study to justify their actions in solving moral dilemmas at school. In the following chapters we highlight the teachers' reasoning in the moral dilemmas they had faced by taking some direct quotations from the interviews. In addition to moral reasoning, we also pay attention to the most common solving strategies used by teachers.

Promoting Moral Learning in Students

In the moral domain students have certain learning challenges in school, in addition to those in the cognitive, affective and social domains. Some of these learning goals are explicitly expressed in the national curriculum, for example, knowledge and application of the Golden Rule (Framework Curriculum for the Comprehensive School 1994). In addition to this very abstract guideline, schools and classes have established their own ethical rules that the students should learn to follow. In the best cases, teachers and students have negotiated these rules together, according to the idea of just community promoted by Kohlberg and his followers (Kohlberg et al., 1975; Oser, 1996). However, a great deal of moral learning takes place unplanned through the general moral messages delivered by teachers and other students in school.

Clark argues that the most effective moral lessons are the virtuous responses to children's needs or the failures to provide those responses. He lists ten basic needs of children: to be loved, to be led, to be vulnerable, to make sense, to please adults, to have hope, to know truth, to be known, to be safe and to make one's mark. Clark has also suggested virtuous responses to each of those needs that every child deserves. He claims that these responses, or the negative manifestation of them, are the educational events that carry moral messages and can change and shape students' lives (Clark, 1995, 25–28).

In addition to implicit moral learning discussed above, we can promote moral learning explicitly through moral education. As mentioned earlier, formal moral education can be a part of all the subjects taught in school. However, religious education and ethics provide a basic knowledge of the concepts needed in discussing ethical issues. In the following section, we give an overview of different approaches to ethics teaching in schools.

Different Approaches to Moral Education

Values Clarification

Values clarification was introduced as a new alternative in the 1970s to teach ethics to any age level (Simon et al., 1972). This approach was claimed to be more effective than the traditional indoctrination, that had been proven to be ineffective in teaching children moral values (Hartshorne & May, 1930). In values clarification, the emphases are not on the content of people's values but on the process of valuing. The three goals of values clarification are choosing, prizing and acting. People involved in the process are encouraged to choose their values freely among as many alternatives as possible, to prize and affirm their choices, whatever they may be, and to act upon their values consistently and with repetition (Simon et al., 1972, 18–22). The approach does not presume to identify or justify the desirable values. The moral values are considered to be personal values, not right or wrong, true or false. Thus this approach can be labeled values neutral and relativistic in the extreme.

The goals of recognizing, articulating and expressing their own and others' views and feelings about values are relevant for students. We can assume that the process of clarifying one's values is a prerequisite for making responsible judgments in the everyday moral dilemmas faced. A values clarification approach has the potential to promote empathy, interpersonal skills and courage that are needed in moral decision-making. On the other hand, the values clarification approach fails to provide students with the cognitive aspects of ethical inquiry also needed in the attempt to combine justice, care and truthfulness. The other danger of this approach is its potential to promote self-regarding, prudential reasoning that may be associated with narcissism and subjectivism. (Howe, 1986, 10). We can conclude that the activities in values clarification are important steps in the students' critical reflection on values, but they are insufficient by themselves in meeting the aims of ethics teaching.

Applied Kohlberg

Unlike values clarification, Kohlberg's cognitive-developmental approach assumes that some moral positions are indeed better than others. Kohlberg's theory of cognitive moral development argues that higher-stage reasoning is uniformly superior to lower- stage reasoning (Kohlberg, 1969). The advanced stages are less self-oriented, solve a wider range of social problems and reflect universal values such as fairness and human rights. In applying Kohlberg's theory to ethics teaching, the aim is to promote moral growth. Typically, this growth process is stimulated in the discussion of moral dilemmas. The task of the teacher is to expose the students to higher reasoning forms in techniques such as "plus one matching." In this technique, the teacher gauges the typical developmental level of a student's judgments. The teacher then introduces an alternative perspective derived from a moral judgment position that is just one level higher than the student's level. The teacher's comments are "matched" to the student's judgmental level but are a bit more advanced. This technique was drawn from experimental research showing that "plus one" exposure is the most effective means of inducing positive moral change (Damon, 1988, 138).

Applied Kohlberg seems to be a very appropriate method in ethics teaching for teachers to adapt in schools. The dilemma discussions used in the applied Kohlberg approach could be modified as a method using case study dilemmas. These case studies can be real-life moral dilemmas that students have faced in their life. Tirri has investigated moral dilemmas identified by sixth-grade students and found that those dilemmas are very different from the original ones formulated by Kohlberg (Tirri, 1996b). The real-life dilemmas identified by students could be discussed in the class giving emphases on both justice and care orientations. In that process, students can practice both deductive and inductive thinking processes in the search of the most appropriate solution.

Discourse Ethics

The concept of discourse was first brought up by Habermas in his theory of communicative action (1984). He has identified two approaches in social action: strategic and communicative. In strategic action, the participants adopt a success-oriented attitude by following the rules of rational choice. In communicative actions, the social interactions are coordinated through co-operative achievements of understanding among participants. Discourse ethics is based on two principles. The principle of universalization assumes that "All affected can accept the consequences and the side effects its general observance can be anticipated to have for the satisfaction of everyone's interests (and the consequences are preferred to those of known alternative possibilities for regulation)." (Habermas, 1990, 65). The principle of discourse ethics contains the distinctive idea of an ethics of discourse: "Only those norms can claim to be valid that meet (or could meet) with the approval of all affected in their capacity as participants in a practical discourse" (Habermas, 1990, 66).

In a moral discourse a communicative action is adopted where all the members participate equally. In order to participate in the moral discourse, all the members are presupposed to be truthfully engaged in an attempt to construct a just solution. Another prerequisite is that all the members want the most justice- and care-oriented decision (Oser, 1986, 919). In an educational setting the teacher has to trust his students in advance to be able to have this kind of moral discourse (Oser & Althof, 1993).

In applying the moral discourse to an educational situation, four principles of discursive ethics should be remembered. These principles are: justification, fairness, consequences and universalization. The discourse is always a step back from the reality of the situation. It is an ideal form of solving a problem, In order to understand the situation at hand, one needs to have an understanding of a person's circumstances, knowledge about his needs and motives and an application of contextual rules. Oser has identified seven elements of moral education to which moral discourse can be applied (Oser, 1986, 921).

Oser advocates the discourse ethics approach in moral education because it has the potential of improving teacher-student relationships and the whole school culture. In adopting the discourse approach, the teachers teach their students both responsibility and justice and at the same time encourage social learning (Oser, 1991, 223–226).

Chapter 6

Rules and Recipes
of 'Good' Teaching

Beliefs about good teaching involve adapting an individual's implicit and practical knowledge of teaching, studying, and learning. Beliefs are like knowledge that a person manipulates to achieve certain ends. Beliefs generally refer to personal commitment, while knowledge usually refers to factual propositions. Making decisions is based on theoretical and experimental knowledge that a teacher has gained in the course of her/his teaching experiences. In the background, different beliefs and opinions also have an effect on these judgments. The teacher possesses this knowledge as a more or less organized implicit theory. In teacher education supervision constitutes a natural context in which to clarify a teacher's pedagogical thinking. The supervisor highlights those things which are important to good and effective teaching. We call such advice recipes and try to discover the justifications behind them. The purpose therefore is to describe a normative didactic phenomenon by means of descriptive didactics and to discover the knowledge-base behind the recipes.

The Concept of Belief

Definitions of the concept of belief are various in the educational literature and often the various definitions have only few things in common. Beliefs of the pedagogical thinking form the combination of subjective and experienced based implicit knowledge of teaching and learning and the whole instructional process. However, conceptions of teaching and learning should be understood as conscious beliefs. In the case of conceptions the cognitive components are emphasized compared to the beliefs and their affective characteristics.

Knowledge and belief have been used in reference to teachers thinking. Research has focused on their many aspects and the two concepts are not easily distinguished. While beliefs generally refer to personal commitments, knowledge usually refers to factual propositions and to the understanding behind skilful action. According to Carlderhead (1993, 15), a variety of content and forms of teachers' knowledge has been identified. In teachers' thinking knowledge and beliefs are used as justifications whenever educational decisions are made. While beliefs considered as individuals subjective knowledge might be logically true knowledge has, instead of that, always this property.

Some relevant questions may be posed about the nature of teachers' knowledge. The most important question concerns the qualitative differences in teachers' knowledge. The studies on teachers' thinking try to answer questions like: What is teachers' professional knowledge? How could it be represented in the practice of teaching.

How does the knowledge of teaching relate to the practice of teaching? Professional knowledge includes various components such as teachers' conceptions and constructs, beliefs and principles, and practical knowledge. It is nearly related to values, attitudes, images, views, metaphors, impressions, and knowledge on the substance of the theme. Also Pajares (1992) points out, a great variety of concepts have been used almost inter-changeable and often it is difficult to identify how beliefs can be discernible from knowledge. Frequently the case is that teachers treat their beliefs as knowledge. Thompson (1992, 130) considers beliefs to have the following features:

1. Beliefs can be held with varying degrees of conviction. This dimension of variations is absent from knowledge systems.
2. Beliefs are not consensual. Knowledge must satisfy a truth condition, whereas beliefs are independent of their validity.
3. Knowledge must meet criteria involving evidence, beliefs are often held for reasons that do not meet those criteria; they include affective feelings and evaluations.
4. The philosophy of science accepts that factual knowledge is dependent upon current theories. What may have been claimed as knowledge may later be judged as belief, and vice versa.

Abelson (1979) defined beliefs in terms of people manipulating knowledge for a particular purpose. Already Rokeach (1968) argued that all beliefs have a cognitive component representing knowledge. In addition to the cognitive components affective and behavioral components are essential parts of beliefs. However, Rokeach (1968) subsumes knowledge as a component of belief, Nisbett & Ross (1980) as cognitive researchers subsume belief as a type of knowledge.

Teachers' pedagogical knowledge is here understood as a belief system because it is more informative than treating beliefs separately. Meyer (1993) uses the term *Unterrichstbild* as a concept of the instructional process when speaking of a belief system. This concept of instructional process is theoretically based on the theory of attitudes (e.g. Statt, 1990) and thus elaborated further.

The area of beliefs is extensive and their components influence each other. In accordance to Green (1971), a belief has a quasi logical structure. This structure follows the individual way of thinking and is closely related to the knowledge system. The beliefs form the common foundation of her/his thinking. When trying to understand some aspect of this totality all the other aspects must be taken into consideration.

Green (1971) describes a belief system as a metaphor for examining and describing how an individual's beliefs are organized. Belief systems are dynamic in nature, undergoing change and restructuring as individuals evaluate their beliefs against their experiences. According to another dimension the beliefs are either central or peripheral in their psychological strength. Beliefs are also held in clusters. This clustering makes it possible to hold conflicting sets of beliefs. Green argued that logical primacy and psychological centrality are orthogonal dimensions, noting that they are two different features of a belief.

Beliefs about Teaching

Hoy & Rees (1977) found that student teachers start with control-oriented belief systems that emphasize the importance of maintaining order and good discipline and importance of guiding the activities of students. These beliefs change slightly during the teacher education developing more liberal and child-centered, but when encountering full-time teaching experience they revert more control-oriented again. Powerful control-oriented ideology in schools usually reinforces the beliefs the student teachers have acquired being students themselves.

The concept of the instructional process is a system of norms, background theories, conviction, attitudes and guiding concepts of teaching. They develop through teaching practice and to a great extent influence the way the teaching task is approached. The theory of teaching (general didactics) aims at identifying the phenomenon of good teaching. Grigutscht (1996) speaks about didactical motivation concerning the good teaching.

The concept of the instructional process is closely related to the theory of attitudes. With regard to the concept of beliefs basic modifications of attitude theories may have an effect on the conceptualization of the instructional process. According to vom Hofe (1995, 98), on the psychological level there are many different and partially contra dictionary concepts, on the didactical level, however, these contradictions are balanced by the theories of teaching.

What is then the functional character of the conceptualization of the instructional process? Of the Törner's (1996, 61) three main structures the regulating system of different beliefs concerning teaching is the first one. Second, the concept of the instructional process usually includes content as a possible indicator of successful teaching. Because the concept of the instructional process is transmitted through different beliefs it gives a relevant estimation of the teachers' experiences of the teaching-studying-learning process. Getting to know the concept of the instructional process offers a method to evaluate indirectly the rules and recipes that have been used. Both are focused on the personal experiences of cognitive elements from the past. The concept of the instructional process may act as an indicator of the teachers' academic studies or their professional development or of their in-service teacher education. It may also reflect students' experiences of the teaching-studying-learning process. It may even be used in considering the educational system in schools. Third, the teachers' subjective knowledge is usually quite stable and has a tendency to remain unchanged. Experienced teachers are no exception in this respect and have, through their long practice, acquired a conviction of effective and good teaching. That is why teaching often is normative and you must act according to some rules to be effective.

Therefore, pedagogical rules and recipes are an essential part of the teachers' beliefs of good and successful teaching (Meyer, 1980, 46–51). Meyer has divided recipes in eight categories. These can be understood as a basis of the concept of the instructional process. There are about four hundred recipes or tips how to act in various teaching-studying-learning situations.

The classification of recipes by Meyer is made in a very intuitive way rising from the teachers' everyday practices. The rules consist of e.g. how to socialize to the role of the student, how to maintain discipline, how to use teaching methods, how to use communication skills etc. (Mitzscke *et al.*, 1984)

The interesting point of view is getting to know what the rules and recipes in the teachers' pedagogical thinking mean. What kind of recipes the concept of the instructional process consists of? How the belief of good teaching is conveyed through good teaching? In German to teach is *Unterrichten*. The word 'right' (richtig) is hidden in this concept. Accordingly *unterrichten* includes the teachers' aim to act correctly. Relying on rules and recipes is doing something correctly and the consequences are satisfactory.

Independent Thinking Through Advice and Guidance

In education, the knowledge and the skills of one generation have generally been passed to the next generation by encouraging the young people to study and develop a critical attitude. This has taken place and still takes place when adopting professional skills to those training for a certain profession. In teacher education this means the practical advice and guidelines given in teaching practice which are supposed to help the student to find her/his own professional practices. The supervisors, often called experts in literature, are expected to possess useful knowledge that novices do not yet have. This knowledge is explicated to the students during supervision.

There are a lot of situations for practicing teaching. For example, the program of class teacher education in our context is based on the idea of integrating theory and practice to develop innovator-teachers who can analyze teaching situations with the help of thinking based on research methodology. Hytönen (1995, 77–83) describes the principles of integrating theory and practice this way: Integration presupposes differentiation and integration must be carried out mainly through practice towards theory. The principles in integrating theoretical studies with practice teaching are:

1. Practice teaching must be started as early as possible.
2. Interaction between theory and practice must be continuous.
3. Each practice period has aims and a character of its own.
4. Practice teaching should progress from simple elements towards complex units.
5. The theoretical studies which give support to a particular practice teaching period must be written out in the curriculum of the teacher education program.

The goal is to make student-teachers capable of reflecting on their actions and aims. Teaching practice is the context for determining teachers' pedagogical thinking. It is a natural situation in which supervisors, as experts, explicate their knowledge in discussions with novices.

The character of a teacher's professional knowledge is implicit. Implicit concepts of knowledge are usually regarded as elements of expertness. Teachers, especially those teachers who work as supervisors of practice teaching, form implicit theories and beliefs about teaching and learning, and those theories and beliefs direct their teaching activities. Teachers' implicit theories are difficult to perceive, except by observing the interaction in an instructional process or otherwise getting to know teachers' thinking. (Clark & Peterson, 1986, 255–296.)

Kroksmark (1990, 12) talks about how everyone, whether s/he is a teacher or not, has a subconscious opinion of what teaching is and how it should be carried out in order for learning to take place. This spontaneous pedagogical knowledge, which we all have a certain amount of is called "*autodidactics*" by Kroksmark . It means the pedagogical knowledge a layman has. It comes "automatically" from our consciousness and it is explicated e.g. when "the man on the street" goes in to a teaching situation and begins to teach. Of course s/he wants to do her/his best to accomplish the teaching activity. Also, when discussing with pupils' parents they often unconsciousness explicate their beliefs or images of good teaching.

Jank & Meyer (1991, 40–45) discuss the conception of teaching (*Unterrichtsbild*). We all have images of what teaching is. These are holistic and practical images of the progress of good or bad teaching, of the atmosphere, the requirements and the results. Literature also mentions subjective theories. Jank & Meyer emphasize that becoming conscious of the structure and quality of one's conception of teaching, internalized during a person's school years, is a condition for goal-oriented improvement of one's teaching activities. This awareness occurs explicitly with the help of pedagogical knowledge.

Everyone has a layman's image of teaching; students starting their teacher education have it as well. A person who has worked as an untrained teacher for many years may have developed a conception of teaching through experience. It would be interesting to know whether it essentially differs from the teaching concept of a so-called professional. In any case, a beginner as well as a professional practitioner produces a *modus agendi* for her/himself and for her/his pupils, based on her/his own knowledge, opinions and beliefs. How does this happen and what are her/his solutions based on?

One way to clarify a teachers' pedagogical thinking is to structure those things that teachers find important in a teaching process—that is, to discover the advice and guidelines the teachers produce, and above all to find out how this advice is justified. Within teacher training the supervision forms a natural context for clarifying a teachers' pedagogical thinking. There a teacher expresses aspects that s/he regards as important in good teaching. This "thinking out loud" takes place when one supervises a student teacher.

From Descriptive to Normative and Vice Versa

In the theory of teaching the question about normativity causes continuous problems. Lahdes (1986, 89–90) says that the normative side of the theory of teaching is usually conceived as the "art of teaching"; the descriptive side again is taken for a descriptive, utmost objective study of teaching. This kind of research can be done without paying attention to normativity, that is, the rules and guidelines on which the teaching process is founded. Forming a brilliant teaching theory, from which to derive teaching advice, however, is difficult. Lahdes states that normative teaching theory is justified if it is supported by a meaningful teaching theory or if the advice is logically-derived from theory. The problem here is the coexistence of educational aims because now we are talking about values, which are agreements by nature.

If normativity is thus understood, it will provide a real possibility for discussion and independence in thinking for all participants. Because every teacher and supervisor has her/his own world of values and her/his own opinions about good teaching, which cannot be denied regardless of their implicity, it is interesting to try to determine the factors behind giving advice. It means that a normative phenomenon will be approached by the means of a descriptive theory of teaching. Lahdes (1986, 88) describes the unity of the teaching theory and empirical reality with the help of the following figure. It shows the structural elements of the research and has been adapted to teaching theory research.

The figure below shows the cyclic nature of pedagogical thinking. Empirical reality and theory are in opposite in the way that it is almost impossible to study theory while teaching. During teacher education studies and working in the field, one has learned a lot of theory on teaching. They help the teacher to think logically and to make decisions when planning her/his teaching. Every time one makes a decision, s/he moves from descriptive to normative. Teacher produces advice to her/himself to accomplish the teaching activities. During teaching, the teacher evaluates her/his teaching and makes new decisions about how to continue her/his teaching. After the teaching activities, the teacher has more time to evaluate her/his teaching, to learn more and to draw conclusions. Then a new cycle restarts. Perhaps we can say that the more a teacher has gone through these cycles the more experience s/he has. Usually this means

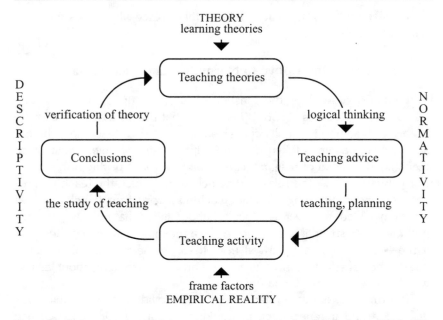

Figure 3. The connection of didactic theory and empirical reality (Lahdes, 1986, 88).

that expert teachers have great many teaching years behind them. But is it possible to become an expert teacher earlier than usual? Perhaps, but does this mean that a teacher must be able to improve the quality of her/his thinking in a relatively short time? That is why we are interested to find out how teachers move in their thinking from the descriptive to the normative. The most interesting thing is—not the advice itself—but the arguments behind it. They hopefully show what can be understood as descriptive and as normative in pedagogical thinking.

Teaching Recipes

Student teachers usually ask their supervisors for confirmation of their own activity in the classroom. Although the supervisor thinks that s/he has already given plenty of advice for carrying out the teaching activity, expressed in simple terms or thus: "I'd like you to think about this yourself. What do you have to do to master the situation in class?", the students repeatedly respond, "Please, tell me what I still have to do." In other words the students are very hungry for recipes. Meyer (1991, 30–51), who has written about "teaching receptology", sees certain reasons for this phenomenon:

Receptes

1. Practice in teacher training is more directed by recipes for teaching than by pedagogically-argued and empirically-verified teaching theories.
2. Giving advice and guiding aim to secure the balance between the beginning teacher and the pupils.
3. The recipes help teachers and pupils in creating sensible circumstances as far as learning results are concerned.
4. The recipes, however, cannot be scientifically defended; their requirements and justifications are generalizations rising from everyday practices.
5. The advice given to the student teacher replaces the lacking routine.

Meyer regards the recipes as unambiguous—or at least meant to be such—operational advice for carrying out instruction. They include explicit or implicit assumptions about situational use and the setting of aims. They have risen from teaching situations and have been generalized. The recipes are not stated as theoretically- or empirically-argued, although this would be possible in many cases. The justification of the recipes arises from their successful use. Meyer adds critical reflection to the use of advice. This means that the advice and guidelines have to be good, in other words pedagogically-legitimate, theoretically-derived and empirically-verified. Secondly, the recipient of the advice has to be sensible in his applications, avoid false generalizations and perceive the implicit conditions of use and aims of the advice. (Meyer, 1991, 46–51.)

Speaking about recipes, it is useful to define what they actually mean. Meyer (1991, 49) collects the previous arguments and displays the following concept:

> "The recipes are meant to be unambiguous operational advice to secure a successful teacher-pupil relationship and positive learning results. The operational advice arises from concrete teaching situations and is universal. It serves classroom routine situations and is not theoretically derived or empirically verified."

The above-mentioned definition is here used as a working definition. Foremost, however, it will be aimed to clarify the argument that the given advice and guidelines are not theoretically-derived or empirically-verified.

Drerup (1988) comments on the recipe literature published in Germany at the end of the 1970s and in the 1980s. He reviews the discussion about the origin, use and functions of recipes for the use of teachers helping them to get started to develop professionally. This type of literature has been commonly criticized because there are so many problems in the use of knowledge and values in the recipe literature.

In German and Dutch recipe literature (see, e.g., Grell & Grell, 1993; Meyer, 1980; Mitzschke et al., 1984; Alfs et al., 1985), the arguments behind giving advice have not been clarified. They have collected recipes, but not assumptions behind them. In this respect we try to penetrate deeper in studying the phenomenon.

In Great Britain Brown et al. (1995) have collected 500 tips for teachers. The idea of the book is to help teachers to provide student-centered and active learning. The book is designed to be dipped-into rather than read cover-to-cover. This purpose of the book shows that it does not include teaching theory and the tips are not systematically-justified or based on research. The themes Brown et al. have in their book are: 1) Techniques for effective teaching and classroom management, 2) planning and assessment, 3) using teaching and learning resources well, 4) supporting pupils' learning, 5) providing personal and pastoral care and 6) being an effective colleague.

Kansanen (1991) suggests that the supervisor has a certain base of knowledge which s/he leans on when giving advice and guidelines. It can be practical in nature but it has sufficient justifications. Is the supervising process scientific in nature and does the supervisor move from the descriptive to the normative when giving advice? He asks which paradigm the supervisor relies on when s/he draws conclusions from the study results. He says that the only way to prove normative advice is discussion between supervisor and student:

> "The advice is always normative and the only way to prove it is through discussion in which both parts have the same right to say what they think. If the arguments are based on the theory of teaching or on the research reports, even better. Can we assume that our supervisors are capable of that?" (Kansanen, 1991, 259.)

Dunn & Taylor (1993) have clarified the giving of advice on a more general level. They have seen the advice in two ways, as so-called teacher advice and consultant advice. In their article they make a reference to studies of expertise, which indicates that competence is acquired in the practice and not during professional schooling per se. The writers have recommended that more advanced professionals use so called advice-strategies in working with novices. These strategies are derived from hierarchical analyses of expertise. They see advice-strategy as "instruction" that encourages a learner to look for relationships or patterns to facilitate development of conceptual knowledge or higher level rules that may be used in subsequent problem solving. Advice-strategies do not teach intellectual skills directly.

When finding out the advice, Dunn & Taylor used such questions as: What is the nature of advice that cooperating teachers give to student teachers? They wanted to know if the advice is primarily "teacher" as opposed to "consultant" advice and if it is likely to promote transfer. They also clarified whether there are differences in the advice that experienced cooperating teachers give to student teachers as opposed to cooperating teachers working with their first student teacher. For their purpose, Dunn & Taylor defined advice in this way: ". . . a recommendation for a decision or course of action coming from the cooperating teacher and directed toward the student teacher". It seems that experienced cooperating teachers give more advice than new cooperating teachers, but the distribution of the advice was quite the same.

Harrison (1978, 71–72) sees recipes as intellectual tools in the process of making, and as such they can be used well or badly. A written recipe is a piece of theory, the theoretical claim that by doing such and such a certain result will follow. Following any recipe is a practical matter and the understanding involved in following it is essentially practical understanding. He says that the recipe itself will not be able to state the criteria of rationality, irrationality, silliness or sense involved. If recipes are practical they are for the practical use of the materials with which they are concerned.

The Place of Recipes in Teachers' Pedagogical Thinking

The following figure shows how we see the relationships between advice, justifications and intentions given by supervisors. We think that the advice is normative, it is hierarchically the most concrete phenomenon when supervizing a student teacher. The advice come from the knowledge base the supervisor has. The justifications are on this level. We suppose that sometimes the supervisors tell aloud her/his justifications and sometimes not, often they lie in the background. The intentions are in this context the broadest concept, and teacher's theories, values and beliefs are in the background when teacher forms her/his intentions.

The advice and guidelines given by supervisors are naturally connected to situations in which they are given, and on the other hand connected to situations where they can be used. (Meyer, 1980, 49; Drerup, 1988, 114.) Part of the advice is anticipated by nature, in other words, it has been given before anything has happened or the student's teaching has been evaluated. It is generalizing by nature. The effectiveness of this advice depends on how the student is able to reflect on it in her/his own

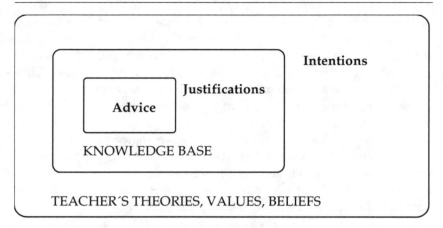

Figure 4. The relationships between the advice, justifications and intentions given by supervisors.

teaching practice. Meyer uses the concept *"Reflexion von Rezepten"*, the reflection of recipes.

Maybe the benefit of the recipes is in the reflection. The advice and guidelines now offer the student reasons to think, not a direct path to effective teaching. The teaching situation seems to be so complex to many a beginning teacher that the planning phase takes a great deal of time. After having lived through the preinteractive phase intensively, the new teacher may find it difficult during the interactive stage to see the reasons why the situation does not work as expected. At the postinteractive phase, when the student evaluates the work together with her/his supervisor, it may be fruitful if the supervisor points out things to pay attention to. Much advice arises in situations when advice is given for the following teaching situation, on the basis of evaluation.

In the worst case, one can suspect that in giving advice and guidelines in a very normative way, indoctrination could even be seen. One main goal of teacher education is to form a teacher capable of independent and critical acquisition of knowledge and its evaluation. To reach this aim, research-based teacher education offers a promising prospect because the student knows how knowledge is produced and also constructs it her/himself.

Chapter 7

Processes of Supervision in Teaching Practice

The topic of this chapter is supervision in teacher education and the identification of the theoretical issues that lie behind all teaching practices. Supervisory discourse is seen as situated cognition, where the supervisor fosters a student's thinking skills. A decisive criterion for the discourse is how we view success in the teaching profession. The number of concrete procedures depends on the understanding of a teacher's independent role in the teaching-studying-learning process. In order to clarify the alternatives, a model of a supervisor's action is outlined. The interaction of a supervisor's viewpoint with the viewpoint of a student teacher is the crucial aspect here, in that it reveals the pedagogical thinking on both sides.

Conceptualizing Teachers' Thinking

Teachers' thinking has become a central issue, also in supervisory settings. The tradition of preservice supervision is as old as teacher education – only the forms and underlying theoretical assumptions have changed during the years. The supervisory model of action has reflected the paradigm that has been in existence in educational research. The empiric-analytical tradition of supervision, that has been common to the positivistic paradigm, has been shifting. This does not mean that the basic assumptions about the normative nature of teaching are not accure today. The normativeness of teaching is still the starting point of research on pedagogy. One of the interesting questions today is how supervisors change from the descriptive to the normative, how they reason and what will count as a good reason. A supervisor's model of action in post-observational conferences can be seen as a reflection of her/his conception of supervision. Conceptions differ; the underlying knowledge base, thinking skills and beliefs are seen as central when trying to understand and interpret supervisors' models of action.

Research on teacher thinking has established a place for itself. As Pope (1993, 21–22) puts it: teacher-thinking research has adopted a different paradigm from that which has dominated educational research in the past. It is an approach where teaching is regarded as actions performed by reflective practitioners. A current core assumption is that teacher-thinking researchers are trying to understand and interpret ways in which teachers make sense of, adjust to and create the educational environment within their schools and classrooms. Yet the field of teacher thinking is diverse in terms of theoretical and methodological approaches. Pope (1993, 23) lists four rationales existing in current research on teacher thinking:

1. To develop conceptual models of teacher thinking
2. To evaluate critically how teachers think
3. To catalog different kinds of thinking among different groups of teachers
4. To help teachers themselves clarify their thinking to form a foundation that enables them to communicate with other teachers and to develop and extend their theories. In this rationale, teachers are seen as active agents in the development of educational events.

The first three of these categories are seen as "outside in" rationales, the fourth as an "inside out" rationale. The focus of research on teacher thinking and the methodology used has shifted. There is much more emphasis on the fourth rationale (Pope 1993, 23). A teacher's voice, as Elbaz (1990) calls it, needs a language, a common framework of concepts. Researchers in this process can be seen as those who make it possible to explicate the implicit by giving an explicit description of and conceptual framework for a teacher's cognitive frame of reference. Academic teacher education implements research methodology and students learn how to think theoretically during their studies. Understanding and discussing research results provides students with the knowledge needed in professional decision-making.

Situated Cognition

The psychological study of cognition and thinking has two parts. Research on topics of productive, higher order, critical, and creative thinking has not been as much in the focus of interest as topics concerning performance on specific tasks. Research on these general thinking abilities has progressed slowly, compared with the progress of the study of cognitive structures and procedures. Greeno (1989, 134) argues that some of the causes of this relatively slow progress may be implicit in the theories and framing assumptions about thinking and learning.

The theory of situated cognition proposes that thinking is situated in physical and social contexts. Cognition, including thinking, knowing, and learning, can be considered as a relation involving an agent in a situation, rather than as an activity in an individual's mind. As well as thinking being situated in physical and social contexts, thinking and learning are situated in contexts of beliefs and understandings about cognition that differ between individuals and social groups. (Greeno, 1989, 135) Considering the ideas of situated cognition, successful thinking consists of aspects of general thinking skills as well as a specific knowledge base.

Although research on cognition, thinking and teacher thinking has been abundant, critics have questioned how its findings can be of use in teacher education. Lampert & Clark (1990, 22) argue that current ideas of cognitive theory and research on teacher thinking lead to suggesting that the conventional academic pattern of producing general principles from particular cases and delivering those principles to novices may not be the most appropriate form for teacher education to take.

Questions about defining or operationalizing the knowledge in teaching have raised discussions of sources and outlines of required knowledge base for teaching and teacher preparation. A common view is that an adequate base of facts are needed, but what these facts are divide teacher educators. If the knowledge base is too narrow, there is a risk that teaching will be trivialized and its complexity ignored (Shulman, 1987, 69).

When considering the general thinking skills the major question in teacher education has been how to educate reflective practitioners. Is it possible to teach student teachers to reflect? Professional practitioners require an academic quality of thinking to see and solve pedagogical problems in their classrooms, schools and in the society. The quality of teachers thoughts interests McNamara (1990), who argues that it is possible to teach how to be critical. The guidance needs to be explicit and detailed. To develop a student's knowledge about teaching requires subjective situational knowledge of the practitioner as a starting point. The theory building in pedagogy can be seen as an implicit process, from practical reflection to theorizing, and back again. Supervisors, when fostering a student's thinking skills, need to identify the problems students attempt to solve and examine the tentative solutions they offer to these problems.

According to Calderhead (1993, 14), much of the debate about whether and how research on teaching might be of use in teacher education rests on narrow, stereotyped assumptions, both about the nature of research and the nature of practice. The development of further understanding of professional development may be dependent on recognizing the complexity and diversity of both research and practice and acknowledging that the relationship between the two is interactive and multifaceted. Floden & Klinzing (1990, 17) identify three ways research on teacher thinking can affect teacher education. First, as a content, secondly as a source to develop methods for teacher education instruction, and finally it can influence educational policies that are important to teacher education. Lampert & Clark (1990, 23) argue that research on teacher thought and action, in the context of practice, has prompted educators to ask and answer new questions about their practices, and to use new methods in examining and reflecting on teaching.

Successful Teaching Profession

Successful teacher education requires a clearly defined paradigm, a rich knowledge base and aims, objectives and methods to foster students' thinking skills. Shulman (1987, 7–8) argues that teacher education, if trying to educate professionals, necessitates a solid knowledge base. Yet the results of research on effective teaching are not an adequate source of evidence on which to base a definition of the knowledge base of teaching. The actual and potential sources for a knowledge base are many. There are seven of these categories: content knowledge; general pedagogical knowledge; curriculum knowledge, knowledge of educational ends, purposes and values; knowledge of contexts; and knowledge of learners and their characteristics. Pedagogical content knowledge is of special interest because it represents the blending of content and pedagogy into an understanding of how particular topics, problems, or issues are organized, represented, and adapted to the diverse interests and abilities of learners, and on the other hand presented for instruction.

Critics say that knowledge base as a basis of good teaching is too intellectualistic and rationalistic in nature. Van Manen (1994a, 138) argues that teaching is difficult, not only because these knowledge bases of teaching are complex; teaching is difficult also, and especially, because it is essentially a normative pedagogical activity. Pedagogy implies distinguishing between what is appropriate or inappropriate, good or bad, right or wrong, suitable or less suitable for children. Van Manen (1994a, 154–155) suggests that the practice of teaching actually relies more appropriately on the unique and particular virtues. Virtues are indications of the educated character of a person. They answer the question of whether a person is well prepared for certain life tasks and responsibilities. The interesting point about virtues is that they cannot be reduced to rules or moral principles. The question of the possibility of the virtuous nature of teaching is a practical concern that introduces itself in situations where teachers interact with students (1994, 162). It requires a practical type of knowledge of how people's actions relate to motives, intentions, emotions, feelings and moods, and that some people possess more of this sensitive insight. Fenstermacher (1994a, 218) in opposition to van Manen, argues that virtues cannot be strengthened or advanced in the absence of practical reasoning. The tendency in modern virtue ethics according to Fenstermacher (1994a, 219) is to employ a non-intellectual concept of virtue, to reject the role of ethical theory and to rehabilitate traditional forms of moral conservatism.

The concept of virtue in the research on teacher thinking is difficult. As Pope (1993, 19–22) argues, language has a central role in the development of a paradigm. In this light, the field of teacher thinking could be assessed as pre-paradigmatic. She questions whether the language used within teacher thinking research is incommensurable. When comparing these two aspects, the knowledge bases and virtues of teaching profession are not necessarily opposites or pejorative domains, rather they can be seen as complementary aspects of teaching profession. In teacher education the context consists of the defined knowledge base and general thinking skills – virtues in this setting can be seen as personal traits.

Kansanen (1993) considers that it is not possible to be in the teaching profession without personal values or without taking sides between various alternatives that continuously come into reflection in a teacher's thinking. The important question he poses is: "How do these values come into the educational process and what is the teacher's role in this process?". The first way for values to come into the educational process is the formal decisions of the curriculum makers. The process gets its steering elements from the curriculum, and the teacher is a link in this process. The teacher must consider and evaluate these values before they are internalized in her/his thinking. If this does not happen, the educational process is steered from outside. The second way for values to enter the educational process is directly through the teacher's thinking, that is guided by various factors like personality, experience, and teacher education. Also, the teacher's personal conception of education, teaching, studying and learning have a central position in this process. (Kansanen, 1993, 51) Questions of ethical theory should be seen broadly. As Fenstermacher (1994a, 219) puts it: it is only reflection, argument and theory that can lead us to fruitful ethical practice. Reason and argument seem more consistent with practice than do habit and non-intellectual orientation. Moral philosophy and virtue ethics are both orientations to reflect successful teaching. In teacher education they should be seen meta-analytical methods to foster student's thinking skills.

Greeno (1989, 134) suggests that successful thinking in specific domains uses knowledge that is specific. At the same time, there are aspects of thinking skill that are common across domains. This possibility has encouraged the idea that there are teachable components of a general thinking ability. What kind of thinking should be taught is a question that can be answered only when knowing the theoretical framework a teacher education program is committed to.

The Supervisor's Model of Action

Individuals are often unable or unwilling to present their beliefs, which makes it difficult to understand beliefs and belief systems. A researcher must make inferences about individuals' underlying states. For this reason, beliefs cannot be observed or measured but must be inferred from what people say, intend and do. One possible way is to ask supervisors to examine the beliefs and assumptions they bring into the supervisory situation and the goals towards which they are working.

Implicit theories have been a common interest of many researchers from the beginning of the tradition. Within this tradition, Handal & Lauvås (1988, 14, 36) have presented a practical theory of supervision. They include in it an integrated but ever-changing system of knowledge, experience, and structures, as well as philosophical, political and ethical values. Handal & Lauvås (1988) place these elements in a three-level model, which is a commonly-known and used way of presenting focuses of abstraction. The first level deals with the action or practice, the second with the theoretical and practical reasoning, the third level consists of ethical reasoning. In supervisory practice, reasons operationalize a person' s practical theory.

The supervisor's model of action (Figure 5) presents four fields of knowledge that supervisors should have a conception of when they are supervising student teachers. The fields of knowledge are drawn from the theories and models of supervision (van Manen, 1977; Schön, 1983; Zeichner, 1983; Zeichner & Tabachnick, 1982; Zeichner & Liston, 1985; Clarke, 1970; Handal & Lauvås, 1988).

1. Concept of the theory of teaching

Theories of teaching give the supervisor the conceptual framework s/he needs in the supervisory situation. The supervisor needs to know theories, models and conceptualizations of teaching to describe and explain the content knowledge of teaching.

2. Concept of the content knowledge (didactics) of teaching
Knowledge of the didactical questions concerning special subject matters give the supervisor the basics for pedagogical problem solving. Shulman (1987, 8) calls this knowledge base pedagogical content knowledge.

3. Concept of development of student teachers personality
The supervisor must have a solid idea of the student teacher's professional development process to know how to help the student to find the right questions and possible answers in the situations of reflecting on teaching. This may happen when the supervisory conferences deal with questions of ethics, values and beliefs, but is clearly dealing with the general thinking skills that are to be promoted.

4. Concept of interaction
To know models of interaction helps the supervisor to identify different approaches in the supervisory conferences, and to orient in the teaching situations.

The supervisors' model of action is based on the idea that the underlying assumptions modify the action in a supervisory situation. How the knowledge base and belief systems are formed depends upon the personal history and manner of orientation a person has. They are connected to the personal theory of education. The implicit theory of teaching is dynamic, like the other elements of the model. The basic underlying assumption concerns the nature of knowledge and the role of the individual in society. These assumptions influence the way supervisors interpret their roles as supervisors and how students interpret their roles in being supervised. The supervisors differ in at least two ways that they understand these fields of knowledge.

1. What is the knowledge base like?
The main difference is the one between theory and experience. Both of these two poles should direct the action. They are not opposites but rather relative priorities and emphases that give the orientation to the action. Supervisors should use both orientations when developing their supervisory skills. The practical knowledge in the situation is not enough; reading educational literature is needed as well.

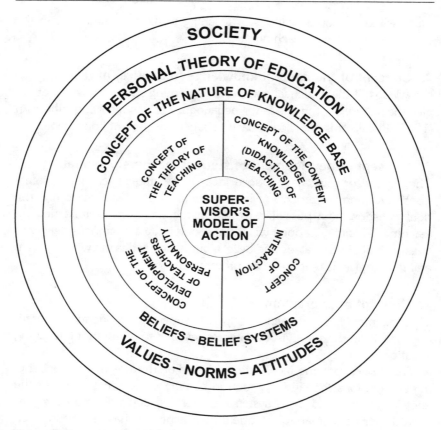

Figure 5. Supervisors´ model of action.

2. How well are they aware of their own thinking and acting?

The more the teacher reflects on the premises of her/his teaching and the whole instructional process, the more the questions of value come into her/his consciousness. The purposes of the curriculum and the teacher's own intentions may integrate into a personal conception of the instructional process. Teachers work with different degrees of consciousness, depending on their commitment to the aims and goals directing their action (Kansanen, 1993, 58). Supervisors should reflect upon their own practical theories of supervision, they should be aware of the premises of their thinking to be able to develop their supervisory skills. This model could be used to give an orientation to the main fields that should be involved when trying to understand a teacher's knowledge base and belief systems in a supervisory situation.

PART III

APPROACHING THE PRACTICE
OF TEACHING

Chapter 8

Teachers' Pedagogical Minds

The chapter presents a generalized overview of teachers' pedagogical knowledge (what is known?) and the processes of knowing (how is it known?). Through consideration of the empirical data derived from narrative interviews of 29 primary school teachers, common features of teachers' pedagogical knowledge and knowing are identified and conceptualized. The chapter divides into two sections. The first section provides the results of the representational analysis (what is known?), and the second concentrates on the presentational analysis (how is it known?). In both sections, which are interrelated, the findings are summarized by means of an interpretative framework meant to identify teachers' pedagogical thinking.

Method and Data Analysis

This section of the study is based on the narrative interviews of 29 elementary school teachers. The narrative interview gave necessary structure while at the same time leaving space for the teachers to tell their stories and narratives in their own words. When this happened the interviewer assumed the role of an active and accepting listener.

The teachers were chosen from a body of teachers that had supervised student teachers in their own classrooms for a few weeks. This selective procedure made it possible to obtain different kinds of teachers for the study. Teachers have reported themselves to be "traditional", "progressive", favoring "alternative pedagogical approaches". The narrative interviews took 1.5–2 hours per teacher and they were conducted by one of the authors. The interviews were tape-recorded and transcribed.

In their narratives teachers talked quite freely and enthusiastically with the interviewer. The data is rich and diverse and in many cases it resembles a sort of "authentic conversation" between the teacher and the researcher. Here the authentic means that the conversation bears a close relationship and resemblance to the tasks typically facing real practitioners. After each interview had been carried out notes were made on the place of the interview. The attitude of the person interviewed towards the interviewer was also noted. A great majority of the respondents were analyzed with positive features (i.e. "very interested" or "showed moderate interest") as well as positive attitudes ("cordial, warm, open" and "kind and polite in a usual way").

Gradually it became more evident that the data can also be interpreted as narrative interviews (Cortazzi, 1993, 55–58); and as teachers' stories (Carter & Doyle, 1987, Carter, 1993; Kelchtermans, 1993; Tappan & Brown, 1989; Mattingly, 1989). Narratives elicited from interviews were usually in the form of a summary, short and to the point. Story telling seemed to be something implicit in teachers' knowledge. After several data analyses the landscape of teachers' knowledge seemed increasingly storied. Bruner's (1986) narrative mode of knowing seemed more and more appropriate to the data.

The analysis was a two-fold process. First, our perspective focused on the current phenomenon: That is, how teachers' knowledge could be represented in an adequately coherent way. The first analysis was labeled as representational analysis focusing on the question: What teachers' narratives represented? The second perspective focused on the interrelated nature of teachers' knowledge: How teachers' knowledge was presented in narrative interviews? The second analysis was labeled as presentational analysis. (Freeman, 1996).

In both analysis the concept of frame was important. According to Goffman (1974, 8), any event can be described in terms of a focus, a certain keynote to understand the whole phenomenon. Frame is the concept Goffman (1974, 10) uses to refer to those basic elements of the data as the researcher is able to identify them. Frames are contextual and practical by nature. Barnes (1992, 18) has developed the idea of frame in educational settings. According to him, teachers' professional frames can be considered by the ways in which teachers perceive and execute their professional tasks. Teachers' frames are not solely made up of information of teaching and learning. In addition, they also incorporate a complex system of teachers' personal values and priorities in general. Frames are often based on teachers' deep-rooted personal assumptions about people and society in general and thus are closely related to teachers' belief systems.

Representational Analysis—What the Data Said?

Basically teachers discussed three issues: 1) their teaching, 2) their students, and 3) themselves as teachers. The issues were not separate, instead teachers tend to discuss them in quite an integrative manner: in teachers' "voices" those three themes could often be heard simultaneously: when teachers were talking about their teaching, at the same time, they told things about their students and about their own character as a teacher. This indicated that these themes were at least partly patterned or organized. Using these three categories the data could be re-read in a way that gave it more coherence and made it more explicit.

Teaching was mainly regarded from two aspects: from 'what' and 'how' aspects. 'What' aspects related usually to the content issues of teaching. 'How' aspects dealt with the issues of teaching methods and methods of the social organization of the classroom. From these two the latter ones dominated the scene. Teachers reported what kinds of teaching methods they favored and for what reasons. These statements were closely related to the more personal views of teaching in general, i.e. what was regarded as good teaching. Some teachers thought that good teaching is the achievement of a mastery of a certain area of knowledge or skill; others reflected that good teaching helps students learn to be independent and healthy individuals, some thought that good teaching helps students learn so that their forms of thinking are broadened. Teachers' personal views of teaching seemed to be related with their practical decisions about what was to be taught and especially how it should be taught.

Teachers could not talk about their teaching without talking about their students—it is the students that they teach. It is the students who practically defined teachers' teaching. According to teachers, their teaching was mainly defined by their students by two means: 1) by students' studying activities, and 2) by student behavior. Both were closely related with teachers' teaching. These themes appeared in each other and they seemed to be nearly inseparable. What is of interest is that when teachers described their students' activities they spoke quite rarely about students' learning. Instead, they talked explicitly and implicitly about students' *studying* and how their teaching was related to their students' studying activities.

Teachers' talk of teaching and of students was closely related with themselves as teachers. Almost every theme of the data was covered by this personal tone of *professional self* but there were some focal points where this personal blueprint was stronger than elsewhere. The question of how the teacher described her/himself as a teacher seemed of great importance here. These self-descriptions were often formulated in terms of general and professional ideals that the teacher wanted to accomplish. The practical school contexts where the teachers were working put severe pressures on these high hopes because teachers had to consider what could be done and in what way. Everything that was regarded as 'good'

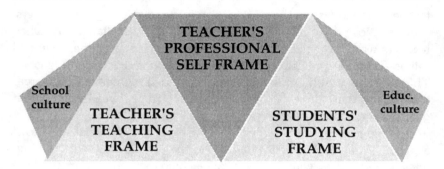

Figure 6. Representational analysis of teachers' pedagogical mind set.

could not be done and many things teachers personally disliked had to be done. This kind of constant uncertainty and doubt on professional issues seemed to be an inherent part of teachers' articulated knowledge.

In the first analysis (see Figure 6) the aim was to grasp the phenomenon examined in order for better practical and conceptual understanding. *Teaching* is the activity of *teachers* and *studying* is the activity of *students*. Both activities belong to each other's professional roles. By using the concepts of teaching and studying the instructional process could be understood as active on behalf of both sides (Kansanen, 1993). It is the active part of the teacher's intention to teach and the student's intention to study which were both reflected in teacher's thinking. These two were linked because it was the teacher's intention to teach which primarily defined the student's situation for her/his studying activities. In this way teaching and studying as active and conscious elements were both pointing to the thing they aimed, learning. Teachers perceived their teaching activities in relation to the their students' studying activities. The interacting network between the teacher and the students in teaching situations was described so enormous that many teachers found it difficult to get a satisfying picture of student learning.

The place and the limits of the *professional self* frame were difficult to define. The teacher as a person was commonly considered by many both within the profession and also outside it to be at the center of the educational process in general and in the classroom process in particular. It matters to teachers themselves, as well as to their students, who and what the teachers are. It turned out that in teaching occupation the self is of major importance because it could not be separated from the craft. As Kelctermans & Vandenberghe (1994, 47) have emphasized: "The self not only influences the way people perceive concrete working conditions and requirements but also the way people act".

The data suggested that the concepts of self and professional self overlapped and their content was related to the context they were used. Hence, what kind of content did educational settings presuppose? In pedagogical contexts we found the concept of manner (cf. Fenstermacher, 1992) useful. In pedagogical practices there seemed to be no special virtues specific to teaching. Rather, the manner of the teacher was more like manner or a virtue in general. And therefore our interest was focusing on the issues how the questions of manner were related to the professional activities teachers performed—i.e. how manner and method were related to each other.

Presentational Analysis—How the Data Said it?

In the first analysis it became evident that the reconstructed framework (Figure 6) could not capture the dynamic nature of teachers' knowledge that could be read out and interpreted from the data. Therefore, in the second analysis the effort was made to seek out more unifying links within the framework. This chapter summarizes some general outlines drawn from the presentational analysis.

In the representational analysis the data was examined for its capacity to reveal what was in teachers' minds and its capability to represent their thinking. According to stance, the words of the language data were assumed to capture teachers' thoughts, beliefs, and knowledge. The "language data" was treated as "data" or information first, and "language" second. The data was studied for what it said, not *how* it said it. Therefore, our next step was to lay open how the language data *presents* meaning in words. In this second analysis, teachers' words were taken for their capacity to reveal some main features how the language data was put together in their presentations.

On the first level teachers mainly *described practical activities* of their teaching, their students' studying activities, and student behavior. Perhaps this is due to the fact that both teachers' and students' professional roles are closely tied with teaching and studying activities constantly examined and controlled in the school context. The data provides numerous cases where teachers' teaching activities could not be separated from particular student activities. Teachers' articulated knowledge reflected a keen interactivity between the teachers and the students and between the tasks both perform in the school context.

On the second level teachers *explain actions* examined on the first level. They offer 'good reasons' for doing things the way they do them. When it comes to teaching teachers do not pay much attention to the 'what' aspects of teaching. They tend to regard the content knowledge of teaching as mostly valid. However, the methods teachers use are lively argued. Our data indicates that teachers do possess different views of knowledge and that these views are related to teachers' views about other educational and pedagogical issues. Students' studying methods are an integral part of these different views of knowledge. The data suggested that when teacher's view of knowledge was treated as external-to-the-knower, subject-centered process, the studying methods the teacher tended to favor emphasized on acquisition and mastery of knowledge delivered. However, when teacher's view of knowledge was regarded as internal, the studying methods the teacher favored emphasized processes of student's self-development. What methods were favored depended also on the contextual issues of classrooms. Teachers displayed their personal preferences that they contextualized by using the 'good reasons' they favored.

On the third level teachers *justify practical actions* and their explanations, i.e. the 'good reasons', they gave to their actions. The scene was mainly dominated by teachers' professional self-image. The statements often concerned issues of 'good teacher', 'good teaching', and 'good learning' and they were contextually bounded to the schools and classrooms teachers were working in. The data suggested that teachers tended to justify their actions to themselves by preferring personal views of teaching and student learning, and that these views were argued by contextually and personally bounded 'good reasons'. It is worth noting that this preference of personal does not mean that teachers argue, nor act, solely on a personal basis. Whenever teachers use 'good reasons' based on educational sciences (and they do use them, too!) they usually tend to utilize them up in order to support their already adopted personal views.

The presentational analysis (Figure 7) aimed to get a conceptually more appropriate picture of the phenomenon. The analysis resulted in three interrelated levels of teachers' thinking (*practics*, *epistemics*, and *ethics*) which had two essential characters: 1) the levels were closely integrated to each other, and 2) the levels took place simultaneously in teachers' thinking. Next, an attempt to explore some main ideas, both practical and theoretical, concerning the three reconstructed levels will be made.

Practics is the level where teachers' thinking is directed at their action. This comes as no surprise because teachers' professional tasks are numerous and the majority of them are practical by nature. Just to mention

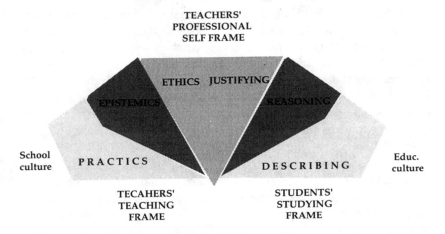

Figure 7. Presentational analysis of teachers' pedagogical mind set.

two fundamental issues: First, in classrooms teachers are in a position where they just cannot stand back and wait—instead teachers have to act constantly. Second, teachers cannot escape their students but stand in relation to them: the pedagogic relation between the teacher and the students is always on. *Practics* is the level of teachers' constant explicit and implicit decision-making in order to keep things going in the classrooms and the schools. This decision-making may be habituated and routinized but, according to teachers' articulated knowledge, it has considerable connections to teachers' general knowledge base.

Teaching is usually associated with epistemological issues due to the fact that teachers perceive their job, at least in part, as having to do with the transmission of knowledge of one sort or another. As the data suggested, teachers do have different views of knowledge and these views are mainly related to the teaching methods they use. Teachers' interest in knowledge is mainly associated with its transmission to students. Teachers are not typically concerned with the knowledge per se, rather than have students comprehended the content taught to them. Instead of knowledge issues teachers turn to their students. Jackson (1986, 56) talks about teachers' "epistemological puzzlement" meaning teachers' psychological orientation to their students in knowledge issues. Teachers' epistemological interest seems to lie in the minds of their students. But what about their own minds? Epistemology deals with knowledge, which is the property of individual minds. For this reason alone epistemology must be interested in the teacher's knowing mind

Goldman (1986) speaks about individual epistemology, or primary epistemology, due to its close connections to the individuals' knowing mind. According to him , individual epistemology is a sort of "architecture of human mind" (Goldman, 1986, 1). Our data indicated that teachers' epistemological dimensions focused on three elements in their knowing: 1) teachers' stance towards the self as a knower, 2) teachers' stance towards students as knowers and learners, and 3) (to a lesser degree) teachers' stance towards the content knowledge of teaching. These epistemological dimensions, implicitly or explicitly, exist in the intellectual and social relationships between teachers and students in their everyday interactions (cf. Lyons, 1990). *Epistemics* describes this many-sided conception of epistemological issues in teachers' knowing mind. Goldman (1986, 9) has presented the concept due to his multidisciplinary conception of epistemology. According to him, *epistemics* is a suitable way of integrating widely shared interests of epistemology

According to Fenstermacher (1994b, 44–45), one way of warranting a knowledge claim in teachers' knowing mind is to offer 'good reasons' for doing something or believing something. The provision of reasons makes the action sensible to those acting. Such reasoning may also show that an action is the "reasonable thing to do, the obvious thing to do, or the only thing to do under the circumstances" (Fenstermacher, 1994, 45). In this way, the 'good reasons' approach integrates the knower and the known together with the specific context the reasoning concerns.

The 'good reasons' teachers provide to support their actions and beliefs often address the ethical aspects, *ethics*, of their teaching. It seems that the criterion mostly used for moral decisions is the teacher's personal preference. Teachers seemed to have a moral vision, a moral sense, however mixed up it may be in any individual person, and this calls attention to the teachers' character. In the school context the teachers' character is of great importance due to the teacher's institutional and practical position. Teachers' personal views of what are the characteristics of a good teacher and how the teacher personally fits them are largely ethical by their nature. The crucial question is in what manner is the teacher performing her/his professional tasks of teaching and organizing students' studying. Teachers' professional tasks are related to the methods they use. In this way methods the teacher uses and her/his personal manner occur together

Summary

This chapter has outlined how teachers' knowledge can be described in a manner that at the same time pays attention to the issues of what teachers' knowledge is about, and how it is organized. We have used an integrated approach to research on teachers' knowledge that uses both the representational approach ("what is said") and the presentational approach ("how is it said"). Before concluding the chapter, an attempt to explore some basic concepts used to describe the teachers' pedagogical mind set will be made.

Why call the mind set pedagogical ? The concept of pedagogy goes beyond teaching to encompass all kinds of encounters where a teacher can contribute to her/his students' upbringing. Defined this way, the pedagogical approach emphasizes the fact that teachers' knowledge is always related to her/his students. Additionally, it means that the pedagogical relationships between teachers and the students are not symmetrical. Teachers are mainly responsible for the pedagogical relationships which occur in schools. Therefore, it is important to study them.

The mind set can be entitled as rhetoric because it is based on teachers' reported views. These do not directly reflect their classroom reality, though they present teachers' perspectives on certain professional issues. According to Packer & Winne (1995), a place or a setting can be seen in teacher thinking itself. The knowledge the teacher thinks about is a joint function of 1) what is in the place of teaching, and 2) what the teacher is capable of perceiving about the place. The framework aims to capture some general outlines from the articulated knowledge provided by the teachers. It is an attempt to describe teachers' knowledge. The framework may be more visual than it is factual in the sense that the framework is not a teacher; it is a visual description of some features that may explain teachers' knowledge its interrelated nature.

Chapter 9

Teachers' Moral Dilemmas

This chapter reports empirical findings on moral dilemmas at school. The data consists of 33 interviews of secondary school teachers. Four main categories of moral dilemmas are formed. These categories are: matters related to teachers' work, pupils' behavior, and rights of minority groups and common rules at school. Special attention is directed to the principles in teachers' arguments that justify their actions. Teachers' reasoning in solving moral dilemmas is investigated with the help of field-invariant and field-dependent arguments. The best interest of a child is found to be the field-invariant argument behind teachers' thinking in all categories of moral dilemmas.

The Data Collection

We started our research on moral dilemmas at school by interviewing all the teachers from a certain school, located close to Helsinki. As mentioned earlier, the school has a very heterogeneous pupil population; from the total of 400 pupils, 15 per cent are foreigners. It has a reputation of an active school, and it has been involved in many projects focusing on improvement of teaching and learning. These earlier projects include curriculum improvement, student assessment and special teaching for foreigners. The teachers are very devoted to their profession, and they made a mutual decision to be involved in our project to identify and solve moral dilemmas in their school. The project started in January 1996 with a preliminary survey. In that first phase of research, 33 teachers were interviewed with a structured interview. The interviews were carried out within four days by the same researcher and each interview lasted approximately 30 minutes. Only two teachers were not able to participate in our preliminary survey due to illness. The research project will continue in the future as an action research in which the teachers participate in ethical discourse of the moral dilemmas revealed in the preliminary survey. In this discourse teachers will together search for better strategies to solve those difficult problems that they regularly face in their profession.

Analysis Methods

In this report we describe and analyze the characteristics of moral dilemmas in this particular school as identified by the teachers. We will particularly concentrate on the solving strategies used and the main principles guiding teachers' decision-making. All the interviews have been recorded and later transcribed. We have adapted a qualitative analysis approach and aimed at increasing understanding of teachers' thinking based on these case studies. The main themes of moral dilemmas in these cases were categorized with content analyses. Special attention was given to the solutions to different dilemmas and the principles guiding them. Although every moral dilemma is unique with its own contextual factors, we have made an effort to identify *field-invariant arguments* in teachers' problem-solving strategies. The field-invariant arguments in our study refer to teachers' arguments that are the same logical type regardless of the moral dilemma in question. We also pay attention to *field-dependent arguments* that are special justifications of certain kinds of moral dilemmas. In these arguments justifications are not the same logical type. The technical term of a field of arguments originates to the work of Toulmin, who made this distinction between two kinds of arguments (Toulmin, 1958). We adapt these and some other of Toulmin's technical terms to analyze teachers' problem-solving strategies and justifications behind them.

The Moral Dilemmas Identified by Teachers

In an interview, the teachers were asked to describe one particular case of a moral dilemma they had experienced during their teaching career. They were encouraged to choose a situation in which they had had difficulties in deciding the right way to act. The teachers were asked to tell about the case in detail, with all important context factors. From each interview, the theme of the moral dilemma was identified. From the total of 33 interviews, we formed four main categories of moral dilemmas. These categories are the following:

1. Matters related to teachers' work (N=11)
2. Pupils' work moral (N=10)
3. The rights of minority groups (N=6)
4. Common rules in school (N=6)

Matters related to teachers' work was the biggest category of moral dilemmas, with eleven teachers identifying a dilemma that belonged to this category. This category include situations where a teacher has difficulties in deciding how to deal with her/his pupils. In two cases the conflict includes teachers' decisions about punishing a particular pupil. In both situations the student is disturbing the class and the teacher makes a quick decision to throw the students out to get peace for the rest of the pupils. In both cases, the teachers are concerned on the appropriate way of doing this and their way of dealing with these particular pupils. In one case, the teacher still remembers a situation from long ago in which she had problems in deciding between two grades for an academically weak pupil. The teacher ended up giving the pupil a failing grade, and she was still concerned about the effects of her decision on this pupil. Another teacher had faced a situation where the contents of her teaching had been criticized. She had to justify to others and also to herself that she was teaching according to the curriculum.

Other important matters related to teachers' work include situations in which the teacher has a problem with confidentiality. In two cases, the teacher knows something about the pupil that even the parents do not know. In both cases, the teachers find this kind of situation very uncomfortable and are mostly worried about the pupils who have confided in them. In three cases teachers find difficulties in dealing with sensitive matters with their pupils. In every case teachers question if their role as a teacher includes handling this kinds of things. These sensitive matters are very personal and include aspects that professional therapists usually deal with. In these situations, teachers have to decide the limits of their professionality in helping their pupils. The teachers who had faced dilemmas with confidentiality and sensitive issues were mostly special education and physical education teachers whose subjects evidently are more prone to such cases as described above.

Things related to colleagues' work include situations in which a teacher sees a colleague doing something that s/he her/himself finds unprofessional. In both these situations the teacher has a problem with loyalty to a colleague. Also in both these cases there is a strong evidence that pupils are suffering from this situation in one way or on other.

The teachers who identified moral dilemmas related to teachers' work varied in their age, sex, subject matter and teaching experience. This category of moral dilemmas seemed to be the other one of major conflicts experienced by teachers regardless of their background. The subgroups of sensitive matters and confidentiality made exceptions to this rule and were identified as common moral dilemmas experienced by special education and physical education teachers.

Pupils' work moral was the second common category of moral dilemmas, including ten case studies. Three teachers complained about some pupils' negative attitude towards learning and schoolwork. Some of the teachers had noticed the same kind of attitude with their parents. These teachers experienced a dilemma between the school's values and these pupils' values at home. Teachers found it very difficult to motivate their pupils in this kind of conflict between home and school. Another subcategory of pupils' work moral was cheating by some pupils. These cases include cheating on a test by showing the right answers to another pupil, forging parents' names on a note to a teacher and a general attitude of lying. In one case study a pupil was denying his obvious guilt till the end and refused to admit his misbehavior. Another kind of conflict occurred with a teacher whose pupil wrote a provoking essay with a very rasistic attitude in it. In all these cases teachers had to deal with pupils' immoral behavior and decide what actions would be the right ones to take.

Another subcategory related to pupils' work moral was harassing. In three cases teachers reported tormenting behavior by some pupils to be the most difficult moral dilemma they had faced in their professional conduct. These situations include both physical and mental harassing towards other pupils. One of these case studies that dealt with impolite speech and behavior towards another pupil was identified as the most common moral dilemma at school that this particular teacher had faced in her teaching profession. The other cases had physical violence in addition to mental harassing of a weaker pupil. In both cases the harasser was bigger and stronger both mentally and physically.

An interesting observation about the teachers who identified conflicts in this category was that they were all females and very devoted to the teaching profession. They also view their role as a teacher to be as much a moral educator as a subject specialist. Half of these teachers were young with less than ten years of teaching experience.

The dilemmas in the category of the rights of minority groups dealt with the problems teachers had had with their foreign pupils. A total of six case studies belonged to this category. All the teachers who had experienced problems related to this category had taught these minority groups. Three of the teachers belonged to some minority groups themselves. Four of the teachers who identified problems in this category were males. The moral dilemmas mainly arose from the cultural conflicts in which religion was identified as a key factor. The pupils in minority groups practiced a religion other than Christianity, and that caused problems at some of school celebrations. Many of them—for example, Christmas—have a Christian meaning, and they include songs celebrating Jesus. One teacher found it problematic to have a school festival that favors one religion even though the majority of the pupils practice it. Another problem with these minority groups dealt with participation in some classes. In Finland pupils should study all the subjects in the curriculum, including music and sports. These two subjects were identified as the most problematic to pupils from minority groups. In their cultural heritage, these subjects are not studied, and they are regarded inappropriate, especially for girls. The teachers also shared two cases of moral dilemmas where trustworthiness of pupils from minority groups can seriously be questioned. In these cases, teachers had problems believing those students in some serious matters. The basic moral dilemma with these minority pupils which was reflected in all these cases was mentioned by the teacher specialized in teaching these pupils. The moral dilemma described by this teacher dealt with supporting the own ethnic identity of the minority pupils. All the other cases shared by the teachers had the basic problem of finding the right balance between adapting to the Finnish culture and being faithful to the pupils' own ethnic identity.

The category common rules at school had six case studies, like the previous category. The cases in this group dealt with forbidden things that usually are such only in theory. These things included smoking and playing cards in the school area for example during recess. In theory, common rules at school are against these things, but in the real life pupils practice both of them. According to these teachers, most of the teachers close their eyes and do not pay very much attention to these practices. However, these two teachers identified this inconsistency as a moral dilemma at school. The other subcategory dealt with pupils' rights in deciding some common rules in their school. These dilemmas included issues concerning freedom of choice in obligatory subjects and school activities outside the classroom. These two teachers found the amount of freedom in making important decisions to be considered as a moral dilemma. Two teachers identified practical matters—for example, common rules in the use of computers at school and problems due to a lack of space in their classrooms—as moral dilemmas. Both teachers from this subgroup were males and had a very practical orientation to their work.

The Solving Strategies and their Justifications Provided by Teachers

The Field-Invariant Arguments

After the teachers had described a moral dilemma they had experienced in their work, they were asked to tell how they had acted in that difficult situation. Some of the cases described were still unsolved or the solving process was still going on without a definite solution visible. However, all the teachers were able to provide some principles that are guiding them in the process of searching for solutions to the moral dilemmas at school. We adapted Toulmin's technical terms "field-invariant" and "field-dependent" to analyze teachers' moral reasoning across the four categories of moral dilemmas reported above. We start our investigation on these solutions and their justifications by analyzing the field-invariant arguments in teachers' stories. In our context the term "field- invariant argument" refers to the same principles by which teachers justify their actions regardless of the category of moral dilemma in question.

Toulmin uses the term *"warrant" to* describe the general legitimacy of an argument. A warrant certifies the soundness of the argument used (Toulmin, 1958, 100). The more abstract justification behind arguments is called *"backing"* (Toulmin, 1958, 105). These abstract justifications include theories or values. Sometimes the difference between a warrant and a backing is difficult to decide. We could identify field-invariant warrants and backings in teachers' reasoning. One of the most often used backing in teachers' justifications for their actions in moral conflicts was the best interest of a child. This principle was used in various conflicts with different context factors. In this principle the teachers adhere to Clark, who wants to highlight the perspective of a child in a moral dimension of education (Clark, 1995, 19–32). Clark has identified some fundamental needs of children that teachers should aim at responding to. These basic needs are: to be loved, to be led, to be vulnerable, to make sense, to please adults, to have hope, to know truth, to be known, and to be safe. Later on Clark has added a 10th need to his list: to create, to construct, to make one's mark in the local world, to make a difference (Clark, 1995, 27). According to Clark the basic question in coping with moral dilemmas of teaching is to think how teachers can respond to these fundamental needs of children.

The most common and ordinary classroom events are often taken for granted, and many times they are the ones that break the spirit, blame the victim, and make cruelty seem reasonable (Clark, 1995, 32). In our case studies of moral dilemmas, these events were found in every category of identified themes. In the dilemmas concerning matters related to teachers' work, several case studies dealt with situations where the teacher's behavior can be questioned. These cases include situations of grading and punishment where the teacher had to reflect on the influence of her/ his actions on her/his pupil. The biggest concern of these teachers dealt with the possibility of being cruel and breaking the pupil's spirit. Some of these cases seemed to be typical ones that every teacher needs to struggle with sometime. Teachers' reflection on these issues can be interpreted as caring and sensitive awareness of the possible negative effects of these things on the pupils they dearly care for. On the other hand, it is always possible that teachers as human beings have lost their temper and let the negative feeling towards a pupil to influence their professional behavior. However, we find this open-mindedness about these situations to be a sign of critical reflection of a teacher (Dewey, 1933). With that kind of open-minded and reflective attitude, a teacher has the potential to grow in handling similar situations in the future.

In some cases the teacher had to question a colleague's professional behavior. In these cases teachers judged their colleagues behavior as immoral by using the best interest of the child as a backing. These dilemmas that involved conflicts with colleagues were among the most complicated ones. Usually the teachers were very reluctant to report their colleague to the principal or to take any actions in the situation. It was typical of these cases that they took very long to solve or they remained unsolved. Nevertheless, all the teachers clearly thought that in these kinds of conflicts it is the pupils' best that should determinate the solution to the conflict.

In cases related to pupils' work moral, especially in conflicts including physical or mental harassing, the teachers always justified their actions with the same backing. That backing was the best interest of a weaker party. In these harassing cases teachers tried to understand all the parties involved but in their solutions to the conflict it was always the weaker pupil whose interest they felt obligated to look after. In a harassing case that lasted for two years, the teacher finally started a process to remove the harasser to another class. The whole process of removing this pupil took about a year, including many conferences between the parents, the principal and teachers. The parents of a harasser were against this removal, and that complicated the situation even more. The teacher who identified the dilemma and suggested removing the student to the other class to protect the rights of a weaker pupil justified this decision as follows:

> "It was very difficult for me to take a side in this dilemma. The parents of those pupils involved took the sides of their own children. However, I took the side of a weaker pupil and said to the parents that even if this pupil has provoked the other pupil it does not give him the right to physically attack him. This harasser was a normal child, even gifted, but he had some problems with schoolwork. The pupil that he was tormenting in every possible way was not normal; he had some kind of brain damage that made it difficult for him to visualize some things. This conflict

was finally solved in such a way that the harasser was removed to the other class. We discussed this together and decided that it is not the pupil who has been harassed that is the guilty one. Even afterwards I do not know what kind of relationship these pupils had; it was a weird one. But I think it was right to take the side of a weaker pupil. I thought that I am a strong one and I have to protect the weak. I also have more experienced that some other teachers and I thought it is my responsibility as a strong person to protect the rights of weak pupils." (Female, 15 years of teaching experience)

In another case in the category of pupils' work moral it is a pupil that the teacher described as "the weakest pupil in the class" who refused to go into the same small group with a fat girl. He had said aloud: "I will not work with a person like that, I can not learn anything with her". The teacher said that this kind of situation is a very typical one and repeats itself every single day. According to the teacher, pupils are cruel to each other and use very hurtful language in evaluating each other's appearance and skills. The teacher did not say anything at the moment this episode happened but she asked both pupils involved to stay with her after the class. The teacher discussed the episode with these two pupils but they did not find any solution then. The teacher asked the pupils to come and talk to her the next day in the teachers' room before class start. The teacher described the conference in the next day like this:

"We went to talk in a private room. Then, in front of the boy, I asked the girl how she feels to hear comments such as the one yesterday by this boy. The girl replied that it does not feel very good, it feels very bad indeed. Then I asked the boy if he has ever paid any attention to the feelings these kinds of comments can cause to the others. I asked him to imagine what it would be like to hear those comments daily himself, to hear things like nobody wants to work with you. The boy was touched by this and told us that he has never thought it in that respect. Then I guided him to make a deal with that girl not to do it ever again. They shook hands and he promised not to do it anymore, at least to this particular girl. After that conference I have never heard that he was mean to this girl again. I think this is very important: always pay attention to these kinds of episodes and do not let them go unnoticed. But it is so difficult because these episodes occur everyday and in every lesson. You do not have time to get involved every time. It is only the meanest and the cruelest things you have time to pay attention to. I think every person is valuable and we should teach the kids not to treat each other in a bad way. The principle behind this view is my respect for other people. Everybody is valuable as a person." (Female, 10 years of teaching experience)

In both cases described above the teacher has a strong warrant for her justifications to act in a certain way. The best interest of a pupil is guiding their decision-making with respect for every pupil regardless of their academic achievement, physical appearance or difficulty in a situation. Another common factor in these cases is the teacher's brave acting to find a solution to the situation. Both of these teachers aim at balancing justice, care and truthfulness in finding the best solution. In respect to Oser's orientations in teachers' attempts to solve moral dilemmas both these teachers adapt discourse orientation in their problem-solving strategies. They both accept their personal responsibility in the conflict situation and explain the justifications behind their actions. In the first episode, our data does not tell how much the pupils in that harassing dilemma were heard. We do know that the teacher arranged conferences between all the parties involved and we can assume that the pupils had a chance to tell their points of view, too. In that respect we can argue that in both of these cases the teachers used discourse II orientation, in which everybody involved in the situation can be heard. According to discourse ethics, every argument should be allowed to be presented and the criterion for the final decision making should be the rationality of the best argument (Oser, 1994b, 112).

In the case of unpolite speaking and behaving towards the other pupil, everybody involved agreed to the same solution. In that situation the teacher could balance caring, justice and truthfulness at the same time. Unfortunately, it is not always possible to be caring to all people involved. As we could see in the case of harassing, the parents of a harasser were against removing their son to the other classroom. In this situation, the teacher had to accept the conflict with the parents to be able to protect the weaker pupil. In this case, truthfulness to the principals the teacher believed in and the right of a person to be safe at school determinated that she care more for the weaker pupil than the other one. We can also argue that her argument was the best argument in that complicated situation. We justify our claim to view her argument as the best with its educational validity and field-invariant nature.

The Field-Dependent Arguments

The field-dependent arguments in teachers' justifications for their solutions in the moral dilemmas they had faced refer to the arguments in some category of dilemmas that are different from the arguments in the other categories. In our data the problems related to the rights of the minority groups shared a common feature in teachers' problem-solving strategies that can be identified as field-dependent. In all the six cases dealing with moral dilemmas concerning foreign pupils, the teachers had used compromises in their solutions. In the other cases discussed above, the teachers had some principals they were not willing to compromise. In the moral dilemmas with minority pupils, the basic question is to find the balance between Finnish culture and the pupils' own ethnic identity. This search for pupils' own identity can be identified as acting in the best interest of these children. In this respect, the backings justifying the compromises can be labeled field-invariant. However, in all these cases teachers' acting for the best interest of the child included making compromises. These compromises include a case in which the teacher did not punish the pupil as severely as she thought the pupil deserved. The teacher justified this solution to punish the pupil in a lenient way by his ethnic background. In this case it was quite obvious that the pupil was lying, but the teacher said she was more careful than with the Finnish pupils to make sure that she is not unjust toward the pupil. Even though most of the pupils know Finnish well enough to know the basic rules at school, they sometimes may take advantage of their ethnic background by arguing that they didn't understand the instructions.

The school and all the teachers involved in teaching pupils from minority groups emphasized that they are willing to discuss conflicts with the parents and try to find a solution that would be acceptable for both parties. In the situations where a pupil refuses to participate to some lessons—for example, music—the teacher has discussed the problem with parents and tried to make a compromise. Usually in these conflicts, the pupil is required to stay in a music lesson only a short time to greet the teacher and maybe to study theory of music. Pupils from the minority groups, especially the Muslim children, do not need to participate in singing or playing musical instruments. The teacher justifies compromises in these moral dilemmas in the following way:

> "Either this or that is a very bad solution in every sense. The pupils should be able to choose both, the Finnish culture and their own ethnic identity. In our society the chance to choose at least a little bit of your own is a big question. It is not easy in the Finnish society to choose your own ethnic identity. The pressures to adapt are very strong. That's why it is good to keep up your own identity. It is a good thing to be able to choose your own ethnic identity but it should not lead to rejection of Finnish society. You can not leave in Finland without adapting to certain things in this culture. This is why these conflicts are so difficult. Even though we try to encourage pupils to choose their own ethnic identity, there is a limit how far they can go. Drawing this line for those pupils is a moral question" (Female, fifteen years of teaching experience)

Discussion and Future Work

In this chapter we have explored the moral dimension of teaching and the concrete moral dilemmas at school identified by teachers. Considering a semi-structured interview, we could detect four main categories of moral dilemmas experienced by teachers. We have given an overview of those dilemmas by describing and giving some more detailed examples of those situations. We have also explored the actions teachers used in solving these conflicts. In addition to the solving-strategies used, we have paid special attention to the principals in teachers' arguments in justifying their actions. Teachers' reasoning in solving moral dilemmas was investigated with the help of field-invariant and field-dependent arguments. The best interest of a child was found to be the field-invariant argument behind teachers' thinking in all the categories of moral dilemmas. Problems related to the rights of the minority groups had field-dependent arguments that differed from the other conflicts. In moral dilemmas dealing with minority pupils, the teachers used a lot of compromises. The justification for their action was an attempt to help minority pupils in finding the balance between the Finnish culture and their own cultural heritage.

The research project will continue as an action research with these same teachers. Our aim is to foster the ethical awareness of these teachers by introducing them with these moral dilemmas in their school. The teachers will be encouraged to participate in ethical discourse on these problems and their solving strategies. In that process we hope to identify solutions that are working well and which do not need much improvement. We also pay attention to those dilemmas that do not have solutions yet or have solutions that could be improved. In that ethical discourse teachers will practice their argumentation skills and take part in communicative action advocated by Habermas (1984; 1990). In that process the moral dimension of teaching will be explicitly discussed.

Chapter 10

The Logic of Rules and Recipes

The results of a deductive and inductive approach to investigate the recipes used in teaching practice are reported. In a study that followed a deductive approach, literature-based collection of pedagogical recipes was collected. The use of such recipes was investigated in two different teacher-education cultures. From the inductive point of view the purpose was to find out what kind of advice and guidelines were given to student-teachers during their practice periods. How the advice and guidelines were justified and what the aims of the supervisor were during the practice period were the main interests. The material was collected in a variety of ways from four different teaching practice periods during one academic year.

Descriptive Overview

The basis for this research was provided by two publications on the logic of recipes used in teaching. Meyer (1980, 30) examined recipes gathered by students at the University of Oldenburg during the 1978/9 semester on the basis of advice and instructions that they received during their period of practice teaching. The advice and instructions thus produced were written down as a catalogue of recipes. A second catalogue of recipes was found from Mitzschke *et al.* (1984). Some of them duplicate those in Meyer's catalogue. The others, however, originate from University of Leeuwarder in the Netherlands. Mitzschke *et al.* do not give any further information as to where or how their catalogue was gathered.

Based on these sources a total of 402 recipes. These were grouped into seven classes according to suggestions made by Meyer and Mitzschke. Although the two classification systems differ, they nevertheless exhibit the same kinds of groupings. The Dutch material also includes instructions on the treatment of subject matter, which are not included in the German recipes.

The catalogue of Mitzschke *et al.* (1984, 88–89) was useful in labeling and arranging the recipe classes into simpler content classes. Thus the following recipe classes were used in this part of the research:

1. The roles of the teacher and pupil
2. Socializing the pupil to become a learner
3. Classroom interaction
4. Classroom discipline and its maintenance
5. Use of teaching methods
6. Implementation of the curriculum
7. Use of the teaching facilities and -space

The first four recipe groups totaling 204 recipes were chosen for this study. The common denominator of these recipes is that they all can serve as tools for carrying out a hidden curriculum (Meri, 1992), where the goal is to make the pupil a good learner. Supervision in teaching practice proceeds from norms and takes the form of clear advice and instructions. Typically a piece of advice or instruction develops from the supervisor's encouragement. Such recipes are for example the following:

Hold fast to the rules you have created.
Loosen the reins as necessary.
Always consider yourself above the pupils.
Remember that the interest of the teacher and the pupil are not alike.
Negotiate an exam schedule for the whole semester.
Avoid forming strong emotional ties to your pupils.

Data for the research was collected in a questionnaire, which included all of the 204 recipes, filled out by 41 Finnish supervisors and 62 class teacher students and 42 German supervisors and 36 student teachers. The supervisors rated how often they give out specific instructions. The student teachers, on the other hand, responded, how often they receive such information. The research interest focused on the actual use of the recipes, not on their importance. The aim was to find out how frequently specific advice and instructions were given, and how often the student teachers reported receiving them.

The following result is based on a mean occurrence value given to each recipe. The questionnaire used a seven-step scale (0–6), according to how often the recipes had been given or heard. Table 1 shows the recipes most often used in both studies. The letters R, S, I and D represent the four recipe classes as follows:

Table 1. Recipes in the order of most frequent use, Finnish data.

Recipe	Class
Speak only when the pupils are listening to you.	Role
Act logically.	R
Consider all your pupils equal.	R
Encourage the pupils to listen to one another.	Interaction
If you cannot answer a pupil's question, resolve the matter in some other way.	R
If a pupil has been given the chance to speak, demand that the others listen.	I
Consider the needs and interests of the pupils.	I
Teach according to the abilities of the pupils.	I
Facilitate the participation of the pupils by varying the form of teaching.	I
Speak clearly.	R
Insist on attentiveness when you make assignments.	Discipline
Encourage your pupils constantly.	R
Begin teaching only when the whole class has settled.	D
Make adequate adjustments.	R
Take positive notice of correct answers.	R

R = Role
S = Socialization
I = Interaction
D = Discipline

Of the 15 most frequently used recipes eight describe the role of the teacher. The teacher is described in the recipes as being logical, fair, flexible, encouraging and able to express themselves clearly. This confirms earlier research, which shows that the teacher who carried out a hidden curriculum was seen by the pupil as being flexible, encouraging and demanding (Meri, 1992).

According to the second group of recipes, which concern the ability of the teacher to see matters from the pupils point of view should show consideration for the needs and interests of their pupils, as well as for their potential, skills, abilities and possibilities. There are also two recipes relating classroom discipline. Both emphasize the importance of concentration as the prerequisite of teaching and learning.

In the German material, there were nine recipes among the fifteen most frequently used that had to do classroom interaction and to take the pupils into account. Listening to the pupil becomes an important goal in this material. In addition, the most frequently used recipes reflect consideration for the needs and interests of the pupils. As was reflected in

Table 2. Recipes in the order of most frequent use, German data.

Recipe	Class
Encourage the pupils to listen to one another.	Interaction
Consider the pupils' suggestions when handling teaching issues.	I
Give enough time for the pupils to prepare their classroom performances.	I
If a pupil has been given the chance to speak, demand that the others listen.	I
If someone is incapable of doing something, let the others help.	I
Facilitate the participation of the pupils by varying the form of teaching.	I
Consider the needs and interests of the pupils.	I
Teach according to the abilities of the pupils.	I
Make adequate adjustments.	Role
If you cannot answer a pupil's question, resolve the matter in some other way.	R
Insist on being attentiveness, when you make assignments.	Discipline
Act logically.	R
Speak clearly.	R
Communicate what you tolerate and what you do not.	Socialization
Concentrate on listening what the pupils have to say.	I

the Finnish material, attention should be given to the potentials, skills and abilities of the pupils and to the differentiation of teaching method. The recipes that describe the role of the teacher, reflect the necessity of logic, flexibility and clarity of speech. One of the most commonly used recipes, that describes the role of the teacher deals with the limits of the teacher's omnipotence. There is only recipe describing classroom discipline and only one referring the socializing of the pupils.

There are several interesting details in the results describing the two different teaching cultures. The most commonly used recipes in the Finnish material describe the role of the teacher, the advice and instructions on classroom interaction, and classroom discipline. The top seven recipes in the German material deal with interaction. Thus we can suppose that in Finnish teacher education the strengthening of the role of the teacher is emphasized, whilst the German way to use recipes refer most frequently to classroom interaction.

The identical recipes listed in both teacher education cultures are listed in table 3.

This list of recipes shared by both Finnish and German teaching culture, summarizes good teaching in well-known pedagogical principles,

Table 3. The identical recipes in both teaching cultures.

Recipe	Class
Insist on attentiveness when you give assignments.	Discipline
Facilitate the participation of the pupils by varying the form of teaching.	Interaction
If you cannot answer a pupil's question, resolve the matter some other way.	Role
Make adequate adjustments.	R
Encourage the pupils to listen to one another.	I
Consider the needs and interests of the pupils.	I
Speak clearly.	R
Act logically.	R
If a pupil has been given the chance to speak, demand that the others listen.	I

that were mentioned by Herbart (1803) in his writings of teaching and its formation into a teaching-studying-learning process.

The next table includes the fifteen least used instructions from both the Finnish and the German material. The recipes included in both cultures are placed at the top of the list.

Among the least used advice and instructions there are mainly those, that concern to socialization of the pupils or maintaining classroom discipline. These instructions are clearly such, that they maintain the teacher's authority. The content of the advice focuses especially the teacher's power to criticize. The teacher's effort to control the situation through authority shows in the maintenance of classroom discipline. Instructions of this type were given fairly seldom by the supervisors, not that the student teachers would have recalled receiving them either. Since the number of recipes that obviously emphasize the teacher's authority was small, it is interesting see how socialization of pupils was described.

According to the Finnish material, the first recipe concerning socialization of pupils was only ranked in 36th place out of 204 items. In the German material the ranking was similar in this respect. In addition, the first recipe containing advice and instructions on classroom discipline is ranked 25th in the Finnish material and 17th in the German material.

The consistency of the use of the recipes concerning the socialization of pupils and classroom discipline in both materials is obvious. In spite of some rare differences, the teacher education cultures resemble one another, based on the advice and instructions used in supervising. If this assumption is valid, corresponding responses should have given by both supervising cultures.

Table 4. The least frequently used recipes.

Recipe	Class	Data Finnish	German
Set the exam papers that are to be returned in sight on the teacher's desk.	S	F	G
Mark a four in your notebook if the pupils aren't working satisfactorily.	S	F	G
Have the pupil stand when answering, as the mind works better.	S	F	G
Make the ones that disturb the classroom discipline look ridiculous.	S	F	G
You are the law, even if you are wrong.	S	F	G
Keep the pupils under pressure.	S	F	G
Resume classroom discipline by comparing the achievements of good and bad classes.	D	F	G
Name aloud the pupils that cannot follow the teaching.	D	F	G
Stand behind your desk while teaching.	R	F	G
Swear when necessary.	S	F	
Do not tell the date of exams.	S	F	
Invite poor pupils to some blackboard work.	S	F	
Try to look more eminent than you are.	D	F	
Do not let late-comers participate in the teaching.	D	F	
Memorize the names of the pupils in the order of achievements.	I	F	
Give the pupil an evaluation of all work done.	S		G
Hold a test during the first lesson of the things you have just taught.	S		G
Adapt the pupils to the possibility of a test at any time.	S		G
Treat the pupils as targets of education.	S		G
Do not allow the pupils to accelerate the work pace.	D		G
Wait for the pupils of an excitable class at the door.	D		G

The Results of the Structure Analysis

Factor analysis was employed to determine the belief systems underlying the teaching-studying-learning process. First an inspection based on correlations was carried out. In this way it was possible to check whether the recipes belonged in different groups of recipes. This was controlled besides factor analysis, through item analysis. In addition, the results of factor analysis should reveal what is shared by the two cultures of supervision, and where are they different. What sort of a teaching world does the obtained result reflect?

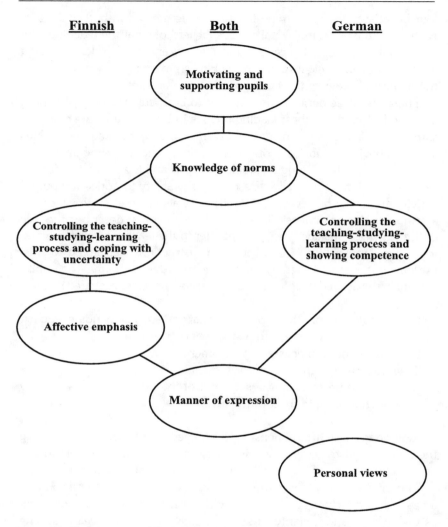

Figure 8. The structures of the belief system concerning the role of the teacher.

Factor analyses were carried out according to the principal component procedure separately for both Finnish and German data sets. Every main recipe class was also subjected separately to factor analysis. The summary of structures obtained through factor analysis is shown in figures 1–4. The number of factors was determined by means of Cattell scree test, and the factors were interpreted and named according to the highest loaded recipes (.300). As a result of the factor analysis, seventeen structures in four belief systems concerning teaching were created in both data sets, each being based on individual recipes (beliefs) of what the teaching process should include. In figures 8–11 the factors are put in order according to the proportional eigenvalues in the Finnish material. When necessary, the numerical order of the factors is shown in brackets.

There are three dimensions common to both cultures of supervision. In these factors the highest loading recipes in both cultures are quite the same. The first dimension, describing *the role of the teacher,* values logical behavior, flexibility, motivation, support and encouragement, fair notice of all pupils, seeking favorable solutions and the ability to adapt to various situations. The recipes describing the ability to notice the pupils' activity and being busy with the pupils were also loaded on this factor.

Another shared dimension, *Knowledge of norms,* describes the role of the teacher. It includes recipes that refer to the teacher's belief in working norms and habits. The advice and instructions pertaining to this, pertains to the model used by the teacher in order to channel the pupils' activity in the desired direction. This dimension includes six shared recipes:

Create in your pupils the impression, that you are a demanding teacher.
Mark the pupils' exams with a strict hand.
Do not give out unnecessary compliments.
Take no notice of the pupils' incitement.
Do not solve personal matters in front of the pupils.
Do not chew gum in front of the class.

In addition to these, this dimension was loaded with the recipe describing the revealing of the way to act in a new class, the recipes demanding equal activity from all pupils alike and taking control over pupils.

The third shared factor, *manner of expression,* had the same content. They included recipes involving the teacher's manner of expression, such as oral presentation, clarity of speech, audibleness and liveliness. The pupil-centered presentation is based on understanding different pupils.

The third factor according to factor analysis of both data sets resemble each other. The Finnish factor was *controlling the teaching-studying-learning process and coping with uncertainties,* and the corresponding German factor was *controlling the teaching-studying-learning process and showing competence.* There were two common recipes, the recipe recommending telling the truth and the advice that the teacher should not show uncertainty. In the Finnish data set, recipes were given not to be uncertain, the German way in recipe recommendation is, that the teacher should demonstrate certainty.

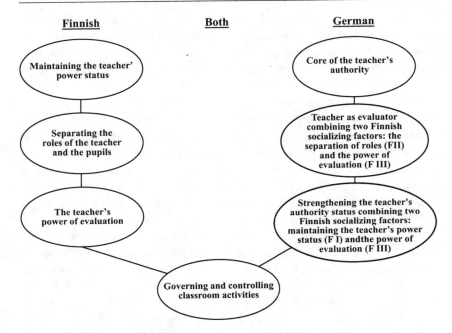

Figure 9. The structures of a belief system concerning the socialization of the pupils.

There were two totally different factors. In the Finnish material, *affective emphasis,* describes the teacher as relaxing and encouraging. Such a teacher tells jokes and tales, allows pupils to carry on their own business, is cheerful and participates in certain activities involving the pupils. It is likely that this advice aims at improving the classroom atmosphere, bringing the teacher closer to the pupil. The recipes in German factor, *personal views,* describe the teacher's political and religious views. Taking sides and expressing courage are also included here. This kind of factor was not contained in the Finnish material. The result most likely means that, students in Oldenburg are encouraged to express their social conceptions or philosophy of life and thus also create an ethical background for their teaching.

In the Finnish material there were three the separate dimensions: *maintaining the teacher's power status, separating the roles of the pupils and teachers* and *the teacher's power of evaluation.* Those recipes were loaded in the first factor, whose aim was securing the teacher's power status. Such recipes included placing oneself above the pupil, maintaining a fast pace in teaching, hitting one's fist on the board, giving out orders and sticking to them, and naming in advance the ones to answer questions.

This factor describes the teacher's authority at its most. In the background is the notion, that the teacher is the utmost and infallible expert of teaching. Solutions to pedagogical problems are based on the belief, that the teacher can control the teaching-studying-learning process and its elements by use of authority.

The second separate factor in the Finnish material, *separating the roles of the teacher and the pupil*, included recipes that described the differences between the roles of the teacher and the pupil. The teacher is to know more, have more skills and have better management skills that the pupils. The pupils are to understand what is allowed, what kind of working habits are favored and when the pupils' behavior exceeds the limits of appropriateness. The model of a skillful, active and knowledgeable pupil is held as a good example for all the other pupils.

The advice and instruction of the third Finnish factor, *the teacher's power of evaluating*, includes recipes for evaluating achievement, accustoming the pupils being evaluated and informing the pupils of the teachers' expectations of achievement for the whole class. The use of a relative evaluation scale makes it possible to compare the pupils' achievements. The recipes loaded here express the use of the teacher's duty of evaluation. They reflects the traditional understanding of the teacher as a critic, the sole evaluator of the pupils' activities. This understanding is in accord with the behavioristic conception of teaching. The teacher teaches and then evaluates.

Only one factor, *core of teacher's authority*, was clearly characteristic of the German data. This factor describes the teacher's unconditional authority in relation to the pupils. This authority also includes the teacher's power of evaluation and duty to oversee pupils' activities.

In the German material the second and the third dimensions are combinations of Finnish factors: The first one consists of *separating the roles of teacher and pupil* and *the teacher's power of evaluating* and the second includes the Finnish factors *maintaining the teacher's power status* and *the teacher's power of evaluation*.

There was only one common factor *governing and controlling classroom activities* in both data sets. This factor was comprised of recipes that describe the teacher as the classroom activity coordinator and controller. The pupils are not to be trusted, their activities must be kept under surveillance, the pupils' actions must be monitored, and the teacher must not be so interested in their affairs as to get emotionally entangled.

The belief system describing teacher-pupil interaction contains two shared dimensions. In both materials, the first factor, *accepting the world*

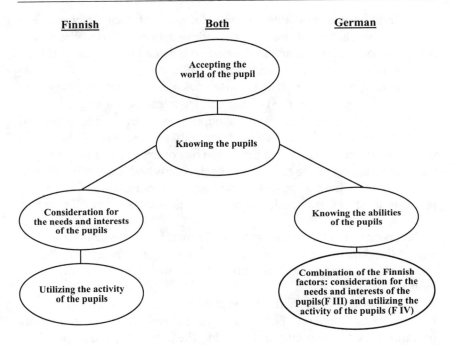

Figure 10. The structures of a belief system concerning interaction in the teaching-studying-learning process.

of pupil, was formed by advice and instructions through which the teacher can recognize the world of the pupils and approve of the events and phenomena that are concerned with it. Examples of this include e.g. the attempt to avoid revealing exam results in the course of returning exam papers, to allow free choice of sitting companion, to allow copying and occasional talking aloud, to reveal the timetable for exams, to give pupils opportunities to tell their own stories and to take notice of the pupils' suggestions, and to take notice of the pupils' opinions. This matter is related to the subject of the pedagogical tact (Meri, 1992).

Another common factor was *knowing the pupils.* This dimension included recipes that aim at knowing the pupils' person. Knowing the pupils includes e.g. the abilities to call them by name.

In the Finnish material *considering the needs and interest of the pupils* and *utilizing the activity of the pupils* were totally separate dimensions. According to the former, the teacher is to respect the pupils' opinions, notices their needs and their interests, adapt their teaching according to the pupils' abilities, provide room for their opinions, promotes the pupils' about the things that interest them during the lesson and encourages the interaction developing between the pupils. A similar factor was found earlier research (Meri, 1992).

According to the latter factor, those advice and instructions were emphasized through which the teacher can try to utilise the originality and special talents that can be seen in the pupils. The instructions that formed this factor, included the idea to use the pupils' activity and helpfulness in order to organize the teaching process. The contents of this factor reflect the understanding of the pupils' activity, business and independent initiatives in making the teaching-studying-learning process versatile. The attempt is to shift from teacher-centered work into using pupil-centered methods.

The recipes loaded in the separate German factor *knowing the abilities of the pupil* pertain to the teacher's knowledge of the pupils' abilities and level of achievement. It is more differentiated than the second common factor.

In the German material there was one dimension, which was the combination of two separate Finnish factors: *consideration for the needs and interests of the pupils* and *utilizing the activity of the pupils*. The content of the factor can be interpreted to mean, that the projection of the needs of the pupils into various meaningful activities is most likely a reality of teaching, that can be rationally described within one and the same dimension.

The content of the belief system pertaining to teacher-pupil interaction reflects the importance of knowing the pupils and their characteristics. The teacher is naturally the second party in the interaction. One dimension that concerned pupil socialization was the dimension of the separation of the roles of the teacher and the pupil. Although the difference between the roles reflects the behaviorist point of view of the roles as giver (teacher) and taker (pupil), the beliefs concerning teacher-pupil interaction guide the nature of the concept teaching-studying-learning process in a constructive direction. According to the constructive point of view, the teacher should recognize those elements through which learning is optimized.

When the recipes regarding *classroom discipline* were factorized, the Finnish and German materials produced three structures what were somewhat alike, and one, which was unique and independent for each respective teacher education culture. The separate factor in the Finnish material was made from recipes through which it is possible for the teacher to

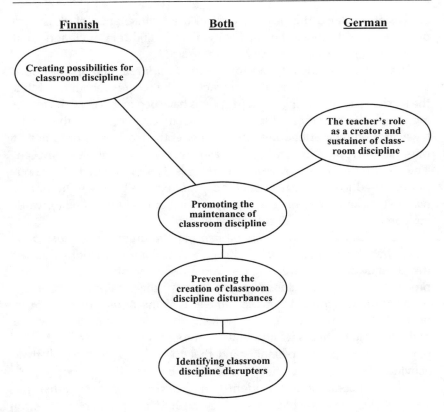

Figure 11. The structures of a belief system concerning the classroom discipline.

create satisfactory classroom discipline. Acting in response to disturbances, the teacher takes special precautions during the first lessons, becomes involved in the disturber's actions right from the first lesson, avoids losing control, realizes the significance of the start of the lesson, and gives the rules for cooperation.

In the German material there was also one unique factor *the teacher's role as a creator and sustainer of classroom discipline.* This factor was loaded with recipes that present different actions the teacher for the purpose of maintaining classroom discipline. The teacher should prevent disorders in advance, keep an eye on the pupils, focus attention to the start of the lesson, evaluate the achievements of the pupils, not argue about following an order, give hints about how matters should proceed, not to rely on a *laissez faire style* but rather to hold the reins firmly in hand and call attention to point out the disturbers of classroom discipline. This dimension included the need to explain the maintenance of classroom discipline, and in these the teacher's influence and role in creating and maintaining classroom discipline is emphasized.

The recipes describing the *promoting of maintenance of classroom discipline* formed the first common factor. The recipes recommend that the teacher begin teaching when the pupils have begun to follow the teaching, when the classroom discipline has been restored, when the pupils have directed their attention to the teacher. If the teaching is disturbed, it must be interrupted. The cause for the interruption must also be removed. The need for adequate control and firmness, is also included. When pupils are used to the teacher's methods, the responsibility can be turned over to the pupils. Attentiveness is demanded of the pupils, and forwarding comments are to be directed individually.

The second common factor, *preventing the creation of classroom discipline disturbances,* included such advice and instructions that lay the groundwork for preventing classroom discipline disturbances. When proceeding along these lines, the teacher keeps the pupils under constant observation, describes what the remedy is if the agreements made in favor of classroom discipline are broken. The teacher should use whole body language while showing how matters are to be carried out. The pupils must be made to understand that the teacher controls all their activities. Rules that have been made are to be obeyed.

The third common factor, *identifying classroom discipline disrupters,* included recipes which give advice on how the teacher can control classroom discipline, involve identifying the disruptive pupils. The teacher should correct individual pupils and not punish collectively. In order to be able to do this, the activities of the whole class must be supervised, the pupils addressed individually and an effort made at identifying the ones disturbing the classroom discipline.

What does control of the teaching actually mean according to the systems of belief expressed in recipes? The Finnish and German cultures of supervision produced so many similar structures that the conception of teaching reflected by the recipes can be regarded as being relatively similar. It is difficult to significant differences in teaching conception, because in both cultures of supervision it is crucial to emphasize the professionality of the teaching in the teacher's actions. The teaching process begins with the teacher's pedagogic authority and full responsibility for the pupils' learning and knowledge. The maintenance of the teacher's pedagogic authority requires interaction between the pupil and the teacher, and good knowledge of pupils and their characteristics. Both teacher education cultures showed also the effort to incorporate elements designed to promote the students' self-orientation.

The conception of teaching that lies behind the recipes presents itself as clearly behavioristic. Perhaps it is safe as such for beginning teachers, to whom the constructive way to act becomes concrete through reflection during their own work. The interaction between the conception logic of recipes and reflective behavior is discussed in Meri (1995). One conclusion of the results of this study is that effective the teacher's pedagogic authority. In that the logic of recipes provides a possibility.

Inductive Way to Approach Recipes and The Knowledge Base Behind Them

In our study we have considered both the inductive and deductive way to investigate the recipes used in teaching practice. The results of the inductive approach are presented here. The supervisors themselves reported on the kind of advice and guidance they had given to the student-teachers and, on the other hand, the student-teachers reported on the kind of recipes they had been given. The purpose of the study was to find out what advice and guidelines were given to student-teachers during the practice period and how the advice and guidelines were divided throughout the different stages of the teaching practice. How the advice and guidelines are justified and what the aim of the supervisor is in her/his work are underlying factors.

Data was collected through a questionnaire administered to the supervisors (N=196) and student-teachers (N=230), altogether 426 subjects, in the Department of Teacher Education. Some student-teachers were also interviewed. In addition, we used tapes of post-observation supervisory discourse between the student-teachers and the supervisors. The data thus gathered was used to clarify the interpretation. Material was collected from four different periods of teaching practice. They are: *field practice I* (orientation practice), in field schools during the first academic year; *basic practice*, in a university training school during their 3rd year; *field practice II*, in a field school in their 4th year; and *final practice period* in teacher-training or field schools in their 4th or 5th year. The idea of our classroom teacher program is to integrate theoretical studies with practice teaching as early as possible to enable continuous integration between theory and practice. At the beginning simple elements are practiced, and in the final practice stage the student-teacher is expected master complex entities. The curriculum indicates which theoretical studies support each practice teaching period. Hytönen (1995, 80–82) describes the curriculum solutions.

One principle is that each practice period contains its own aims and character. The focus in *field practice I* (orientation practice) is on pupils and on the interaction between the teacher and the pupils. The second practice teaching period, the *basic practice*, emphasizes student-teachers' instruction of school subjects. Supervisors, specialized in the didactics of the subject in question, pay attention to the special character of each school subject. In the fourth academic year, the student-teachers have the possibilities to explore their own personal ways to function as a classroom teacher. This happens in *field practice II*, by offering the student-teachers experiences in practicing in schools which encourage innovations or experiments. In the last practice teaching period, the *final practice*, student-teachers are quite independent. They are reflecting the whole area of the teaching profession. Student-teachers plan and carry out all teaching activities during this period. Of course the supervisors help and give as much feedback as the student-teachers need. The focus is on considering, from many angles, the questions arising in the teaching profession.

The material in this study was collected in a variety of ways from the above-described teaching practice periods throughout one academic year. This part of the study reports the findings gathered through the questionnaire. The questions asked were:

1. What kind of advice and guidelines have the supervisors given/ have the students received during training?
2. How was the given/received advice justified?
3. What was the aim of the supervisor in her/his work?

The advice given in connection with practice teaching supervision is seen as a reflection of what the supervisor as a teacher regards as good teaching. Thus, each supervisor's personal teaching theories, values and beliefs are underlying factors. The supervisor somehow clarifies to her/ himself why s/he does something in a specific way in her/his teaching. In other words, her/his knowledge base is linked with her/his personal teaching theory. The aspects mentioned above are reflected in the advice and guidelines that the supervisor gives to the student-teacher. If we take a typical teacher, s/he would naturally produce this advice and guidelines for her/himself, even though s/he might not refer to them aloud.

The open answers have been classified into different content classes, according to what elements the statement included. The bases of the classification are founded on the material. Content categories were established inductively, based on the raw data. The data is described using seven main classes, dividing the advice and guidelines into a new structure. The 118 minor content categories contain recipes related to the teaching of a certain subject. For statistical usage the categories were combined into about 40 classes. The raw data consists of more than 6000 units set in different categories.

In addition to the contextual division, which is the focus of the advice and guidelines, we will clarify how extensively they are used. Some advice is very concrete and focuses on a very small area of teaching, while other advice is of a principal nature. Some advice includes justification, but in most cases the justification is implicit; it should be self-evident to the expert if not to the novices.

What Are Teaching Recipes?

Referring to recipes, it is useful to define what they actually mean. Meyer (1991, 49) defined recipes as following:

> The recipes are meant to be unambiguous operational advice to secure a successful teacher-pupil relationship and positive learning results. The operational advice arises from concrete teaching situations and is universal. It serves classroom routine situations and is not theoretically derived or empirically verified.

A philosophical point of view to the recipes is to view them as intellectual tools in the instructional process. A written recipe is a piece of theory, the theoretical claim that by doing such and such, a certain result will follow. Following any recipe is a practical matter, and the understanding involved in following it is essentially practical understanding. Because recipes are practical, they relate to the practical use of the materials with which they are concerned. Behind the practical and normative advice is a teacher's knowledge base and subjective theories.

In teacher education, the purpose of the practical advice and guidelines given in teaching practice is to help the student-teacher to find her/his own professional practices. The supervisors as experts explicate their own professional knowledge to the student-teachers during supervision.

One way to clarify a teacher's pedagogical thinking is to structure those things that teachers find important in a teaching process—that is, to discover the advice and guidelines the teachers produce to carry through effective teaching and learning, and above all to find out how this advice is justified. Within teacher education the supervision forms a natural context for clarifying a teacher's pedagogical thinking. Here a teacher voices aspects that s/he regards as important in good teaching. This *thinking out loud* takes place when one supervises a student-teacher and offers the researchers some possibilities to clarify how a teacher moves from the descriptive to the normative in her/his thinking.

The Results of the Inductive Approach

Data was described in seven main classes. The two data sets from supervisors and student-teachers were compared with each other with a factor analysis, and were tested with a transformation analysis to ensure that the two sets of answers were sufficiently uniform so to be combined. The method used was the Kaiser-Hunka-Bianchini method. (Kaiser *et al.*, 1971, 409–422; Fleming, 1992, 113–115.) The answers of the supervisors and the student-teachers were quite similarly divided, which seems to point to good validity and reliability.

Teaching methods and *teacher-pupil interaction* are the most frequently mentioned recipe areas. Next, advice was given in questions concerning the *supervision process,* which was therefore separated into a main content class of its own. Thus, the advice offered directly on the teaching-studying-learning process can be studied separately from the questions of the supervision itself. This main content class includes, among other things, a minor category called *giving positive feedback to the teacher* meaning the praise expressed in the *supervision process.* If the positive feedback included something clear and concrete belonging to another content class, it was also recoded in that class. Praise focused on something specific can be considered a clear piece of advice to the student-teacher to act according to the guidelines given.

The Division of Recipes into Different Practice Teaching Stages

This comparison concerns the percentage division between the different periods of practice teaching. Figure 12 shows the amount of advice given in different practice periods in the main content classes.

During the first practice period, most recipes refer to *teacher-pupil interaction*. The students are guided to plan their lessons and are given advice to help them survive the practice. It is natural that *subject matter* is almost lacking, because the focus in this period is on the questions concerning pupils. The second practice period takes place in the university's teacher-training school and, according to the curriculum, it is subject-oriented. At this stage, when compared to other practice stages, most

Table 5. The division of the advice and guidelines into main content classes (%).

Main content classes		Supervisors	Student teachers	All %
100	Planning	9,6	5,2	7,4
200	Teaching methods	23,4	24,8	24,1
300	Subject matter	7,4	10,5	8,9
400	Organizing	12,8	14,4	13,6
500	Teacher-pupil interaction	25,5	21,1	23,3
600	Evaluation	3,5	2,1	2,8
700	Supervision process	17,8	21,9	19,9
		100	100	100

advice belongs to the main class consisting of the *subject matter. Evaluation* is another focus during this practice period. Less attention is paid to *teacher-pupil interaction,* perhaps because it was emphasized during the previous practice period. The second field practice period is supervised by the field school class teachers. The number of recipes is not very large and they do not clearly emphasize any particular main content class.

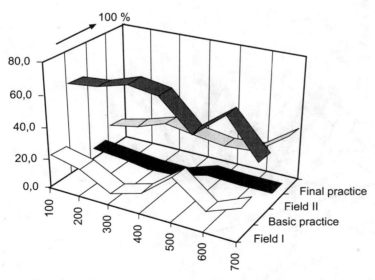

Figure 12. The division of all advice in main content classes between different practice-teaching stages (%).

Perhaps only *teacher-pupil interaction* and *planning* receive somewhat more attention than the other classes. During this period, the student-teachers have traditionally been very free to experiment with their own ideas on teaching. The relative lack of advice may also depend on this. Most of the recipes in the final practice period seem to be survival recipes concerning the *supervision process*. Due to the nature of the instructional process, the *subject matter, teaching methods* and *organizing* are emphasized.

The Division of Recipes within the Different Teaching Practice Stages

This comparison concerns the percentage division within the different periods of practice teaching. Figure 13 shows the amount of advice given in different practice periods in the main content classes.

When studying the division of recipes within each practice period, high priority on *teacher-pupil interaction* recipes can be seen in the first field practice. *Teaching methods* have also been given a lot of attention. During the basic practice period in the university training school, most recipes concern *teaching methods, teacher-pupil interaction, organi-*

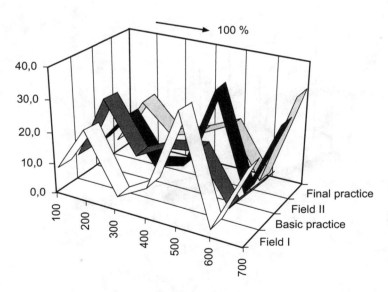

Figure 13. The division of all advice in main content classes within different practice-teaching stages (%).

Table 6. The division of all advice in main content classes within different practice-teaching stages (%).

Main content class		Field I	Basic practice	Field II	Final practice
100	Planning	7,3	7,1	7,0	4,0
200	Teaching methods	21,9	27,9	18,3	19,9
300	Subject matter	3,0	12,1	4,3	10,4
400	Organizing	8,8	16,8	6,7	13,4
500	Teacher-pupil interaction	34,7	18,7	33,4	18,3
600	Evaluation	1,5	2,8	3,0	2,3
700	Supervision process	22,8	14,5	27,2	31,8
		100	100	100	100

zation and *subject matter*. In the second field practice, *teacher-pupil interaction* has the same priority as in the first field practice period. The division of the recipes in both field practice periods looks very similar. In the final practice period, the main emphasis is on the *supervision process*, and the whole instructional process is emphasized, too. The result shows that the objectives of the four different practice periods are fulfilled quite well. An interesting notion is that the two field practice periods are quite similar, maybe too similar, when comparing the focuses of the recipes, although the aims of the two are a bit different. The more-detailed results, with percentages divided within different teaching practice periods, are presented in Table 6.

A more detailed scrutiny of the table above shows how *teacher-pupil interaction* is in a central position in the field schools. This result follows the aims of the curriculum in teacher education, but the emphasis on *interaction* is clear when comparing the division of recipes in those practice periods which are carried out in the university training school. In basic practice and in final practice, which are mainly done in a university training school, *subject matter* and *organizing* are emphasized much more than in field schools.

Most Frequent Recipes Used by Supervisors

The most and least frequent recipes were collected from the data in order to compare them with the deductive material. The list of the most frequent recipes is as follows:

Table 7. Fifteen most frequent recipes.

Recipe	Main content class
You taught well, go on in the same way.	Supervision process
Quite a nice lesson!	Supervision process
Learn to know your pupils.	Interaction
Vary different teaching methods.	Teaching methods
Learn to ask logical questions.	Organizing
Give your pupils clear working instructions.	Teaching methods
Vary different illustrating tools.	Teaching methods
Learn to use the different teaching and illustrating tools.	Organizing
Be a friendly, consistent adult.	Interaction
Ensure a peaceful working environment in class.	Interaction
Guide and motivate the pupils to plan and draw conclusions.	Teaching methods
Pay attention to the special character of each school subject.	Subject matter
Outline the subject matter didactically-correct.	Subject matter
Analyze the structure of the lesson carefully.	Organizing
Be positive and respectful towards your pupils.	Interaction

Most recipes belong to *teacher-pupil interaction* and *teaching methods*. The recipes concerning interaction seem to emphasize the warmth in the personal relations in the instructional process. *Organizing* is emphasized too. The main classes of *planning* and *evaluation* are totally lacking from the top of the list. It seems that the most important guidelines are connected to the same dimensions which Ryans (1960) had already found when studying teacher characteristics. He identified three major classroom behavior patterns: *empathetic, systematic and stimulating*. The fifteen most frequent recipes include these elements. In particular, a teacher's empathy, warmth, responsibility and kindness comes out clearly.

Least Frequent Recipes Used by Supervisors
The least frequent recipes are in the inductive material as shown in Table 8.

In the list of the most frequent recipes there were none belonging to the main classes *evaluation* and *planning*, but in the list of the least frequent recipes there were many belonging to these classes. Of the main classes, only the *supervision process* is totally lacking. It seems that the student teachers require survival recipes during the practice periods. The least used recipe was *evaluate the content of your teaching*. Perhaps this is a more detailed question, and the idea of it is included in such

Table 8. Fifteen least frequent recipes.

Recipe	Main content class
Evaluate the content of your teaching.	Evaluation
Define the cognitive goals.	Planning
Ask the pupils to speak clearly and in a loud voice.	Interaction
Emphasize co-operative learning.	Teaching methods
Pay attention to the general goals.	Planning
Plan together with your pupils.	Interaction
Pay attention to educational goals.	Planning
Learn to prepare a test and the required answers.	Organizing
Use project work in your teaching.	Teaching methods
Help and guide your pupils during individual work.	Teaching methods
Make the pupils practice together.	Teaching methods
Make sure you find the material you need for the lessons.	Organizing
Keep in touch with your pupils' parents as much as possible.	Interaction
Form concrete skill-related goals.	Planning
Include the affective goals as well in your teaching.	Planning

recipes as *outline the subject matter didactically-correct.* The emphasis does not seem to be on evaluation but on outlining the content. The recipes concerning *planning* are guidelines divided in to different goals: *general, educational, cognitive, skill-related* and *affective. Teaching methods* apply to separate methods, such as *co-operative learning, project work, individual work* and *pupils' practicing together.* These are details and not-so-often-used recipes. A more common and general recipe concerning teaching methods was fourth on the list of most frequent recipes: *Vary different teaching methods.* The advice concerning contact with pupils' parents is perhaps important for the teacher in her/his work in her/his own class, but not so important when practicing in a supervisor's class.

How Can A Teacher Use Recipes as Intellectual Tools?— Some Discursive Thoughts

Both the deductive and the inductive material show that a great deal of teaching recipes are given during teaching practice periods, although the supervisors sometimes claim that they not give recipes, they only want to get the student-teacher to think independently. When reflecting on the recipes, the supervisors offer the student-teacher reasons to think, not a direct path to effective teaching. Here is the real benefit of advice and guidelines.

The keyword to benefit from the advice and guidelines is reflection. It should be noticed that the *right* questions asked by the supervisor will help the student to think the *right things.* In other words, the supervisor advises the young teacher to pay attention to certain things, and this advice is based on the supervisor's observations during the lesson. In a way, the supervisor's feedback is indirect: A *right* question leads to a *right* idea. It is, however, important to notice that there are several *right* ideas or *right* ways to teach. Since the teacher's personality plays such an important role in teaching, it is all right for the student to discard the advice and guidelines that s/he is not comfortable with. On the other hand, a skilful supervisor focuses her/his advice to suit the personality of her/his student-teacher.

Giving advice and guidelines is normative. Education is always normative. It is important for the teacher and the student to be capable of acquiring independent and critical information and of evaluating it. Research-based teacher education offers the students possibilities to find out how scientific knowledge is produced, and, in turn, they can produce it themselves. This offers the student the tools for critical reflection on the advice and guidelines given to her/him during the training, and s/he can apply the advice in the right context.

Chapter 11

Reflection in Counselling Situations

Three models of action in supervisory discourse in which the level of practical reflection differs are presented. Forty supervisory conferences were tape-recorded. Using a category system, thought units in the discourse were classified into factual, evaluative, justificatory, or critical main classes. Continuums of thought units were drawn into profiles in order to illustrate visually the progress of the discourse. The profiles were qualitatively classified into three groups, and the classification was tested by discriminant analysis. Groups of profiles differed from each other in their focus and their level of reflectivity. They were named descriptive, normative, and reflective models of supervisory discourse.

General Framework

The general purpose of this part of the study is to understand, explain and interpret the substance and form of the discourse during the supervisory post-observation conferences in an elementary student teaching program. The aim is to make implicit theories of supervision explicit by studying the models of action in supervisory discourse.

The classroom teacher education at the University of Helsinki was originally based on the principles of humanistic psychology. A student teacher's personality and identity as a teacher were in a central position in the supervisory settings. Gradually the scope of reflection was found to be too individually centered. The educational goal based on humanistic psychology had to be broadened with the aspect of educational psychology. Future teachers were seen as critical professionals who must be able to analyze and develop the school as a part of society. Theoretical grounds for this kind of teacher education can be found in the ideas of the social-reconstructionistic tradition of teacher education using an inquiry-oriented student teaching program. The main idea is to propose a conceptual apparatus for prospective teachers to use in thinking about education. It is seen as important that students learn to consider and discern what will count as a good reason for appropriate educational action.

The knowledge base in the classroom teacher study program can be described as critical in nature. The goals and practices of the curriculum are seen as problematic according to ethical and social criteria, and as reflexive according to the criteria of the role the prospective teacher is supposed to take as a student. The knowledge base in itself is similar to the one Shulman (1987, 8) has represented. Yet there is one important difference: Because of the paradigm adopted, the student is seen as an important element; the understanding of basic instructional elements and a personal way of teaching are fostered through reflective practice. These principles are very much in coherence with the ones Hatton & Smith (1995, 44) describe as the major features commonly shared across by teacher education programs. The only difference is that theoretical and methodological studies are more intensively represented; classroom teacher education aims at the M.A. degree. Students work extensively with their thesis, using a wide range of methodologies.

Theory building in teacher education is often seen as implicit rather than explicit. This is an important point of view when organizing teaching practice as a part of teacher education. Subjective experiences are seen as an important starting point when integrating theory and practice. To give meaning, to conceptualize experiences of student teachers', is one of the tasks a supervisor is committed to in a supervisory situation. When examining the actions, thoughts and intentions of the student teacher in a dialectical manner, the aim is to give her/him theoretical tools to reason pedagogical events and actions. The integration principles between theory and practice are quite simple: practice teaching starts in the first study year, interaction between theory and practice is continuous and the practice-supporting theoretical studies are written in the curriculum. There are four practice periods, each having aims and a character of its own; they start from simple elements and expand towards more complex units.

The general framework is in line with the tradition of the research on teacher thinking. The study could be seen as an "inside out" rationale (Pope, 1993, 23), because the main interest is to help supervisors themselves to clarify their thinking and develop and extend their theories. The main theoretical assumptions underlying the empirical inquiry are drawn from studies of reflection by Schön (1983; 1987), levels of reflectivity by van Manen (1977), paradigms of teacher education by Zeichner (1983), supervisory-belief systems by Zeichner & Tabachnick (1982), discourse in supervisory conferences by Zeichner & Liston (1985), and the strategy for supervision by Handal & Lauvås (1988).

We tried to understand the form and substance of the supervisory discourse. Data was collected during the second practice teaching period, from post-observation conferences carried out by supervising teachers. In the study program, this practicing period is due when student teachers have finished their basic instructional studies and the aim is to practice, analyze and conceptualize teaching in an ordinary practice school setting. The research questions posed were:

1. What kind of focuses appear in the supervisory discourse?
2. What kind of profiles appear?
3. What kinds of models of action do the profiles represent?

Design and Method

The data is based on 40 supervisory conferences from 24 supervisors. Supervisors were asked to record two post-observation conferences during a practice teaching period lasting eight weeks. These tape-recorded supervisory conferences consisted of ten hours of supervisory discourse. Conferences were analyzed by qualitative and quantitative content analysis. The idea was to find various types of supervisory discourse and describe its character and quality. The main interest was to find qualitatively different forms of supervisory discourse and interpret the underlying belief systems and concepts of supervision.

The discourse during the tape-recorded, post-observation supervisory conferences was analyzed by a special category system. Categories for the classification of the discourse were drawn mainly from a study by Zeichner & Liston (1985) and adjusted to our supervisory customs. We adopted a procedure used in several other studies of this type (Zeichner & Liston, 1985; Haggarty, 1995), and employed a "thought unit" as the basic unit of analysis. The data consisted of ten hours of supervisory discourse which were divided into 2324 thought units. The thought unit as a coding unit was seen to represent a very precise description of the content characteristics.

According to Zeichner & Liston (1985, 160), Bales (1951) defines the "thought unit" as the smallest discriminable segment of verbal behavior to which the observer, using the present set of categories after appropriate training, can assign a classification under conditions of serial scoring.

Zeichner & Liston (1985) developed an instrument for the analysis of verbal behavior during supervisory conferences. Their major concern was to employ a system of analysis which would enable them to assess the quality of thinking exhibited during supervisory conferences. The primary concern in the analysis was to understand and distinguish types of reasoning used by supervisors and student teachers in deciding how to handle practical problems. They constructed a set of categories by applying Gauthier's (1963) and van Manen's (1977) categories of thinking and reasoning. Zeichner & Liston developed new categories where neither framework could adequately differentiate the quality of thought exhibited by supervisors and student teachers.

Gauthier (1963, 1) distinguishes between practical and theoretical reasoning: "A practical problem is a problem about what to do. Practical problems may be contrasted with theoretical problems whose solution is found in knowing something, in understanding." In other words, theoretical reasoning concerns knowledge about "what is the case", and practical reasoning concerns " what action ought to be taken".

The concept of 'practical' has been contrasted with 'theoretical'. According to van Manen (1977, 220), practical knowledge, in a communicative sense, is provided by phenomenological and interpretative bodies of knowledge. Coming to understand is a sense-making and interpretative enterprise. In this context, practical knowledge does not consist of technical-practical recommendations derived from empirical-analytic theory and research.

In van Manen's (1977) notions of "levels of reflectivity", he adopts the tripartite division of rational analysis by Habermas (1971). In Habermas' division the rational analysis is divided into empirical-analytic, hermeneutic and critical modes of reasoning. Van Manen (1977, 226–227) argues that on the first level of deliberative rationality, the practical is concerned mainly with means rather than ends. On the first level, the practical refers to the technical application of educational knowledge. On the second level of reflectivity, it is assumed that every educational choice is based on a value commitment to some interpretative framework by those involved in the process. The practical refers to the process of analyzing experiences, meanings, perceptions, assumptions and prejudgements, for the purpose of orienting practical actions. At this level of the practical, the focus is on analyzing interpretative understanding of both the nature and quality of educational experience, and of making practical choices. On the third level of deliberative rationality, the practical addresses itself to the question of the worth of knowledge.

Zeichner & Liston's conceptual framework for analyzing practical reasoning during supervisory conferences distinguishes among four types of practical discourse:

Practical Discourse

1. *Factual Discourse* is concerned with what has occurred in a teaching situation or what has happened before or what will occur in the future;
2. *Evaluative Discourse* revolves around suggestions about what to do or around evaluations of what has been accomplished;
3. *Justificatory Discourse* focuses on the reasons and grounds used for discourse concerning facts or evaluations;
4. *Critical Discourse* examines and assesses the adequacy of the reasons offered for the justification of pedagogical actions or assesses the values and assumptions embedded in the form and content of curriculum and instructional practices.

Each of these primary categories was further divided into several subcategories. In the final category system, there were four main categories which were adopted from Zeichner & Liston (1985). Only the name of the second category was changed, from prudential to evaluative discourse. All the categories were divided into four subcategories. Together there were 16 categories into which the thought units were divided. These categories addressed the logical dimensions of supervisory discourse—in other words, how thinking occurs. Two new subcategories were included

QUALI-TATIVE	**CRITICAL DISCOURSE** *Quality of personal theory* *Intrinsic: value of the educational theory* *value of experience or universal knowledge* *Value of the pragmatic rationale*							
FOCUSES	**JUSTIFICATORY DISCOURSE** *Extrinsic rationale* *Intrinsic rationale: educational theory /* *experience, universal knowledge* *Pragmatic rationale*							
OF THE	**EVALUATIVE DISCOURSE** *Support* *Judgement about value, worth or quality* *Advice/Opinion* *Instruction*							
DISCOURSE	**FACTUAL DISCOURSE** *Hypothetical* *Explanatory* *Informational* *Descriptive*							
		T H O U G H T U N I T S						

Figure 14. The category system used to analyze the data.

to get a more specific picture of the nature of the justificatory and critical discourse. According to Handal's & Lauvås' (1988) theory of supervision we wanted to make a distinction between the intrinsic rationales drawn from theory and those from experience and practice. The final category system is presented in Figure 14.

Two persons were trained to categorize the data. After an adequate level of agreement (75%) was reached, tapes were divided between them. The coders listened to the tapes and coded each thought unit to one of the 16 subcategories. The reliability of the categorizing was examined by studying the coefficient of coincidence. Relative frequencies were calculated to get a picture of the discourse as a whole.

After the discourse was categorized the continuum of thought units was drawn into profiles. Altogether 40 profiles were drawn. Profiles of the discourse were classified qualitatively, and the classification was confirmed by discriminant analysis. Three models of supervisory action were named.

Results

Discourse and Subcategories

The character and quality of the supervisory discourse is reported here at a general level. The supervisory discourse was categorized into four main divisions. These categories represent the main focuses of the discourse which are seen as qualitatively different perspectives. Evaluative discourse has the greatest number of thought units (Table 9), justificatory and critical discourse show a higher level of abstraction. Thirty percent of all the discourse reached this reflective level. When comparing the amount of this higher level reflective discourse to the results Zeichner and Liston (1985) got, it is interesting to notice that the amount is a little higher compared to their data, where it was 19.6%, although they had included two subcategories from the factual discourse in this higher level reflective mode of discourse. When examining the individual discourses, great differences in the amount of higher level reflective discourse existed. The variation was from 8.5% to more than 50% of the discourse during the supervisory conference.

The greatest difference between the study of Zeichner & Liston and the results of this study was in the amount of factual discourse. Twenty-nine percent of all the discourse was coded as factual, when they had 63.2% coded as factual. Still in this material there were also discourses which were very concentrated on factual discourse. In these cases the amount of factual discourse was around 50%.

Table 9. Four categories of the supervisory discourse in frequencies and percentages.

The focus of the supervisory discourse	f	%
Factual discourse	675	29
Evaluative discourse	959	41
Justificatory discourse	583	25
Critical discourse	107	5
Total	2324	100

Percentages of each subcategory are illustrated in Figure 15. As seen, judgmental evaluative discourse is the most common category; 71% of all the evaluative discourse is judgmental by nature. Another important notion is that only 4% of the justificatory discourse is based on theoretical grounds. Almost one half of the reasons underlying the evaluative and factual discourse used are based on experience or universal knowledge about the matter.

To get a picture of the qualitatively different focuses of the discourse, a few examples of thought units coded into categories are given. Supervisors' comments are in italics, to differentiate the speakers.

Well, it was me who started by telling first the story of the backyard cat, and it was kind of a motivating start. (Factual discourse, descriptive) *You have been watching these other mathematics lessons and noticed that the same idea has been used on the two previous ones, too.* (Factual discourse, informational) Yes, and it has worked very well. (Evaluative discourse, judgement) *Why do you think it works?* It has become familiar . (Justificatory discourse, pragmatic rationale) The blackboard is simple enough; although there is beginning to be quite a lot of information, most of it is already known to pupils. It doesn't matter if you put some more. (Justificatory discourse, experience, universal knowledge).

It's better to quote the Bible just as it is. (Evaluative discourse, instruction) I felt very good about the lesson,(Evaluative discourse, judgement) because I think they were very interested. (Justificatory discourse, pragmatic rationale) I have never before used this tell and draw method, and especially the video everybody was watching it, (Factual discourse, descriptive) although I didn't know how they understood it. (Justificatory discourse, experience) I think the lesson was very nice. (Evaluative discourse, judgement)

I think you managed very well to outline the content of the subject. (Evaluative discourse, judgement) *But the pedagogical outlining of the*

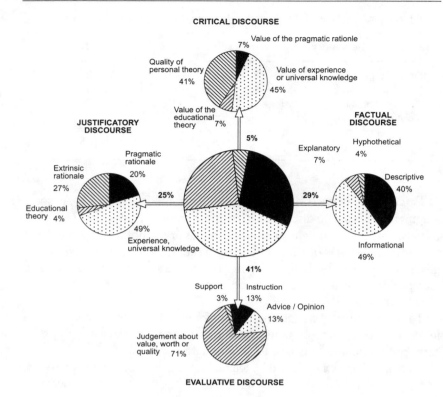

Figure 15. Percentages of main categories and subcategories of the discourse.

instructional process, that is something you should practice some more.
(Evaluative discourse, judgement) *When you have a class of your own,
you should use pupils' feelings more when teaching* (Justificatory discourse, educational theory) What do you mean by that, why? (Critical
discourse, educational theory) *Well, maybe it is more a matter of teaching method, to get pupils to discuss with each other, to doubt what
you tell them. Partly, I think it is a skill a teacher needs.* (Critical
discourse, personal theory)

   *What kind of basis can you find for this new constructivistic theory
of learning? Why has it been taken as the basis of a whole curriculum?* Well, maybe because what's ahead is changing, the world is in a
state of change all the time, nothing stays still here. (Justificatory discourse, extrinsic rationale) Well, you can see it, what we had ten years
ago and how it is now, there is not much left there. (Factual discourse,

informational) You have to be very extrovert with the knowledge, you have to find new information in new and different sources and I think that's as it should be, it's all right like that. (Critical discourse, quality of personal theory)

Profiles

The continuum of thought units was drawn into profiles to get a more specific picture. There are sixteen possible turning or stopping points in the scale, according to the number of subcategories. The idea of the profiles is to illustrate visually the advancement of the discourse. Altogether 40 profiles were drawn. They differed from each other in two main aspects: the situation in the scale varied as did the width of the profile.

Three examples of typically different profiles are presented. They are called descriptive, normative and reflective models of profiles. The reflective profile differs from the other two. The range is wider and it covers the whole scale. The descriptive profile is more concise and is situated at the lower part of the scale. The normative profile is quite concise as well, but its position is in the middle of the scale.

The descriptive profile describes a supervisory action that focuses on factual and evaluative discourse. Descriptive elements of the discourse are central, and a great deal of time is spent on discussing observations made during the lesson. It is also characteristic that there is not much justificatory discourse, and critical discourse is often totally missing.

To get a picture of the discourse visualized in the profile, an example of the discourse is presented. The example is from the beginning of the framed area in the profile and it consists of twenty thought units.

Descriptive profile

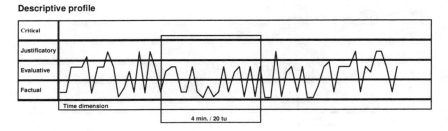

Figure 16. Descriptive Profile.

— *Let's go back to the session where they worked according to themes from books in pairs. How did you succeed with that?*
— Directions should have been clearer. They were uncertain about what to do next.
— *Although everything looked good.*
— Yes, but there were a few groups who did not know what to do.
— And they did not know what to do with the notebooks. They thought they should write down the arguments they gave.
— *Well then, what happened when they worked in pairs when you controlled that?*
— As a matter of fact, I was actually a partner to one of the pupils, so I did not control the work of others much . Me too.
— There was an odd number of boys, and when I asked Jari to go as a third to some group, he did not want to. I suppose some kind of social discrimination was going on . . .
— *What was the pupils' attitude to this work in pairs, did they like to go . . .*
— Well, I think normally it is quite easy, of course there are always those to whom it is difficult to find a partner.

This example shows very typically that discourse does not proceed to judgemental or critical modes although it would have been possible. The supervisor changes the topic after students have noticed that the given advice was not good enough. Other possibilities would have been to ask why it was not good enough, how to better it or what the principles are behind the instructional process when giving directions to pupils.

The normative profile describes supervisory action which focuses very clearly on evaluative and justificatory elements of the discourse. Observa-

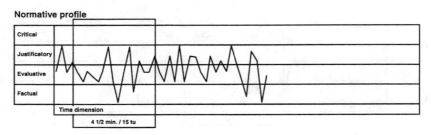

Figure 17. Normative profile.

tion of the lesson is inferred from this context; exact descriptions of the lesson are not central. Critical discourse is missing totally or there are very few critical comments. The discourse is limited to the observed lesson and follows it quite closely. The example is again from the beginning of the framed area in the profile and consists of 15 thought units.

— *As a first lesson of the period, this was on the whole very clear. There was much good in it.*
— *The objectives you had chosen you reached quite well.*
— *Well, what I thought, considering those objectives you have for the whole period, you could have had some affective objectives, too, because you had quite a lot of that kind of discussion.*
— Yes, we were talking about this nature protection and clean water, that's true.
— *But otherwise these formal and skill objectives are quite good.*
— *Well, in the beginning , this looking at the slides was all right – well of course you could have found out a bit more . . . if you want to get everything out of it.*
— *And also that was good, you did have only few slides, not too many . . . and don't start to explain if you do not have those slides you intended to show. You don't have, and that's it.*
— *And then, what I noticed here and a few other times, too: don't repeat pupils' answers. That's unnecessary. If they don't hear, ask the pupil to repeat the answer. This is something you just have to kind of recognize . . .*
— Well, I have recognized that, but somehow it is so automatic, it just happens . . .
— *And then, when children are commenting a lot, try to keep in mind turns and ask them to put up their hands.*

Normative discourse in this example shows that the supervisor is speaking quite a lot. She gives advice and justifies it with her own experience, common knowledge or pragmatic rationale. Typically she does not ask questions like why or how. There would have been opportunities to go deeper into the situations by asking the student teacher to give reasons for her action, but the supervisor did not comment on student teachers' notions. Very often she just went on, changing the subject.

The third profile, the reflective one, describes a discussion where evaluative and justificatory elements of discourse are followed by critical

Reflective profile

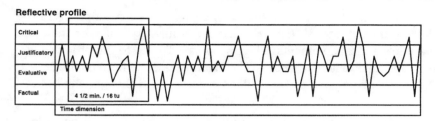

Figure 18. Reflective profile.

discourse. The emphasis is not on descriptive discourse. A broader scope of discourse brings to the discussion elements concerning matters of education and teaching on a common level. It is also distinctive that the discourse is dealing with matters like aims, objectives and methods, or personal theory of education and disconnects from time to time totally from the actual observations of the lesson.

— *Did you feel that your role in the lesson was different from before?*
— I don't know. Well, of course it was less giving instruction, it was different, more like guiding, not formally instructing.
— *Yes.*
— I was kind of guiding them to find information from different sources.
— *Well, if you think of these two ways of teaching, which of these saves your resources as a teacher?*
— I think the case is a bit two-sided. I think it saves your nerves when you do most of the work ahead. When you are well prepared you notice that pupils do not need you all the time, you just give some guidance if they need it. Well, I really liked this.
— *Can you find any negative sides to this kind of method?*
— You can't do this all the time because this requires lots of work.
— *That's what I meant, there is lots of work before teaching.*
— That's true, but when you have done it, it is very easy to be here. During the lesson, it's the pupils who are working.

Quite often in a reflective supervisory discourse the supervisor asks questions which encourage the student teacher's reasoning. As in this example, the student teacher talks quite a lot. She is reflecting on action; the supervisor helps her to describe her thoughts. In many cases supervisor leads the discourse to ideas behind the reasons and gives theoretical terms to the issues the student teacher is interested in.

Models of Action in the Supervisory Discourse

The profiles were qualitatively classified into three groups, and the classification was tested by discriminant analysis. We found three groups of discourse that differed in their focus and their level of reflectivity. Groups were named as descriptive, normative and reflective supervisory discourse.

Table 10. Descriptive, normative and reflective models of supervisory discourse in frequencies and percentages.

The supervisory discourse	f	%
Descriptive	10	25
Normative	21	52
Reflective	9	23
Total	40	100

The focus in the descriptive model of supervision is mostly on the factual discourse; in the normative model, the focus is on evaluative and in reflective model of supervisory discourse the focus is on critical discourse (Fig. 19).

When visualizing and comparing the relative frequencies of the three models of action (Fig. 20), it is interesting to see that all the models have strong evaluative elements in them but the amount of factual, justificatory and critical elements differs quite clearly. When the reflective discourse concentrates on justification and critical elements of the discourse, descriptive discourse at the same time has strong factual elements.

As a conclusion, the study has shown that there are interesting differences in the focuses of the supervisory discourse. The normative nature of the supervisory discourse is obvious. An interesting notion is that reflective and critical elements are quite well represented. As Zeichner & Liston (1991, 38) put it: ". . . since teachers are responsible for key educational decisions and actions within the classroom, it is important that prospective teachers begin to consider what will count as a good reason for effective educational action". That means that in supervisory situations discourse should have justificatory and critical elements in it.

		THE MODEL OF ACTION		
		DESCRIPTIVE	*NORMATIVE*	*REFLECTIVE*
THE FOCUS OF	*CRITICAL*			■■■
	JUSTIFICATORY		▒▒▒	■■■
DIS-COUR-SE	*EVALUATIVE*	▒▒▒	■■■	▒▒▒
	FACTUAL	■■■	⠂⠂⠂	⠂⠂⠂

Figure 19. The focus of the supervisory discourse in the models of action.

Conclusions

As Calderhead (1993, 14) has noted, it is extremely difficult to find examples of teacher training programs that typify only one paradigm of teacher education. It is far more likely that they reflect a combination of these paradigms, described by Zeichner (1983, 7). Zeichner's classification reflects different epistemologies of practice, different ways of thinking about the nature of knowledge prospective teachers should possess

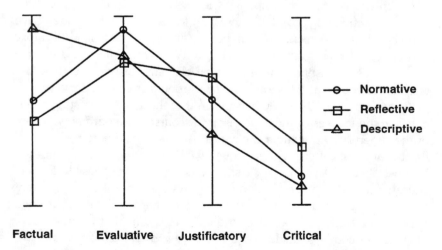

Figure 20. Relative frequencies of models of action in each discursive focus.

Table 11. Models of action in supervisory discourse compared with terms from the theoretical assumptions of the empirical study.

	The level of reflection	The quality of reflection	The paradigm of teacher education
Descriptive model of action	The hermeneutical-phenomenological rationality	Practical reflection	Personalistic paradigm (Personal growth-centered supervision)
Normative model of action	The empirical-analytical rationality	Technical reflection	Behavioristic paradigm (Technical-instrumental supervision)
Reflective model of action	The critical-dialectical rationality	Critical reflection	Inquiry-oriented paradigm (Critical supervision)

and also different ways they should acquire it. The fundamental questions are related to purposes and ends which differ in behavioristic, personalistic, traditional craft and inquiry-oriented teacher education programs.

Although our paradigm in the teacher education program defines its epistemology as social-reconstructionistic and the program as inquiry-oriented, results of this study point out that in supervisory settings three of the four traditional paradigms are represented. Table 11 summarizes the theoretical assumptions found behind the classified models of actions supervisors had.

One of the main ideas of this study is to clarify the conceptual field of supervision to help supervisors to clarify their thinking and to develop and extend their personal theories. The descriptive model of action was based on the hermeneutical-phenomenological rationality, reflection was practical by nature and it reflected the personalistic paradigm of teacher education. The normative model of action was based on empirical-analytical rationality, reflection was mainly technical and it reflected the behavioristic paradigm of teacher education. The reflective model of action used critical-dialectical rationality, reflection was critical, and teacher education was seen as inquiry-oriented.

Although the idea behind the teacher education program is defined, it would be idealistic to think that all educators and supervisors should think and act like-mindedly. They are and they should act differently. If we are true to our ideals, the central question is: Are supervising teachers aware of their conceptions of practice and knowledge? Can they explicate their personal theories and values behind them? Can they defend and give reasons for their way of supervising? These are basic questions if the idea behind the teacher education program is to give a conceptual apparatus which helps student teachers to learn to think theoretically. It is not possible to guide students in their thinking if you are not aware of your own thinking.

According to Zeichner (1983, 1–7), *behavioristic* teacher education emphasizes the development of specific skills of teaching. Issues prospective teachers are to master are limited in scope and are fully determined in advance by others. Performance is assumed to be the most valid measure of teaching competence, and observable skills are assumed to be related to pupil learning. *The personalistic* paradigm views teacher education as a form of adult development, and it seeks to promote the psychological maturity of the prospective teacher. The knowledge and skills prospective teachers are to master are not defined in advance. Students are encouraged to find their own best ways to function as a teacher. A particular set of behavior for all teachers is seen as anti-ethical, success within the personalistic orientation is measured primarily in terms of effects upon individuals, not in terms of effects upon social systems. According to *teaching as a craft*, knowledge is often seen as tacit, and teaching skills are accumulated largely by trial and error by a craftsperson. Teaching is seen as the "wisdom of an experienced practitioner" and teacher education as a process of apprenticeship. The method is to elaborate sequences of skills to learn how to perform routines. However, the whole is more than the sum of the parts, and even more, close scrutiny of the particulars of a comprehensive entity runs the risk of destroying the conception of the entity itself. *Inquiry-oriented* teacher education prioritizes the development of inquiry about teaching and about the context in which it is carried out. The fundamental task is to foster prospective teachers' capacity for reflective action. Technical skills of teaching are highly valued, not as ends in themselves, but as means for bringing about desired ends. The development of technical skills in teaching and the mastery of content knowledge is always addressed within a broader framework of critical inquiry.

Our teacher education curriculum has taken questions of research methodology as one of the central issues when trying to foster prospective teachers' theoretical pedagogical thinking. A theory of education as well as a theory of teaching are the main conceptualized sources of knowledge we have backing up our actions. As Kansanen (1991, 258) notes, the question "How do we know?" cannot be answered without one's being acquainted with the research process or how the knowledge has been sought. In this study very little of the reflective element of the supervisory discourse was theoretical by nature.

Clarke (1995, 258–259) concludes his study by providing ways in which teacher educators might foster reflective practices in supervisory settings. A supervisor should provide students with opportunities not only to practice teaching but also to theorize about that practice. Multiple perspectives from which students might examine their practice should be available. In this reflective examination, students should be encouraged to tolerate uncertainty. Reflection on action seemed to be more effective in intense longer time periods than in short after-lesson discussions.

When student teachers theorize about their teaching, it is very often the case that they are not reflecting on broad educational issues, but rather on problems within their day-to-day practice. If supervisors want to encourage dialectical supervisory discussions, they should be aware that giving advice is always a normative process. In this light it is important that supervisors understand and can explicate their knowledge base and the educational paradigm behind it. If using the concept of pedagogical level thinking (Kansanen, 1993), supervisors should help student teachers to realize the relations between action level, object theories as conceptualizing elements and metatheory as the relative value basis behind all the action.

PART IV

PRACTICAL ARGUMENTS
IN TEACHING

Chapter 12

The Nature of the Teaching-Studying-Learning Process

The viewpoint of the art or science of teaching is briefly examined in order to understand better the requirements of the teaching-studying-learning process. Reflection is considered a means of understanding, and can be analyzed in the teachers' interviews and reports. Two systematic approaches are described. The first is the analysis of arguments by Toulmin, and the second is a variant of it presented by Deanna Kuhn. (P.151)

Spontaneous Forces as a Starting Point

The promotion of learning is usually a process where a lot happens in a short time as the students and their teacher aim at common understanding. How much of this process is planned beforehand, and to what extent are the activities spontaneous? Both features are obviously needed. Involvement in the instructional process does not allow time to reflect and make rational decisions; such an activity presupposes distance-taking. A teacher's work is not satisfactory without a solid professional foundation, however. Combining the features needed for making educational decisions is what we in everyday school life look at as teachers' practical theories.

Much is learned without any specific purpose and much is not learned in spite of a very definite purpose. In describing the joint activities of parents and child John M. Stephens uses the terms 'natural forces' or 'spontaneous forces' (1965, 436–438). For thousands of years and in all cultures, children have learned the language of their parents. This process has usually succeeded without the mother really knowing how it happens. Stephens presumes that some primitive tendencies are at work and that such tendencies can, in general, be found in all adults. He claims further that such spontaneous forces "automatically come into operation whenever an adult, enthusiastic about some field of knowledge, regularly consorts with growing children" (1965, 437).

Spontaneous forces are rarely sufficient, but with the help of them, what happens in the classroom may be described as spontaneous and not too inflexible, although the instructional process as a whole run may be seen as highly systematic and methodical. This is also in line with the common-sense understanding of the teacher's work, where interaction takes place rapidly and where making educational decisions is mostly unconscious, although the decisions may be justified afterwards. In addition to arousing discussion of the nature of teachers' thinking, the teacher's way of acting in the instructional process provokes the question of the teachability of teaching and of what kind of teacher education is necessary to successful teaching.

The Art or Science of Teaching

Because of its fleeting and volatile nature, teaching and the teacher's thinking may be described as intuitive, instinctive, creative, improvised, spontaneous, impulsive, etc. This is due to the lively interaction during the teaching-studying-learning process, which also makes it difficult to estimate the course of events or to plan it in detail. On this basis, teaching is often compared with art. This may be in conflict with the requirements of the learning objectives. The point, however, is that the teaching-studying-learning process cannot be explained using only technical terms. The concept of teaching as an art may consequently be understood in contrast to the scientifically defined idea of teaching.

In addition to the artistic interpretation of teaching, the 'art of teaching' has also been used for the German *Didaktik*, especially when referring to the practical or normative side of teaching (cf. Smith, 1961, 88; Iisalo, 1979, 74), following the tradition of *didactica magna* of Comenius. The contrast of the two sides of teaching, the normative and the descriptive, is also effectively presented by William James when he states that "Psychology is a science and teaching is an art;" (James, 1899, 8). In spite of this, James adds that psychology is no guarantee of good teaching; this particular justification is often used to contrast the two sides of teaching. Skinner (1954) stated the same, using the expressions 'the science of learning' and 'the art of teaching.'

Teachers have also been compared with artists, although this has mainly been done in a metaphoric sense (Delamont, 1995). Didactics has been considered dramaturgy as well (Hausmann, 1959), and the work of teachers is said to resemble that of actors. Gage has presented a kind of compromise by combining the two sides and calling it 'the scientific basis of the art of teaching' (1978). This expression emphasizes that practical classroom life, nevertheless, can be studied systematically. It seems, however, that the understanding of the artistic nature of teaching is increasing along with the generalization of the qualitative approach in educational research. An adherent of the artistic viewpoint, Eisner, has recently directed attention to literature research, although this represents the research perspective in contrast to the practical situation (Barone & Eisner, 1997). Teaching as an art has long been a fascinating topic in researchers' minds (cf. Highet, 1951), and it seems regularly to regain their attention (Woods, 1996, 14–31).

Reflection and Making Educational Decisions

Making educational decisions in the classroom means reflecting continuously and flexibly without consciously and systematically taking a stand. The flow of situations in the teaching-studying-learning process is usually extremely rapid and too changeable to think of placing possible alternatives against each other. The systematic way of teacher thinking takes place in curriculum writing or when the teacher reflects on her/his work afterwards. In the midst of the process, there is no time to stop to think; making decisions must happen quickly and spontaneously. However, this does not mean that thinking is irrational or without reason. The idea behind making educational decisions in the teaching-studying-learning process is that the more solid the professional competence of the teacher, the better the quality of the process as evaluated in the students' activities and learning outcomes.

Although we view the teacher's activities as continuous decision-making, this does not mean that the teacher reflects or contemplates her/his actions during the teaching-studying-learning process. As Bengtsson (1995, 27,29) notes, reflection means that "thought dwells a longer period of time on an object in order to get a better and deeper understanding of it" and further, "But to react on or interact with a situation is not the same as to reflect upon it." Making educational decisions needs distancing. This can happen either during the preinteractive phase or during the postinteractive phase of interaction.

Reflection in itself hardly guarantees any better quality in the teaching-studying-learning process; it is, however, a necessary condition for development in the profession, we claim. In any case, through reflection it is possible to get to know the differences and typical features in teachers' thinking. The research on teacher expertise (Berliner, 1995) resembles the problems that become evident in the teachers' thinking as well.

Educational decisions may be justified in various ways. Beliefs supporting the justification are also varied. A clear division into empirical and philosophical beliefs can be made (Fitzgibbons, 1981, 23–33). Both can be attained by intuition or reasoning. Usually this is not known until the teachers have reflected and stated their justifications. The purpose here is to use argument analysis to clarify how the teachers justify their educational decisions.

Argumentation and Justification

The analyses of discussions in our various data material were made according to the principle that the way of argumentation used by the teachers was of concern. The viewpoint of argumentation and justification were not emphasized or sought directly in the interviews in order to avoid hindsight and the desirability effect. We were interested in unconstrained reflection and spontaneous personal thinking as it was expressed in the teachers' talk. The starting point in the analysis was Toulmin's argument pattern, which we apply to educational decisions (Toulmin, 1958, 94–145).

We look for a claim or a conclusion (C) based on data (D). If the conclusion has been justified, this is expressed as a warrant (W). Behind the warrant there may be some assurances and justifications, and these are called backings (B). The conclusion may vary in quality, and qualifiers (Q) indicate the strength of the conclusion. Although the qualifiers usually express the probability or credibility of the conclusion, a rebuttal (R) may also disqualify it to some extent. To take an example: Jim is expected to do well in the next examination (C) because he is working hard (D), and experience shows that preparing for the examination has a positive correlation with success (W); Jim's parents have promised to supervise his homework because this belongs to the principles of co-operation with the school (B); but since there are many situational variables, the estimate cannot be particularly reliable (Q) — for example, Jim's falling ill before examination may destroy the result (R).

A variation of this analysis of argumentation is presented by Kuhn (1991). It is based on the idea that second-order reflective thinking ability, ability to reflect on one's own thinking, is necessary in argumentative

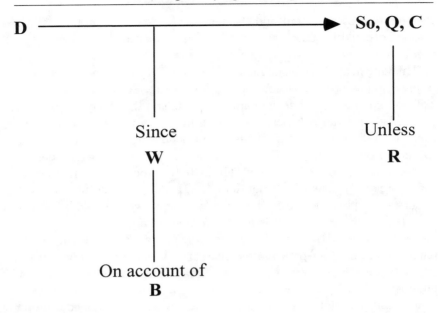

Figure 21. The layout of arguments (Toulmin, 1958, 104).

analysis

reasoning. This means that a person uses her/his metacognition and is aware of her/his own thoughts. Although much of the thinking we do involves arguing silently with ourselves, formal logic has been regarded as the preferred model of thinking. Kuhn (1991, 3) points out, however, that there is not much knowledge about the process of rational argument, and he asks several interesting questions:

> "Do people know why they believe what they do, in a way that they can justify to themselves or to others? Do they even know what they believe, in the sense of being consciously aware of these beliefs as choices they have made among many different beliefs they might hold? Do they understand what sorts of evidence bear on the correctness of their beliefs and what sorts of evidence would indicate that a belief should be modified or abandoned?"

Categorization or concept formation has been investigated extensively, and substantial progress has been made in studying basic cognitive processes as well as in building models of their operation. Yet, as Kuhn (1991, 9) remarks, the extent to which this fundamental knowledge has provided a pathway to understanding more complex forms of thought remains uncertain. When investigating an individual's thinking processes, the structure of argument and the nature of competent argumentative reasoning could be taken as central issues instead of using logic as a model of thinking.

Thinking in arguments, defined by Toulmin (1958), means the process of justifying assertions. According to Kuhn (1991, 264), the elementary skills of argument can be summarized as entailing the ability to contemplate whether what one believes is true, in contrast simply to knowing that it is true. Knowing what values are included is never certain. Instead, this is a product of hard cognitive work in which possibilities are generated, contemplated, and evaluated. Through this process, reasoned judgements are reached, which is what Kuhn (1991, 265) calls 'epistemological understanding.' Without this, the practice of argumentative skills is likely to be lacking. When thinking is seen as competent argumentative reasoning, knowing could be defined as an ongoing process of evaluating possibilities where the ever-present possibility of new evidence and new arguments means it is never completed. The basic elements of Kuhn's argumentative reasoning are seen in Figure 22.

Increasingly, thinking ability has become the central aim of education. The model of argumentative reasoning skills emphasizes accurately what

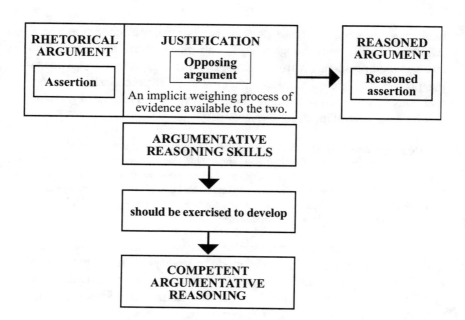

Figure 22. Model of argumentative reasoning skills (Kuhn, 1991).

educators refer to as critical thinking. According to Kuhn (1991, 12), in the study of informal reasoning, the structure of an argument can be defined as an assertion with accompanying justification.

Justifying means relating evidence to the assertion and its opposing argument. Justification as a part of a rhetorical argumentative reasoning process can be described as an implicit weighting process of evidence. By justifying the rhetorical argument, one makes it a reasoned argument. How well a person can justify shows how well her/his reasoning skills are developed. This is a central issue when considering teacher thinking as a focus of teacher education. Argumentative reasoning skills should be exercised to develop competent argumentative reasoning. Defining the thinking skills presupposes any attempt to teach thinking skills. According to Kuhn, causal theories, supporting evidence, alternative theories and counterarguments as well as their rebuttals are all elements a person considers when argumentative reasoning skills are well developed. Kuhn argues that the educational challenge in teaching thinking is one of reinforcing and strengthening skills already present in at least implicit form. Once a skill is in place, in even rudimentary form, the most obvious method of strengthening it is that of practice. Most educational programs designed to teach thinking skills have focused on teaching students about thinking. Engaging them in the activity of thinking has not been so usual. According to Kuhn, social dialogue offers us a way to externalize the internal thinking strategies and this ". . . externalization serves not only the research objective of analysis but also the practical objective of facilitation." (Kuhn, 1991, 293)

Chapter 13

Empirical Findings of Teachers' Argumentation and Justification

Teachers' arguments are first analyzed on an intuitive and rational basis with the help of Toulmin's framework. A mixed pattern of justifying is also applied, and the text of teachers' interviews is analyzed qualitatively as well. The text from the supervisory discourse sessions is analyzed by means of a framework developed by Deanna Kuhn. Some examples of the text data are presented. Finally, some common components behind educational decisions interpreted as latent belief systems with the help of factor analysis are discussed, and the Finnish and German belief systems are compared.

Intuition and Reasoning

In this section, we present some empirical findings of teachers' argumentation and justification. The arguments teachers use to justify their actions can be studied in the conceptual framework of practical arguments defined by Fenstermacher and Richardson (1993). According to these researchers, practical arguments in teaching are post hoc examinations of teachers' actions. Their main functions are to explain or justify what the teacher did and why s/he acted as s/he did (Fenstermacher & Richardson, 1993, 104). Practical arguments can be viewed as formalization of teachers' practical reasoning with specific components and a definite structure. In our study, teachers' practical arguments are used as an analytical device for understanding how teachers think when they decide what to do as suggested by Pendlebury (1990). As Pendlebury (1990, 175) argues, practical reasoning is always moral reasoning according to the Aristotelian tradition: it is concerned with the commitment to the Good Life, the demands of the teaching profession and the role teachers have undertaken.

The findings related to the moral dilemmas and their solving strategies indicate that teachers' actions in these situations are very context relative. The relevant features of a situation demand perception from the teacher which in the Aristotelian tradition means the ability of a teacher to see fine detail and nuance. Pendlebury (1990, 176) uses the concept 'situational appreciation' in referring to perception or in responding to the particularity of each hard case. In our study, the hard cases teachers reported had involved difficult moral dilemmas. Here, we investigate further teachers' argumentation and justification in these dilemmas using practical arguments as a device for understanding teachers' thinking. We adopt Toulmin's model for analyzing teachers' arguments. To avoid too narrow a conception of the practical argument, we have paid special attention to both the intuitive and the rational basis of the arguments presented. In the following section, we give some empirical examples of analyzing teachers' intuitive and rational arguments in the framework presented by Toulmin (1958).

Intuitive Basis of Justifying

In a case that belonged to the category of matters related to teachers' work, a male teacher had thrown one pupil out of the classroom in a violent way. This particular pupil did not belong to the group the teacher was teaching, and he was continuously disturbing the lesson. First, the teacher had politely asked the pupil to leave, but he did not obey the teacher. In fact, the pupil started to make fun of the teacher, who became very angry at this behavior. The teacher got so angry that he picked up the pupil and carried him out of the classroom. During this episode, the teacher had pushed the pupil against the wall a couple of times and made some unfriendly comments. In an interview, the teacher reflected on this episode in the following way:

> "It was a situation that made me think about my behavior afterwards. I thought I went too far and I did wrong. You should never go that far in your behavior. However, I was so angry that I could not help myself. I think nothing else would have worked in this situation. It was such a spontaneous act in that situation." (Male, eight years of teaching experience)

This case was a typical situation in a classroom where a pupil misbehaved and the teacher needed to decide on an appropriate way of dealing with his misbehavior. We have presented a quotation from an interview to describe the teacher's point of view in a reliable way. We have analyzed

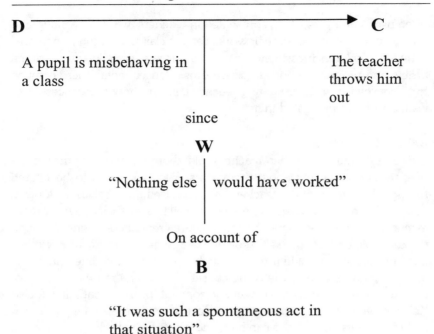

D ─────────────────────────► **C**

A pupil is misbehaving in   The teacher
a class   throws him
                                   out

since

W

"Nothing else │ would have worked"

On account of

B

"It was such a spontaneous act in
that situation"

Figure 23. The layout of an intuitive argument.

the teacher's arguments with the help of technical terms developed by Toulmin. As Figure 23 shows, the data (D) provided by the teacher can be formulated as "a pupil is misbehaving in a class." The teacher tried to be friendly and asked the pupil to leave the classroom. According to the teacher, the pupil started to make fun of the teacher, making him very angry. The teacher made an intuitive decision and carried the pupil out of the classroom. In our analysis, "the teacher throws him out" forms the conclusion (C) of this episode. We can justify the intuitive base of the teacher's decision-making by his warrant (W) given in this episode. The warrant the teacher used was an intuitive judgement, *"nothing else would have worked."* The more abstract principle behind the teacher's argument, backing (B), confirms our analysis of the intuitive base of reasoning: *"It was such a spontaneous act in that situation."*

The claim that teaching is personal activity is often advanced as some sort of common-sense understanding of the teaching profession. According to the claim, teachers build a store of practical knowing mainly from personal experiences. This knowing is not usually made explicit, but it is often useful and powerful, represented in teachers' ways of working and their ways of talking about their work. Yet this claim, teaching as personal activity, is seldom investigated as to how it serves to justify teachers' beliefs and reported actions in classrooms. Consequently, there is much to be learned from investigating teacher talk and how the processes of justification are presented in it.

Being Themselves

Throughout our data, when teachers told about instances of their practice, they were talking about themselves. Events seemed to be filtered through the person of the teacher. Teachers used their 'selves' as tools to manage both the problems and the possibilities of their work. A great extent of teacher talk contained some self-referential comment. Through the data, aspects of the 'self' repeatedly emerged as the central experience in teachers' thinking, even though each 'self' was different. Since one never has access to the complete set of teachers' representations of themselves, we have used the heuristic concept 'professional self' (cf. also Kelchtermans, 1993) to describe that part of teacher talk where justifications for beliefs and actions can be found. Professional self-concept is not a monolithical unity, but rather a collection of different types of teachers' self-representations. These self-representations illuminate the problem of how teachers conceive of themselves as teachers.

Our data shows that these self-descriptive statements are often formulated in terms of the general principles and images that govern teachers' professional behavior. These statements are often used to justify both the general approach to the teaching profession and the particular practices teachers are dealing with in their classrooms. One teacher explained why she uses a particular teaching method:

> I am that kind of a teacher myself. Every year I have to learn something new, even if I do not have any practical use for it in my work. I just love to know new things. I guess it keeps me professionally alive and progressing. And at the same time I get good opportunities to exercise my very own curiosity . . . All in all, I think that a teacher must get some ideas and methods for her work. Otherwise it may happen that a teacher doesn't know what's old and new, what's coming and going . . .

Social Selves

In the person of the teacher, pedagogical knowledge is justified according to the ideas that are meaningful to the teacher him- or herself. Claiming that those ideas are often intuitive by their nature does not mean that they are unsound for the practices of teaching. Rather, they present and justify pedagogical ideas in a way that is socially useful. Teachers have learned this 'language of practice' in classrooms and staffrooms together with their students and their peers. It indicates that teachers' knowledge is justified much in the same ways that they experience the people and things with which they come into contact. Accordingly, teachers' 'selves' in the processes of justification are inescapably social (cf. Nias, 1989, 20). Very often teachers also refer to the way they think they are perceived by others (colleagues or parents). One teacher explicitly states:

> I am quite sure that the other teachers in our school know what and how I am teaching my class. Of course, some know more than the others. I know that there are teachers who regard the methods I use as simply ridiculous, even if they really do not want to know why I am teaching the way I do. . . . and every time we have guests in our school the headmaster together with local school authorities want to present my classroom as an example of good work. And of course it flatters me, even if I simultaneously get envious comments from my own colleagues.

The frustration deals with the teacher's task perception: the way the teacher herself has defined her job. Here the judgements of significant others (school leaders, colleagues, parents) are used as arguments to support or suppress the teacher's pedagogical ideas and actions. The teacher's personal agenda is, at least to some extent, justified by the attitudes of others in the school context. However, the main reason to legitimate ideas and actions seems to be their value for the classroom. The experience that "it works" seems to be the most important criterion for justifying them on the teacher's personal agenda. The same teacher continues:

> According to my own view, I see that I have progressed quite well, and I am pleased with the situation. And now I am not talking only about myself. According to my experiences, pupils also feel the way I do . . . During our discussions, I have told my pupils that I can't go back to the 'old days' and old ways of teaching, and they have told me that neither can they. They told me that they do not want to study according to the old methods, but instead they want to proceed in their studies individually.

According to the teacher, the 'others' that matter the most are her pupils. Ultimately, the teacher's ideas and actions are justified by how well they work with students. However, it is not a matter of formal teaching only. Teachers report that their personal agenda must help to *"establish all in all a good relationship with pupils."* They also maintained that *"a teacher must get co-operation from the pupils"*, and *"teaching is a joint effort between you and them."* Teachers' pedagogical ideas and actions were often justified by their experienced worth for teacher-pupil relationships. Nevertheless, teachers found it quite hard to describe what they meant by their 'relationship' with pupils. Occasionally it was seen as playing a parental role: *"I want my classroom to become a sort of home to my pupils."* Some teachers wanted to relate as peers: *"I like to be very close to my pupils, like a grown-up friend. I do not want to take the formal teacher role."* One teacher described teaching as *"communication with another human being."*

Teachers tend to justify their ideas and actions according to the possibilities of 'being themselves' in the classroom. Many saw little distinction between their 'selves at work and outside of it'; as one said, *"What's happening to you outside school as a person can't be separated from what's happening to you as a teacher in the classroom."* Teachers often experienced the blurring of personal and professional boundaries as being very satisfying. They felt a sense of unity in school, particularly with their classes. The desire to create 'wholeness' was also shown in teachers' attempts to be an integral part of their pupils' learning experiences. Many talked with enthusiasm about their involvement in their pupils' curricular activities: they wanted to be an integral part of *"their pupils' journey of discovery and learning."* The teacher's pedagogical agenda was justified on account of feelings of shared understanding with pupils.

Commitment and Hopefulness

Many teachers felt that they were committed to their work. The notion of 'commitment' was obviously central to how teachers reasoned and justified their pedagogical ideas and actions. However, they do not use the concept of 'commitment' frequently in their talk. Rather, teachers report the amount and quality of thought and energy they put into their work. One teacher said: *"Now I have worked with these pupils over five years and I am gradually starting to see where all my efforts are leading us. And it is quite akin to what I hoped for."* Teachers are committed not only to their pupils, but they also care for the development of their school, and they strive to reach higher professional standards in their own work. When teachers talk about their pedagogical agenda, they seem to feel that their personal strivings serve as adequate justifications for their actions, although it looks as if their 'intuitive high hopes' are often placed above the 'reasoned facts.' One teacher explained: *"I am not at all sure about the way I am teaching my class. Ultimately, I can only hope that it will bring some good results."*

The commitment to teach calls for hope. Often it requires placing personally relevant and optimistic beliefs above 'the facts'. Zeuli & Buchmann (1988, 142) call it the 'triumph of hope' in teachers' thinking. According to them, as a basis for action, the hopes that pupils can learn and change must be upheld whenever test scores, the opinions of parents, and even the firsthand experiences of the teacher may imply the contrary. Spontaneous feelings of hope over reasoned experiences are justified, not because they can fit with our data, but because teachers think that their hopes can create new and more desirable results in their pupils as well as in themselves. As one teacher said: *"Even if you can't see the positive results, you must still hope for the best."*

This hopefulness has a moral character in teachers' thinking. It can be seen in two ways: on the one hand, as relative passive willingness to wait and see how things turn out, and, on the other hand, as a more active tendency to foster pupils' growth. About the former, one teacher said: *"You must give enough time to your pupils and also to yourself to develop as a teacher."* Another teacher commented on the latter: *"(as a teacher) you just can't sit still and wait, you've got to help your pupils (in their growth)."* Elbaz (1992) stresses that this hopefulness in teachers' thinking should not be interpreted merely as naive or sentimental. It rests not on teachers' idealized images of their work but often on a detailed perception of their pupils' life in their classrooms. Accordingly, teachers (hope to!) know more than they can express.

So far we have dealt with the intuitive basis of justification in teachers' thinking. We have called attention to many non-cognitive elements in the background of thought, such as teachers' personal experiences, the social nature of teachers' selves, teachers' feelings, commitment, and hope. They all belong to the intuitive context of justification that precedes and interacts with the more rational areas of teacher knowledge. This background of thought (cf. Garrison, 1996) is not a consistent whole because it contains many illogical relations and is filled with many contradictions. Being a teacher means living with paradoxes because teaching presupposes inventing personal strategies for working with many inconsistencies that cannot be finally resolved (Lampert, 1984). However, even if we regard the intuitive basis of justification as inconsistent by its nature, we argue that it is coherent enough to be labeled a 'basis.' Here we adhere to Buchmann & Floden (1993, 5), who look at coherence as allowing for many kinds of connectedness, "encompassing logic but also associations of ideas and feelings, intimations of resemblance, conflicts and tensions and imaginative leaps."

The knowledge on these intuitive levels of justification is often loose and infinite by nature. Therefore, this background of teacher thinking is viewed according to the Aristotelian tradition of knowledge as phronesis. It is mainly concerned with the understanding of concrete cases and complex situations, and it is primarily formulated in concrete and context-related terms.

Rational Basis of Justifying

The intuitive aspects of justification focused on a broad range of mental states of teachers that arose from their selves, personal experiences, and reflections that frequently did not have a solid rational basis. They can be characterized by the phrase 'what it feels like to be a teacher?' In teachers' thinking, these intuitive feelings do not take a very outward form. Rather, they were interpreted from the data by using the concepts that transformed teachers' implicit and scattered knowledge into a more explicit and coherent form. Our aim was to present this mostly non-rational background of teachers' thinking that precedes but also partakes in more rational forms of thinking.

Epistemological Standards

Teachers' justifications also comprise more rational forms of thinking and knowing. If the knowledge claims are made with the intent of having rational characteristics, then there must be a way to justify them. Such justification requires some notion of epistemological standards that must be met before they can properly be regarded as rational. According to Kuhn (1991, 172), these epistemological standards answer to the question: what basis do teachers have for knowing what is appropriate and true in matters they face in their work? Thus, epistemological standards involve issues of how the knowledge in teachers' thinking is used and constituted.

A rational basis of justification presupposes that the knowledge claims which teachers use have epistemological standards which the teachers regard as adequate for justifying their pedagogical ideas and actions. Kuhn (1991, 23–28) speaks about sufficient causes that justify people's knowing and knowledge. She argues that people hold explicit or implicit epistemological standards according to which they treat their arguments as worthwhile, as personally accepted paths to their knowing (Kuhn, 1991, 201). Here we do not follow this path all the way. Instead, we concentrate on the questions to be answered in its first two steps: i.e., how do people explain their ideas and actions, and how does a teacher's pedagogical agenda become a justified true belief for her/him.

Although, the concepts and their variants which we present in the following may sound very linear, we only use them as working tools to explicate the practical rationality in teachers' justifications. Therefore, we emphasize that the teaching situation itself, and the reflective talk about it, is mainly nonlinear. But it is difficult to describe and make sense of teachers' thinking that is related to complex settings without having some conceptual landmarks. Otherwise, we might run the risk of getting lost in teachers' nonlinear paths of knowing.

Rational Arguments

The case concerns the category of pupils' work moral. A pupil described by the teacher as "the weakest pupil in the class" refused to go into a small group with a fat girl. He had said aloud: "I will not work with a person like that, I cannot learn anything with her." The teacher stated that this kind of situation is a very typical one and repeats itself every single day. According to the teacher, pupils are cruel to each other and use very hurtful language in evaluating each other's appearance and skills. The teacher did not say anything at the moment this episode happened, but she asked both pupils involved to stay after the class. The teacher discussed the episode with these two pupils but they did not find any solution. She asked them to come and talk with her the next day in the teachers' room before classes began. The teacher described their conference thus:

> "We went to talk in a private room. Then, in front of the boy, I asked the girl how she feels to hear comments like the one by this boy yesterday. The girl replied that it does not feel very good, it feels very bad indeed. Then I asked the boy if he has ever paid any attention to the feelings these kinds of comments could cause to the others. I asked him to imagine what it would be like to hear those comments daily himself, to hear things like, 'Nobody wants to work with you.' The boy was touched by this and told us that he has never thought about it in that respect. Then I guided him to make a deal with the girl not to do it ever again. They shook hands and he promised not to do it anymore, at least to this particular girl. After that conference I have never heard that he has been mean to the girl again. I think this is very important: always pay attention to these kinds of episodes and do not let them go unnoticed. But it is so difficult because these episodes occur every day and in every lesson. You do not have time to get involved every time. It is only the meanest and the cruelest things you have time to pay attention to. I think every person is valuable and we should teach the kids not to treat each other in a bad way. The principle behind this view is my respect for other people. Everybody is valuable as a person." (Female, ten years teaching experience)

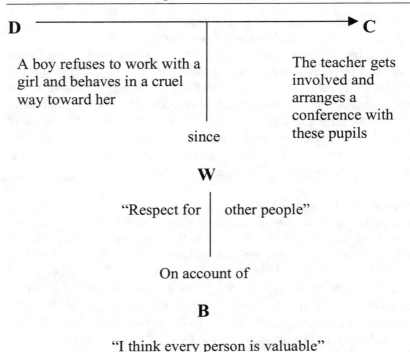

D ──────────────────────────▶ **C**

| A boy refuses to work with a girl and behaves in a cruel way toward her | The teacher gets involved and arranges a conference with these pupils |

since

W

"Respect for | other people"

On account of

B

"I think every person is valuable"

Figure 24. The layout of a rational argument.

This case reflects the rational basis of justifying practical arguments. The teacher in this episode had observed a very typical moral dilemma in her work, when one pupil behaved in a cruel way toward another pupil. The data (D) in this case is the actual behavior of the boy "a boy refuses to work with a girl and behaves in a cruel way toward her" (see Figure 24). The conclusion (C) of the episode was that the teacher was involved in the situation, and she arranged a conference with these pupils the next day. In this episode, the teacher did not act in an impulsive way. She did not say anything at the moment the episode happened but she made a rational choice to talk with these pupils later. The justification the teacher provided for her actions was her warrant (W) "respect for other people" that did not allow her to ignore cruel behavior in her classroom. The teacher had a philosophical backing (B) in her rational thinking; the value of a human being was the ethical standard guiding her decision-making.

Rules of Practice

In analyzing the process of justification and to identify its structure, we are at first inclined to look for some "straight" reasonings that can be read out from the data. One teacher stated that:

> "When it is a question of my pupils' safety, I always prefer clear and clean-cut rules and guidelines on how to act in those situations. And that is because I have seen what can happen if you don't do it."

The statement is straightforward and its content is simple: as a teacher you must protect your pupils from getting into accidents and getting injured. The teacher does this by giving *"clear and clean-cut rules"* to her pupils and ensures that her pupils act accordingly. In the case of safety issues, this is the most common rule of practice teachers use. The reasoning here goes along a single line: if a teacher does not do her work properly, she might cause accidents and injuries to her pupils. Therefore, the single causal line in reasoning is included in the rule of practice: give clear and clean-cut rules and guidelines to your pupils.

The rule of practice is simply what the terms suggest: a brief, clearly formatted statement of what to do in a particular situations frequently encountered in practice (Elbaz, 1983, 132). In the case of a safety rule, the rule of practice can be applied to broader situations, but the rules of practice can also be highly specific, relating to, e.g., how to deal with conflicts a teacher faces with a pupil. As one teacher reported:

> "I have one pupil that really gets on my nerves. He just can't sit still and wait his turn. He wants to be noticed immediately; he can't stand the fact that there are others in the classroom, too. What I have tried to practice with him is that he will get my attention after I have finished my instructions and other pupils have made their comments on the subject at hand."

Here also the reasoning goes along a single line: the pupil must wait his turn. Only then can he get attention from the teacher. In this case, the single causal line in the teacher's reasoning is included in the rule of practice: in the classroom pupils, must learn to wait their turn.

Good Reasons

As presented, the rules of practice make reference to the details of the situations to which they relate. In both cases, the reasoning goes along a single causal line: the following of the rules promises good results. If the teacher discards the rules, s/he might get into trouble. Therefore, following the rules is a good thing to do. Not only is it a good thing to do, it often seems to be the only thing to do under the circumstances. The rules of practice appear rational because they contain good reasons to think and act accordingly.

But what kind of evidence serves to justify the reasoning according to the rules of practice? How do the rules of practice offer good reasons for teachers to believe them? According to Fenstermacher (1994b, 44), justification can take place when reasoning may show that "an action is the reasonable thing to do, obvious thing to do, or the only thing to do under the circumstance". Each of these is a contribution to the justification of a rule of practice. Notwithstanding, the evidence supporting the rules of practice must come from the practice of teaching itself. The rules are justified because they have proven their worth and got approved. Teachers think, both implicitly and explicitly, that the rules of practice work. And because they work, they act accordingly. Teachers are justified to reason that there is a connection between the rules of practice and their supposed or intended outcomes. In this way, the rules of practice are backed by genuine evidence (Kuhn, 1991, 54–56).

In our two examples, this rational line of thinking presents itself in counterfactual terms. In the case of the safety rule, the teacher explicates that *"I have seen what can happen if you don't (follow the rules)"*. The rule is justified by personal security based on practical experiences. The waiting rule shows the same implicitly: when the teacher states that the pupil must learn that *"there are others in the classroom, too"*, she bases her rule on her justified belief in what would happen if she acted counter to the waiting rule. In both cases, the rules of practice seem to necessitate both the thinking through of the practical matter, and the acting according to the rule. The rules of practice are justified because they meet the standards held by the teacher.

Principles of Practice

Teachers' practical reasoning also consists of more inclusive statements. One teacher commented that:

> "I do not have a huge amount of pedagogical ideas guiding my work with my pupils. I'll try be fair and honest towards every one of them; I try to guide them to do their studying work in an appropriate manner and so on . . . but all this can happen only if they really like to come to the school and your classroom. If you (as a teacher) have failed to create that sort of good mood among your pupils, then even a great many of your sincere efforts are useless. And as a teacher you must yourself act accordingly."

Compared to the rules of practice, this statement is more comprehensive. Here, the reasoning does not go along a single causal line, as was the case in the two rules of practice presented earlier. Instead of one causal line, the statement now consists of multiple causal lines. We can identify at least three rules of practice: First, when the teacher states that she tries to *"be fair and honest towards every one of them"* she expresses her rule of justice. Second, the aim *"to guide them to do their studying work in an appropriate manner"* refers to the rule of diligence. Third, the rule of a moral example is exemplified in the expression *"as a teacher you must yourself act accordingly"*. As stated earlier, each of these three rules of practice can be justified separately by their own external evidence. However, here the three rules of practice find their justification in the phrase *"all this can only happen if they (the pupils) really like to come to the school and your classroom"*. This statement is more inclusive than the rules and it implies what the teacher should do, and how to do it, in a given range of practical situations (Elbaz, 1983, 137). The above three rules find their justification in this more general principle of "pupils' pleasure in attending."

This principle of pupils' pleasure in attending gives the teacher a good reason to act according to the three rules that are related to the principle. But the rules must be practiced in a manner that accords with the pedagogical idea and the agenda of the principle. It is the practical principle of pupils' pleasure in attending that provides the epistemological standards for the three rules; these standards must be met before the rules can be considered rational in the teacher's thinking. Thus, what finally makes sense for the teacher is that the rule of justice, the rule of diligence, and the rule of moral example are practiced according to the principle of pupils' pleasure in attending.

The principle of practice is justified by practical evidence: the teacher's personal experience demonstrates that the principle of "pupils' pleasure in attending" should provide the guidelines for putting the three rules into practice. Counterfactual evidence proves that if teachers don't act according to the manner of the principle of pupils' pleasure in attending, the mere following of the rules does not bring the intended outcomes. Consequently, teachers are justified in reasoning that pedagogical principles make sense in their work. In this way, the principles are backed by genuine evidence (Kuhn, 1991, 54–56).

The principle of "pupils' pleasure in attending" offered us a case in which it was possible to analyze the practical principle and to relate it to its specific rules. This can't be done in every case. As Elbaz (1983, 143) notes, even if the principles may be quite clearly held, the complexity of the situation, the teacher's inexperience, the lack of necessary means, and many other factors, may prevent the formulation of the explicit rules.

Nevertheless, teachers construe the use of practical principles as a vehicle for their reflective activity. Practical principles can be derived quite formally from theoretical viewpoints, they can grow out from personal experiences, or, most often, they can develop from a conjunction of the rational and the intuitive bases of reasoning.

Mixed Patterns of Justifying

In the interviews analyzed above, the justifications were not purposely requested. Instead, the flow of teachers' talk was followed, and the arguments which were presented in the course of talking were analyzed as justifications for decisions. Here we present some results of another approach where the teachers, mostly supervisors, were in specific asked for their justifications and could write them down. In a supervisory discussion, it is usual that the supervisors use a great number of normative arguments and give direct advice which they back mostly with intuitive reasons. These are usually based on personal and practical experiences, and we can interpret them as common-sense expressions. *"Because I have found them good"* is an example of this kind. In another longer example, the same kind of experiential knowledge is exposed as follows:

> In my opinion all advice is derived from practical situations. They have not been drawn at the desk. They are not opinions of a supervisor but observations based on student behavior from countless lessons. The things dealt with in the supervisory process are thus the result of a long 'product development.' The students notice this quite rapidly when they see that the advice work in practice. Differences of opinion of good teaching among supervisors are not a problem because the supervisors know that practical knowledge cumulates through practice.

In addition to personal and practical experiences, habits and routines are also found in the justifications: *"The reason for this was how to get things to work in practice."* Examples and generalizations also turn up to some degree: *"I justify the advice with examples from my own work. Or I tell how and in what situation I myself have acted as I have described."*

In addition to intuitive arguments, another category of justification is theoretical knowledge, or rational thinking in general. This may also be called reasoning. Cause and grounds as a subcategory of rational arguments may turn out as follows: *"I indeed give direct advice and guides in questions of safety."* Sometimes the supervisor has found facts to be sufficient justification: *"Physiological arguments (the function of the brain, the function of the eyes, the function of the ears)."* An argument quite close to the physiological one is ergonomy: *"The technical and economic reasons – reasonable conditions of work."*

One of the most central rational arguments is research knowledge. Here we can find such topics as developmental psychology a justificatory basis when making decisions on aims and goals, content, and teaching methods. *"Children's learning strategies"* is a typical argument. The knowledge acquired in one's own studies is also common: *"When we talk about teaching methods and about their usefulness etc., I apply the knowledge I have got in my own studies."*

In various situations during practice teaching and in evaluating learning results, the aspects of evaluation and reflection are also mentioned. *"I have understood it as my duty in supervision in general to reflect my decisions with questioning — for example, why the various decisions are justified."* When one's own behavior is expanded to act as an example for the students, we can think of it as a rational way to back the advice: *"You are a model for your students. The students easily do the same as you do."*

In these examples we have deliberately sought intuitive or rational arguments in the advice given in the supervisory discussion. Quite often both kinds of justifications were given in the same discussion; such mixed patterns contained many-sided arguments like the following: *"My arguments vary according to the topic of action which is under discussion. I try to differentiate my views depending on their being generally accepted or only subjective, or if it is possible to find knowledge which is based on research."* In practice, however, the supervisor and the teacher act all-inclusively without thinking about how each piece of advice may be justified:

> "Generally I justify my advice by appealing to general didactical and educational conceptions concerning the problem presented. I make use quite a lot of use of my somewhat short but fruitful experience. Sometimes balanced adult common sense is helpful for observing things which are brought to a discussion; advice and justifications are not needed."

In some cases, the supervisor has specified more accurately both intuitive and rational justifications and has also mentioned some details. These kinds of arguments may contain almost all possible ways of justifying the decisions, and they reflect a deep thinking over teaching:

> There are some things (the use of blackboard lights, the use of an overhead projector, the things which are connected to the size of the text on the board, to the clarity of making the presentation concrete) which I indeed justify by saying that it is a fact that writing on the board in big letters is more visible than writing

in small letters or that I myself have found the argument to be true or someone else has found it true. Of some things I say that there is no one right way to teach, everyone has to choose the one which is in line with her/his personality; on the other hand, I have arrived at my own way of action from my experience of fifteen years as a teacher: the base is thus the practical experience and in particular my nine-year experience in practical field work. I suppose that I know quite well what is waiting my student teachers. In the course of years and in my studies, I have, of course, happened to read many kinds of texts; various kinds of research results give hints. I sometimes cite them or I tell my students that I have read that somewhere. The years of supervision have naturally taught me, or at any rate I hope they have.

In short, when both ways of arguing are used, the expression may be quite simple: *"I justify the advice I give with my experience of teaching and on the basis of my knowledge."*

Justification of advice is a moral and responsible way to act. In this way, the student gets the opportunity to understand where the point of view of the supervisor originates. The argumentation can be developed to pedagogical discourse by means of which the typical terminology for the profession comes into being. The main interest examining the advice and recipes which are presented in student teaching is how they are justified or whether they are justified at all. Usually the teaching recipe does not include justifications. These are expressed separately if necessary. If the idea of a recipe is made conscious and if its justification is insisted on, the teacher's pedagogical thinking may become more advanced. Only some justifications are clearly based on theorizing of teaching. Instead, they usually reflect the teacher's personal beliefs about good teaching and are intuitive by nature. Behind these recipes may lie reasonably good knowledge of educational theory and thus a rational basis for the justification of the recipes. Our results indicate, however, that teachers justify both intuitively and rationally, and usually they have a mixed pattern where both sides are combined into an integrated whole.

Kuhnian Framework

In this section we present some empirical findings of argumentation and reasoning in supervisory discourse. The argumentative process in supervisory discourse is studied in the conceptual framework of argumentative reasoning skills presented by Kuhn (1991).

According to Kuhn, competent argumentative reasoning rests on a person's ability to develop supporting evidence to an assertion in question. When the reasoning process goes on, alternative theories and counterarguments are brought into consideration. Rebuttals are generated,

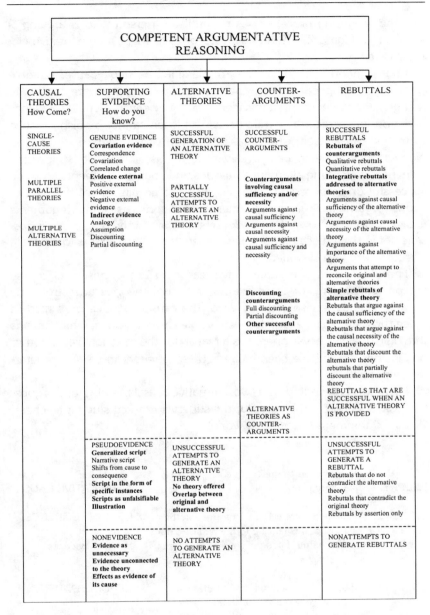

CAUSAL THEORIES How Come?	SUPPORTING EVIDENCE How do you know?	ALTERNATIVE THEORIES	COUNTER-ARGUMENTS	REBUTTALS
SINGLE-CAUSE THEORIES	GENUINE EVIDENCE **Covariation evidence** Correspondence Covariation Correlated change **Evidence external** Positive external evidence Negative external evidence **Indirect evidence** Analogy Assumption Discounting Partial discounting	SUCCESSFUL GENERATION OF AN ALTERNATIVE THEORY PARTIALLY SUCCESSFUL ATTEMPTS TO GENERATE AN ALTERNATIVE THEORY	SUCCESSFUL COUNTER-ARGUMENTS **Counterarguments involving causal sufficiency and/or necessity** Arguments against causal sufficiency Arguments against causal necessity Arguments against causal sufficiency and necessity **Discounting counterarguments** Full discounting Partial discounting **Other successful counterarguments** ALTERNATIVE THEORIES AS COUNTER-ARGUMENTS	SUCCESSFUL REBUTTALS **Rebuttals of counterarguments** Qualitative rebuttals Quantitative rebuttals **Integrative rebuttals addressed to alternative theories** Arguments against causal sufficiency of the alternative theory Arguments against causal necessity of the alternative theory Arguments against importance of the alternative theory Arguments that attempt to reconcile original and alternative theories **Simple rebuttals of alternative theory** Rebuttals that argue against the causal sufficiency of the alternative theory Rebuttals that argue against the causal necessity of the alternative theory Rebuttals that discount the alternative theory rebuttals that partially discount the alternative theory REBUTTALS THAT ARE SUCCESSFUL WHEN AN ALTERNATIVE THEORY IS PROVIDED
MULTIPLE PARALLEL THEORIES MULTIPLE ALTERNATIVE THEORIES				
	PSEUDOEVIDENCE **Generalized script** Narrative script Shifts from cause to consequence **Script in the form of specific instances Scripts as unfalsifiable Illustration**	UNSUCCESSFUL ATTEMPTS TO GENERATE AN ALTERNATIVE THEORY **No theory offered Overlap between original and alternative theory**		UNSUCCESSFUL ATTEMPTS TO GENERATE A REBUTTAL Rebuttals that do not contradict the alternative theory Rebuttals that contradict the original theory Rebuttals by assertion only
	NONEVIDENCE **Evidence as unnecessary Evidence unconnected to the theory Effects as evidence of its cause**	NO ATTEMPTS TO GENERATE AN ALTERNATIVE THEORY		NONATTEMPTS TO GENERATE REBUTTALS

Figure 25. Competent argumentative reasoning and its subcategories (Kuhn, 1991).

and the weighting process goes on until the person who is arguing is satisfied. In Figure 25, Kuhn's subcategories to these argumentative elements are presented.

Causal theories in Figure 25 are classified as single-cause, multiple parallel or multiple alternative theories. Supporting evidence can be either genuine evidence, pseudoevidence or nonevidence. Genuine evidence bears on its correctness, while pseudoevidence cannot be distinguished from the cause itself, and it takes the form of a scenario or script. Nonevidence as evidence is irrelevant to the assertion. Like supporting evidence, generating alternative theories and counterarguments could be successful or unsuccessful. The possibility of no alternative theories or counterarguments is likely, too. Alternative theories as counterarguments is a category of its own. Successful rebuttals are numerous, but it is possible not to have success in providing a rebuttal. Nonattempts to generate a rebuttal are also classified.

Three examples of argumentative reasoning in supervisory discourse are presented here. In these examples, causal theories arise from the question the supervisor asks. Two of the causal theories presented in these three empirical examples were single-cause theories, which means that only one cause was offered as a reason for the question asked. Other possibilities would have been multiple reasons, either in parallel or alternative possibilities.

There was one finding with two alternative causal theories for the question asked. As seen in Figure 26, the supervisor asked student teachers, "Why did the method you used work?"

CAUSAL THEORY	It has become familiar. The blackboard is very plain.	MULTIPLE ALTERNATIVE CAUSE
EVIDENCE	Although there is lots of information there, most of it is familiar to the pupils. It does not matter if you put some more there if you replenish it.	GENUINE EVIDENCE External evidence
EVIDENCE	If you give something new all the time, there would be too much information and it would take too much time to interpret it all. The main points could even get lost there.	GENUINE EVIDENCE Negative external evidence

Figure 26. Example of student teacher's argumentative reasoning in a supervisory discourse setting: Why did the method you used work?

Student teachers gave two alternative causes and began to find evidence for their assertions. The evidence they offered is genuine external evidence because they try to invoke some additional external factor; they are talking about the idea of replenishing when using a blackboard. They continue with new evidence, which is also genuine but this time negative external evidence. Student teachers try to point out something that is absent rather than present.

In the next example (Figure 27), student teachers are trying to justify their response to the question the supervising teacher asked. The question was: "Did pupils understand what it means when matters, not persons, conflict with each other?"

In this example, student teachers gave only one cause as the answer. Their evidence for this assertion was genuine but this time different compared to the example presented in Figure 27: they used correlated change to justify their assertion, giving an example of the case. The supervising teacher gave a counterargument by giving an alternative theory to describe the situation. She said that Mary, one of the student teachers, noticed what was going on and showed the limits to the pupils. This is the point where discussants had an interesting opportunity to generate an argumentative reasoning process that could have gone deeper into the situation, but student teachers did not continue to generate rebuttals to the alternative theory. Nor did the supervising teacher go on by asking student teachers more questions about the situation. Instead, they changed the subject.

In the final example of argumentative reasoning interpreted by Kuhn's classification (Figure 28), argumentation goes from assertion and evi-

CAUSAL THEORY	Well, maybe there were a few who understood, but not all.	SINGLE CAUSE
EVIDENCE	Well, you can notice that when they argued with each other—it's so easy to take it personally. Somebody told Jack that he was a bit stupid.	GENUINE EVIDENCE Correlated change
COUNTER-ARGUMENT	Yes, but Mary noticed that quite soon and showed where the limits are.	ALTERNATIVE THEORY AS COUNTER-ARGUMENT

Figure 27. Example of student teachers' and supervisors' argumentative reasoning in a supervisory discourse setting: Did pupils understand what it means when matters, not persons, conflict with each other?

CAUSAL THEORY	Instruction could have been better.	SINGLE CAUSE
EVIDENCE	They were not sure what to do.	GENUINE EVIDENCE Correlated change
COUNTER-ARGUMENT	Everything looked all right, though.	ALTERNATIVE THEORY AS COUNTERARGUMENT
REBUTTAL	There were a few groups who didn't know what to do. They understood incorrectly that they should write these arguments in their notebooks. And that was a problem.	SUCCESSFUL REBUTTAL Rebuttal that contradicts the alternative theory

Figure 28. Example of supervisory discourse where all the basic argumentative reasoning elements are presented: How did they succeed when working in pairs?

dence to counterarguments and rebuttals. This example has all of the argumentative elements presented by Kuhn. The supervisor asked student teachers how pupils succeeded when they worked in pairs.

As seen in Figure 28, student teachers assert that working in pairs did not succeed very well, because instructions were not good enough. This was the only cause they gave. Student teachers gave evidence for this assertion. Evidence was again genuine and can be classified as correlated change, because they gave an example of the situation by saying that pupils did not know what they should do. The supervising teacher gave a counterargument to this by saying that everything looked all right. This alternative theory as counterargument was the basis for a successful rebuttal. Student teachers gave a specific example of a few groups who were working incorrectly because they misunderstood instructions. The supervising teacher could have asked why the instructions were not good, but she didn't. This question would have given the argumentative reasoning a new focus of a more theoretical or critical nature. Instead, the supervising teacher changed the topic.

The findings related to argumentative reasoning in supervisory discourse indicate that in these examples the reasoning occurs on the factual level; it does not go into the theoretical or critical elements of teaching. The reasoning and reflection can be said to be practical. Normative elements are also few; only in the first example (Figure 26) do student teachers try to reason why something happened. If supervisory discourse aims at developing student teachers' reasoning skills, there should be more reasoning that looks for answers to why questions rather than to how and what questions. Practical reasoning should go further, through technical to critical reasoning. Reasoning skills should be strengthened through argumentative discussions between experts and novices in practice teaching situations. Competent reasoning develops through practice.

Background Belief Systems

In other parts of our data, we have directly asked teachers about their experiences, their motives in making educational decisions and, to some extent, the reasons for them. We have also interviewed teachers in various situations and contexts. The arguments and justifications are concrete talk and real verbalizations. In addition to this approach, we have tried to go behind these kinds of concrete explanations and belief systems. We have also asked teachers about their views of some matters concerning teaching in general, as well as in different situations and curricular contexts. In this part of the study, we have used a list of rules and recipes and advice which are supposed to be presented in teacher education and especially during the supervising process.

The idea in using this alternative is to identify common components behind educational decisions as latent belief systems with the help of factor analysis. The teaching recipes are supposed to reflect the common conception of good teaching and to manifest direct recommendations and advice without any justification about their origin. The recipes have been enacted during a long time of practice and experience, and their use has gradually developed into common-sense application, which means that their justification is no longer problematized. Apparently, the thinking behind those recipes reflects a common core of understanding concerning good teaching, and the latent dimensions structured by factor analysis may be considered the hidden justification for the manifest recipes.

The first analyses contained the original four recipe categories by Meyer (1991) with their ideas of good teaching: "Role of the teacher," "Socialization of the students," "Interaction and caring for students," and "Discipline". The analysis introduced earlier in the chapter 10 brought out seventeen dimensions or structures to be used as descriptors for these belief systems. In these belief systems, common features in the Finnish and German teacher education cultures were found, as were some differentiating structures, as mentioned in the Chapter 10.

In order to help the comparison of the latent belief systems, a second-order factor analysis was made separately for the two data. The seventeen first-order structures from both the Finnish and the German data sets were used as the basis for this second-order analysis. These factors were transformed into factor variables by summing the appropriate recipe variables (cf. Meri, 1998) and these factor variables were factor analyzed again. Three second-order factors were obtained in both data sets (see Chapter 10).

The similarities of the three belief systems in both data sets as presented by second-order factors are apparent. It is also to be seen how the original recipe lists are organized into broader concepts and where the recipes are supposed to get their justification. The concept of good teaching is fairly similar in spite of the fact that the teacher education of the participants in this study differs as to the content and extent of the curriculum as well as to the realization and practices of the curriculum. The common goal of both the Finnish and the German systems is to develop readiness for good teaching, and this goal seems to be quite universal in the everyday thinking presented by the teaching recipes.

The new dimensions in the German data set were "Pedagogical authority of the teacher," "Role of the teacher in socializing the students to learners," and "Interaction between the teacher and the students." "Discipline" as a separate dimension was not constructed as it was in the Finnish material. The phenomena belonging to its range were described through other structures, particularly through the items in the pedagogical authority of the teacher. This fact may be interpreted as emphasizing the competence and capability of the teacher. Good teaching is characterized by a teacher who knows her/his profession and functions without problems. In the belief system concerning the role of the teacher, the pedagogical competence is characteristic of a knowing and capable expert who manages various situations and circumstances in the classroom. Comparable descriptions can be found in the definitions of pedagogical authority by Mitchell & Spady (1983) and Burbules (1995).

The pedagogical expert also functions in the role of socializing the students and s/he thus understands the importance of guiding the growth of the students in the teaching-studying-learning process. In the original list of recipes by Meyer, the instructions and advice concerning socializing were called "taming rules." The idea of "taming" is to guarantee that the students understand what kind of activities form the basis of studying which leads to learning. The role of the teacher is to function as a help in this understanding. Interaction may be conceived as a mediating process where the pedagogical authority regulates the activities in the teacher's role of socializing the students.

In the Finnish data set, the first dimension of the second-order structures can be described as belief systems that are composed of the role of the teacher in motivating the students and maintaining interaction. In the Finnish data set, it is interesting that the first dimension also contains some recipes from other the two main dimensions, socializing the students and the items relating to discipline. These two dimensions, socializing and discipline, get their particular characteristics through active incidents and real events. In other words, there are elements related both to the personality and activities. Consequently, the dimension concerning socializing the students has components connected to the position of the teacher's role and its consequences in action. Characteristic to the third dimension, discipline, is that competence and role are not emphasized in this dimension, but instead teaching and educating are defined through a certain content that the teacher should be aware of and become acquainted with. The recipes belonging to the concept of discipline as a belief system of its own indicate at the same time a central topic of discussion in Finland today: how to succeed in restless classrooms where management of discipline and interaction are becoming the most important requirements for effective studying.

When comparing the Finnish and German belief systems, one can notice that they are fairly similar. The Finnish belief system describing interaction and motivating the students has a connection to the German pedagogical authority. The Finnish belief system concerning discipline has elements in common with the German belief system of pedagogical authority and the role of a socializer. Socializing the students as a Finnish belief system is parallel with the corresponding German belief system.

The results regarding the belief systems indicate quite well the similarity between the German and Finnish teacher education cultures. The pedagogical world that forms the atmosphere of the activities may be understood to contain the same kind of background thinking. The result is also understandable if we remember the origins of the Finnish educational background with its close relations to the German history of pedagogics. The differences are also reasonable considering the strong influence from the Anglo-American research on teaching during the recent decades. The contemporary Finnish research on the teaching-studying-learning process relates almost totally to Anglo-American studies with its results as well as to its theoretical background and assumptions. The belief systems behind the conception of good teaching may be relatively similar in different teacher education cultures although the everyday behavior and manners may seem to be fairly dissimilar, as Giangreco (1996) argues when analyzing receptology in the American teacher education culture.

PART V

TEACHERS' PRACTICAL KNOWLEDGE LANDSCAPE

Chapter 14

Justification of the Knowledge Claims

This chapter presents a conceptual framework of teachers' practical knowing. Through consideration of the empirical findings, the common features underlying teachers' thinking are identified. The empirical findings indicate that teachers share field-invariant epistemological standards that guide their practical knowing. The intuitive and rational basis of teachers' justifications are interrelated and cannot be separated from one another. In this chapter, these two epistemological dimensions in teachers' reasoning are brought together. The intuitive and rational stances of reasoning have the potential of combining vocational and professional aspects by establishing epistemological standards in teachers' pedagogical thinking.

Epistemological Uncertainties

Greene (1994) has analyzed different approaches to educational knowledge and concludes that there has been relatively little inclination to pose epistemological questions. These questions would involve what constitutes knowledge, what validates knowledge claims, how social and cultural ties affect knowledge, what the connection is between the knower and the known, and how belief systems have to do with the determination of what is taken to be "real" and "true." The questions open a number of perspectives on epistemology in its relation to educational research.

Epistemology, viewed as a normative action to evaluate knowledge claims in terms of their relation to "the truth," is generally understood to have reached its end. Many have joined Rorty (1979, 315–317) in his belief that so-called "foundational epistemology" has suffered a demise. "Foundations" in educational research means "a framework of beliefs governed by certain agreed-upon rules that ensured the commensurability of dependable beliefs (like Thorndike's and Skinner's) and points of view" (Greene, 1994, 426–427). Consequently, we are now in the midst of epistemological puzzlement with few generally approved standards to value our knowledge claims. As Fenstermacher (1994b) has shown, we have a number of possibilities for using the term knowledge when we refer to the mental states and activities of teachers. But whatever possibilities, formal or practical, we use, some kind of epistemological stance should be required if we intend to keep up with the concept of knowledge.

When knowledge is viewed from the phronesis perspective, we need to define teachers' thinking much in terms of teachers' personal experiences and their reported doings and its results. The perspective presupposes, as Dewey (1929) also notes, that we should avoid the assumption that "what knowledge must be had to be known in advance" (Greene, 1994, 434). For the most part, our attention has been focused on what teachers need to know, rather than on *what* they actually know and *how* that knowledge is acquired and further justified (Carter, 1990, 291).

In *Art as Experience* (1931), Dewey rejected any conception of mind that isolated it from persons and things. According to him, "mind is primarily a verb. It denotes all the ways in which we deal consciously and expressly with situations in which we find ourselves" (Dewey, 1931, 263). Thus, the concept of the knowing mind brings the situatedness into the consideration of epistemological issues. In the exercise of the mind, the concern of rationality must also be dealt with. As Greene (1994, 434) interprets Dewey, there can not be any supreme devotion to a single truth and, consequently, to the dominance of the scientific method over all other modes of knowing. Science should not be treated as truth meaning over other experienced meanings.

As Dewey (1958, 411) stated, "poetic meanings, moral meanings, a large part of the goods of life are matter of richness and freedom of meanings, rather than truth; a large part of our life is carried on in a realm of meanings to which truth and falsity as such are irrelevant." What science in general, and perhaps its educational approaches in particular, should do is to clarify meanings. As Greene (1994, 435) argues, the stance leads to "view knowing primarily as a search for the meaning of things with respect to acts performed and with respect to the consequences of those acts when performed."

Those who investigate social phenomena should come to terms with *verstehen* (Schutz, 1970), a kind of knowing by which persons in their everyday life interpret the meanings of their actions and those of others with whom they interact. Understanding is "an experiential form of common-sense knowledge of human affairs" (Schutz, 1970, 323). Thus, scientific educational understanding is the result of a researcher's subjective interpretation of the phenomena of human conduct which s/he studies. Its results belong to the intersubjective, and when succeeded, more objective realm of the interpretative method and theory.

Eisner (1988, 15) distinguishes two factors central to all experience: the experiential qualities themselves and the conceptual structures we bring to them. We construct knowledge from experience and produce different versions of knowledge depending on the conceptual structures we choose. Different conceptual structures value different kinds of authorities of knowing.

Authorities of Knowing

Bruner (1986) presents two ways of knowing, the paradigmatic and narrative modes, which provide different answers to the epistemological question: "What is the relationship of the knower to the known?" The paradigmatic mode of knowing "deals with general causes and makes use of procedures to assure verifiable reference and to test for empirical truth" (Bruner, 1986, 13). It is based on the authority of reason assuming that some sort of framework or a structure exists behind knowledge, upon which what we know is built, and which assures its certainty or truth (Bruffee, 1986, 776). The paradigmatic mode of knowing easily leads to the authority of decontextualized reason.

The narrative mode of knowing "leads to conclusions not about certainties but about the varying perspectives that can be constructed to make experience comprehensible" (Bruner, 1986, 37). According to the stance, our stories are authored from the particulars of experience and are expressions of our personal practical knowledge (cf. Connelly & Clandinin, 1990). As Olson (1995, 122) states, "The view of knowledge as embodied within individuals who interpret experience through personally and socially construed symbolic forms is foundational to the conceptualization of narrative authority." Each person both shapes his or her knowledge and is shaped by the knowledge of others. Knowledge is personally and socially constructed and reconstructed as people share their ideas with others. Thus, the narrative mode of knowing presupposes the authority of the person.

Narrative authority presupposes narrative epistemology. Its task is to help us transform teachers' personal narratives into the ideas of professional insight. According to Whitehead (1995), this transformation process requires epistemological capacity to use personal values and understanding as the standards to test the claims of knowing. In the case of narrative authority, what is known, and how the knowing is justified, both raise epistemological issues that are related to the person of the teacher. It is a question of a teacher's individual epistemologies.

Goldman (1986) speaks about individual epistemology or primary epistemology. The term primary epistemology is used due to its close connections to the individual's knowing mind. According to Goldman (1986, 1), it is a question of "the architecture" of the human mind, and an understanding of this "architecture" is essential for individual/primary epistemology. The task of the primary epistemology is to identify basic belief-forming processes. Once identified, these processes can be examined according to some evaluative standards: justification rules and principles. In teachers' narrative authority, we aim at 1) identifying teachers' basic belief-forming processes, and 2) developing descriptive categories with which individual epistemology operates.

The Knower and the Known

In looking for justifying evidence, we were not interested primarily in statements having an external form. Rather, we concentrated on determining how such statements operate in structuring teachers' thinking. Our data indicated that teachers used two different kinds of epistemological standards in structuring their thinking. Practical reasoning is an interrelated entity (cf. Hollingsworth *et al.*, 1993; Webb and Blond, 1995). In order to present this entity, the conceptual frameworks of both teachers' character and teachers' principles should be brought together. This interrelated nature of teachers' practical knowing is presented in Figure 29.

The personal context of justification precedes and interacts with the more rational areas of teacher knowledge. As presented, when teachers talked about their work they also talked about themselves. Events were filtered through the person of the teacher. Teachers used their selves as

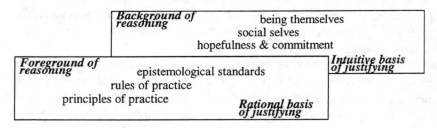

Figure 29. The interrelated nature of teachers' practical knowing.

tools to manage their work, and a large proportion of teacher talk contained some self-referential comment. The aspects of the self emerged quite implicitly, without much conscious thinking, in teachers' practical knowing. This reasoning closely connected to teachers' character provided the overall context of thought, and it seemed to regulate the determination of a principled reasoning, whether in the way of terms or the relations that became perceived and therefore objects of thought.

This accords with Dewey's (1926) notions concerning people's selective attention and its intuitive base. He maintained that our primary relation to reality is not cognitive. Rather, the experience of the situation, i.e., what is perceived from the contextual whole, is immediate. According to him, the word intuition describes that "qualitativeness underlying all the details of explicit reasoning" (Dewey, 1926, 249). This intuitive background may be relatively simple and unexpressed and yet penetrating: it often underlies the definite ideas, which form the basis for explicit reasons and justifications. However, it directs attention and thereby determines what is perceived. For example, hopefulness and commitment set a teacher's mind to seek "weak signals" to prove that at least some learning and progress has taken place in their pupils. It often implies that some personally relevant and optimistic beliefs are placed above "the reasoned facts" of explicit and formal reasoning. But without hopefulness and commitment, those "weak signals" of learning and progress would not even get recognized. Therefore, the intuitive, personal aspects are crucially important: they justify and compel teachers to perceive their pupils with greater care.

The knowledge of these intuitive levels of justification is often loose and indefinite by nature. It is mainly concerned with the understanding of individual cases and complex situations, and it is primarily formulated in concrete and context-related terms. The intuitive base is not a consistent whole because it contains many illogical relations and contradictions. This is because being a teacher means living with paradoxes that cannot be resolved (cf. Lampert, 1985). Teachers are in a position where their own learning never ends. Every time teachers try out something new, they seem to meet new challenges.

The intuitive, personal way of knowing seems to lack the epistemological standards that can be applied to more rational ways of reasoning. Because events are filtered through the person of the teacher, no event or process has any single and unambiguous description and interpretation. Events are described and interpreted in different terms depending on the standpoint from which the teacher is considering it. The teacher intuitively relates events to the contexts in which the action takes place. But note that here the context must be understood to cover far more than the physical setting of the action. The phrase 'cultural context' is closer to what is meant here. According to Jackson (1986, 96), "it includes the awareness, presuppositions, expectations, and everything else that impinges upon the action or that contributes to its interpretation by the actors themselves and by outsiders as well."

Consequently, the epistemological dimension means the use of the teacher's own values and understandings as the standards for testing the claims of knowing. It focuses on the question of how teachers justify their ways of knowing. Here our purpose has been to explore more general ways in which teachers' minds can be conceptualized and to explore the pedagogical practices that are tied to and follow from these ways of thinking.

Chapter 15

Towards Balanced Educational Decisions

Finally, several conclusions are drawn. Our empirical studies seem to confirm our original conception of the moral nature of the teachers' pedagogical thinking. Our purpose has been to deal with the teaching-studying-learning process as a totality. There are, however, numerous different aspects contributing to this process, all at the same time. As teachers speak about their thoughts, they have to choose and leave something out. During the instructional process incidents are strongly lived and experienced. However, when the same incidents are analyzed, they are decontextualized. To understand the totality from as many sides as possible, we refer to the three kinds of moral languages presented by Robert J. Nash. As a final, positive point of view we hope and believe that developing teachers' pedagogical thinking will lead to a better understanding of the teaching-studying-learning process in general.

The Contextual Conditions for Teachers' Pedagogical Thinking

Thinking in educational situations is an integrated whole which is difficult to divide into categories to be formally analyzed. That is, due to its practical character, thinking occurs in circumstances where the teacher is hardly able to think consciously about alternatives. In the instructional process, innumerable and unexpected incidents follow each other, and usually the teacher does not have time to ponder various possibilities and alternatives in the middle of the process. The teacher is, however, responsible for the learning and personal development of the students and much in this striving can be done rationally and systematically. The pedagogical context brings with it certain frames that practically and symbolically form the borders of teachers' thinking and action. The aim of autonomous and independent action and decision-making may become a serious problem when considering the requirements of commitment to the values of the curriculum. The degrees of freedom are clearly restricted, although the feeling of freedom may be unrestricted in spite of this. In the world of values defined by the curriculum, it is possible for the teacher to act without knowing her/his own grounds for thinking and acting. The more the teacher acts technically in the sense of following certain material or authoritative advice as well as manners that are defined by the atmosphere of the local community and school, the more the danger of indoctrination and external guidance threatens her/his autonomy.

The problem of autonomy is in all probability not settled with the help of systematic planning or advice seeking without penetrating in to a teacher's own thinking and the premises and arguments that form the justification for it. In the teacher's mind we can differentiate only theoretically descriptive and normative sides, or knowledge from feelings and emotions. In practice they are mixed and impossible to define. When describing the process of making educational decisions, we may classify various factors and build potential models to better understand a teacher's thinking. Such models may also be helpful in getting the teacher her/himself to understand the instructional process and her/his own position in it. It must not be forgotton that the value of such models is secondary: They are meant to help and structure research questions and to illustrate the starting point of the research project; they are not meant to restrict the approach and creativity of the inquiry but to open various ways to progress.

We have also started with such a model in our minds (p. 17). It is relatively usual to consider the thinking and action from various levels or angles. When drawing pictures to describe its main features and ideas, the design is often simplified and distorted although this has not been the purpose of the researchers. It is evident that it is difficult to describe and design complicated matters; therefore the result is usually simplified. When speaking of levels, a system of a certain hierarchy is often implied although the levels could be described horizontally as well. When analyzing ethics and moral thinking, Nash (1996) uses the expression of different moral languages that we consider a parallel way of examining the same kinds of problems.

We have claimed from the very beginning that teachers' pedagogical thinking is normative by nature. Making educational decisions means taking a stand, choosing between alternatives. That makes the pedagogical thinking moral thinking as well. On the action level, the instructional process is continuous. Reflection is difficult during the process; we must be content with teachers telling about their thinking and decisions afterwards. In these narratives the different aspects, levels or languages are revealed. In addition to personal matters, be they rational or intuitive, descriptive or normative, cognitive or affective, etc., the whole personal history and the larger context of the local community come to the fore. The challenge of the holistic interpretation of a teacher's thinking means that in the middle of the instructional process the incidents are strongly lived and experienced. When the same incidents are analyzed and interpreted by the researcher, they are decontextualized at the same time. Some theories may be developed with these concrete facts and interpretations, and the link to the practice may be lost in the meanwhile. Our purpose has been to keep this totality undivided as far as possible and to describe and analyze it in parallel from different angles, levels, or languages and with various kinds of material.

The Moral Languages on Different Thinking Levels

Research on teacher thinking is methodologically problematic, while thinking is examined through the stories and narratives that teachers relate to their action. Actually, we are drawing a parallel between telling and thinking. Is there any better method? In addition, telling is not enough in the sense that telling is also choosing what to tell. We know from our own experience that thinking may be fast and can be verbalized only partly. Perhaps, only a very small part of it can be expressed verbally. If we want to enrich the telling about thinking it may be done by some non-verbal means. These may clear the emotional and affective side of the expression, but in clarifying the exact meaning of this telling it is no longer as useful. That is why in examining teacher thinking it is necessary to ask additional questions and to try to concentrate on those aspects that may be of interest in that particular inquiry.

The central interest in our investigation has been the question of how teachers argue and justify educational decisions. This is a research approach that is difficult to realize because argumentation in narratives is not automatic. On the contrary, any kind of argumentation and justification is rather unusual. To know more, additional questions must be asked. Another point of view is that the questions should be indirect in order to avoid any desirability effect. This approach means discussions and interviews with cautious questions and as little interfering as possible. The result is a large amount of talk, usually transliterated on paper. As a matter of fact, the analysis of teacher thinking begins at that point. We can wonder further how authentic it is when we have reached that point.

The material reflecting teacher thinking in that way may be considered quite realistic in any case because arguments and justifications are exactly in the form in which the teachers have told them. When the researcher interprets those narratives and draws conclusions and interpretations from them, a possible misunderstanding of the text we call teacher thinking can take place. In any case, all types of classifications, be they descriptions by languages, levels, or other viewpoints, are theoretical or symbolic representations of the original narratives which are based on what we suppose thinking to be. There is a warning point here because now we have departed from our original material. Is it possible to reduce these interpretations to original intuitions, explanations, or rational arguments? What we call teacher thinking at this phase is mainly symbolic. But are there any other possibilities?

In order to find different aspects of arguments and justifications, we have followed quite a typical approach by looking at the research material from different angles according to the research problem considered. It is relatively common in the research literature to approach the narratives from different theoretical sides (Handal & Lauvås, 1988; Guhl & Ott, 1985) which may be considered levels when they resemble some hierarchy or as different thematic angles; or we can describe the material with different theoretical aspects which Nash (1996) calls languages. The approach presented by Nash is highly interesting and invites a possible comparative concluding description of the model applied in this inquiry.

Although making choices between alternatives means taking a stand, teachers seldom consider it normative by nature. Our data have indicated that justification by one's own experiences or by some rules and principles is not often conscious. Teachers may have the insight that their decision-making is normative on the whole or that it belongs to the realm of pedagogy where nearly all action is normative. In spite of that, the very incidents during the teaching-studying-learning process flow continually with no conscious normative insight and reflection. When it later occurs, it is not even then experienced as being normative or moral by nature. This applies to educational decision-making in general, but when we add certain content to it, the insight of decision-making may change. If the content of teacher thinking is clearly moral education or concerns some moral dilemma, the nature of justification also changes. While the justification in general questions and in the cognitive content usually refers to pedagogical experience or educational literature, in moral questions ethical justification is common.

We claim cautiously that in pedagogical questions teacher education has given some preparedness to make decisions, but in moral questions teachers refer more to common-sense thinking without any theoretical ideas. The methods of teaching and other content areas of educational psychology may seem self-evident because they have become known during the teacher education, but moral content may not be so familiar. If we try to go behind the everyday thinking which various recipes and traditional manners represent, the difference between cognitive content and moral content becomes more distinct. The practical theories or object theories, if they can be found, are for the most part content-centered. To take some examples, the focus may be on learning and its principles, discipline problems with suggestions for their solution, teaching some subject and its problems, or evaluation of the instructional process, and they refer to the consequences of this process. Usually these results are expressed as test results or grades, with evaluation according to more general aims and goals being infrequent. The criteria are usually learning results, and although moral development is part of total personal development, it is usually not graded, as we know.

Nash (1996) presents three kinds of moral languages. Comparing our thinking levels with these languages opens some interesting perspectives for future research. If we start from the teaching-studying-learning process which presents the concrete world, we are on the action level. That means concrete action and a constant flow of pedagogical interaction. In the educational literature, what may be divided into different phases with planning and evaluation included. This corresponds to the second moral language presented by Nash. There is a real moral problem or dilemma, and the person lives with it and needs a solution to regain mental balance. In such a case, the person behaves according to his character. In the context of the teaching-studying-learning process, this person has certain frames and resorts to the world of education. The person using of Nash's second moral language may be in any context and the emphasis on character may be understood as a common aspect which applies to all possible contexts. In any case, Nash points out the role of moral intuition as a first approach for solving the problem. Listening to one's own moral intuition raises possible conflicting moral feelings and incongruencies that may clarify the nature of the problem. The decision must be made in character in contrast to out of character (Nash, 1996, 72–84), and in order to determine it some frame factors it should be analyzed. The solution must be in line with surrounding moral communities. That is no problem in education because the curriculum also sets the moral frames for action, but when we go outside of the school and look at the families of the students, the situation changes. Here we see possible differences between cognitive content and the broader context of the curriculum.

A person is not able to avoid his or her personal history in decision-making. In the context of teaching the teacher is a professional, but every teacher is also a unique teacher. This is also true when considering the personality and especially the virtues of each teacher. This aspect brings the discussion close to the earlier topic of teacher personality, which has not been particularly central in the teacher thinking research. The viewpoint of personal virtues may, however, help one to understand the differences of justifications, and the background of object theories as well.

The expectations of the teachers' profession contain at least teacher education, workplace norms and role expectations. Nash (1996, 94–99) emphasizes the code of ethics as a source of finding a solution. He claims that the code of ethics is not well known by different professionals, and this is certainly shown in our material. In everyday teaching, the code of ethics may be of little help but in moral dilemmas it should be considered. In any case, the second moral language refers to many frame factors which we also find in the teaching context. To combine these aspects with educational decision-making may help in structuring the teachers' pedagogical thinking and finding grounds for its justification in usual educational questions, as well.

The first moral language of Nash deals with background beliefs held by individual persons. This is quite close to our search for justifications behind educational decisions. The knowledge of existing background beliefs is meant to deepen, explain, and reveal the motives for action. In our investigation, the aim has been to find out if there are any justifications and if it is possible to consider them beliefs. The implication for teacher education could be a program which could be used in making these beliefs conscious. A common hypothesis may be expressed with the intention that being aware of one's own beliefs may improve the quality of making educational decisions (Fitzgibbons, 1981, 18–19). Our data indicates that possible object theories are not only situation-based or common-sense theories but that there are certain belief systems, various kinds of arguments and justification, behind them.

Nash's third moral language has moral principles as its object. Comparing the first moral language of background beliefs with level thinking leads to our first thinking level while the third moral language with moral principles corresponds our second thinking level. On this level, the content divides fairly naturally into two parts: facts and norms. The descriptive part may contain an empiric-based belief system which is mainly comprised of educational research results and which is constructed by the teacher with the help of professional experience. The normative part deals with value questions regarding aims and goals of education and their consequences. This level, which we call the level of metatheory, corresponds to ethical theories or moral principles as explained by Nash. In practice, it is not so simple because the division on the metatheoretical level is artificial. In the teacher's mind, metatheory is an integrated whole where the named parts interact continuously.

It should be noted that in this discussion when we have drawn certain parallels between the moral languages of Nash and our model of teachers' pedagogical thinking, the first two languages are person-based and the third moral language represents general moral principles or ethical theories. Our model of teachers' pedagogical thinking is totally person-based, and the possible generalizations and theories are explored in teachers' narratives that represents thinking. In spite of this, the belief systems that we claim we have found may be looked at through certain educational or ethical theories that clarify their interpretation and prospective application.

As to the belief systems of the authors of this book, we hope that developing teachers' pedagogical thinking leads to better teaching in general. This is why we believe in teacher education where both intuition and rationality are represented in a balanced way. Teachers' pedagogical thinking is one variation of doing educational research. The implication is that to be able to perform adequate pedagogical thinking, teachers should also be trained to do educational research.

References

Abelson, R. (1979). Differences Between Belief Systems and Knowledge Systems. *Cognitive Science, 3*, 355–366.

Alfs, G., Wagener, W., Wierdsma, T. & Wilbers, H. (1985). *Rezepte im Schulpraktikum II. Berichte—Anregungen—Reflexionen*. Materialien Universität Oldenburg.

Anderson, L. W. & Burns R. B. (1989). *Research in Classrooms. The Study of Teachers, Teaching and Instruction*. Oxford: Pergamon Press.

Aristotle (1975). *The Nicomachean Ethics*, Books I-X (D. Ross, Trans.). London: Oxford University Press.

Bales, R. (1951). *Interaction Process Analysis*. Reading, MA: Addison-Wesley.

Barnes, D. (1992). The Significance of Teacher's Frames for Teaching. In T. Russell & H. Munby (Eds.), *Teachers and Teaching: From Classroom to Reflection* (pp. 9–32). London: The Falmer Press.

Barone, T. & Eisner, E. (1997). Arts-Based Educational Research. In R. M. Jaeger (Ed), *Complementary Methods for Research in Education*. Second Edition. Washington, DC: AERA.

Bengtsson, J. (1995). What is Reflection? On Reflection in the Teaching Profession and Teacher Education. *Teachers and Teaching, 1*(1), 23–32.

Berlak, A. & Berlak, H. (1981). *Dilemmas of Schooling: Teaching and Social Change*. London: Methuen.

Berliner, D. C. (1995). Teacher Expertise. In L. W. Anderson (Ed.), *International Encyclopedia of Teaching and Teacher Education* (pp. 46–52). Second Edition. Cambridge, UK.: Pergamon.

Brown, S. & McIntyre, D. (1993). *Making Sense of Teaching*. Buckingham: Open University Press.

Brown, S., Earlam, C. & Race, P. (1995). *500 Tips for Teachers*. London: Kogan Page.

Bruffee, K. A. (1986). Social Construction, Language, and the Authority of Knowledge. *College English, 48,* 773–790.

Bruner, J. (1986). *Actual Minds, Possible Worlds*. Cambridge, MA: Harvard University Press.

Bruner, J. (1990). *Acts of Meaning*. Cambridge, MA: Harvard University Press.

Buchmann, M. (1987). Teaching Knowledge: The Lights that Teachers Live by. *Oxford Review of Education, 13*(2), 151–164.

Buchmann, M. (1990). How Practical Is Contemplation in Teaching. In C. Day, M. Pope & P. Denicolo (Eds.), *Insights into Teachers' Thinking and Practice* (pp. 43–56). London: The Falmer Press.

Buchmann, M. & Floden, R. E. (1993). Coherence, the Rebel Angel. *Educational Researcher, 21*(9), 5–9.

Burbules, N. (1995). Authority and the Tragic Dimension of Teaching. In J. W. Garrison & A. A. Jr. Rud (Eds.), *The Educational Conversation. Closing the Gap* (pp. 29–40). Albany: State University of New York Press.

Calderhead, J. (1991). The Nature and Growth of Knowledge in Student Teaching. *Teaching and Teacher Education, 7,* 531–535.

Calderhead, J. (1993). The Contribution of Research on Teachers' Thinking to the Professional Development of Teachers. In C. Day, J. Calderhead & P. Denicolo (Eds.), *Research on Teacher Thinking: Understanding Professional Development* (pp.11–18)) London: Falmer Press.

Calderhead, J. (1995). The Development of Initial Teacher Education: Insights from Research on Learning to Teach. In P. Kansanen (Ed.), *Discussions on Some Educational Issues* VI (pp. 63–75). Research

Report 145. Department of Teacher Education, University of Helsinki. (ED394958)

Calderhead, J. & Robson, R. (1991). Images of Teaching: Student Teachers' Early Conceptions of Classroom Practice. *Teaching & Teacher Education, 7*, 1–8.

Carlgren, I. & Lindblad, S. (1991). Teachers' Practical Reasoning and Professional Knowledge: Considering Conceptions of Context in Teachers' Thinking. *Teaching and Teacher Education, 7*(5/6), 507–516.

Carter, K. (1990). Teachers' Knowledge and Learning to Teach. In W. R. Houston (Ed.), *Handbook of Research on Teacher Education* (pp. 283–310). New York: MacMillan.

Carter, K. (1993). The Place of Story in the Study of Teaching and Teacher Education. *Educational Researcher, 22*(1), 5–12.

Carter, K. & Doyle, W. (1987). Teachers Knowledge Structures and Comprehension Process. In J. Calderhead (Ed.), *Exploring Teachers Thinking* (pp. 147–160). London: Cassell.

Carter, K. & Gonzalez, L. (1993). Beginning Teachers' Knowledge of Classroom Events. *Journal of Teacher Education, 44*, 223–232.

Clandinin, D. J. (1985). Personal Practical Knowledge: A Study of Teachers' Classroom Images. *Curriculum Inquiry, 15*(4), 361–385.

Clandinin, D. J. & Connelly, F. M. (1987). Teachers' Personal Knowledge: What Counts as Personal in Studies of the Personal. *Journal of Curriculum Studies, 19*(6), 487–500.

Clandinin, D. J. & Connelly, F. M. (1992). Teacher as Curriculum Maker. In P. W. Jackson (Ed.), *Handbook of Research on Curriculum* (pp. 363–401). New York: Macmillan.

Clandinin, D. J. & Connelly, F. M. (1995). *Teachers' Professional Knowledge Landscapes.* New York: Teachers College Press.

Clark, C. M. (1986). Ten Years of Conceptual Development in Research on Teacher Thinking. In M. Ben-Perez, R. Bromme & R. Halkes (Eds.), *Advances of Research on Teacher Thinking* (pp. 7–20). Lisse: Swets & Zeitlinger.

Clark, C. M. (1995). *Thoughtful Teaching.* New York: Teachers College Press.

Clark, C. M. & Peterson, P. L. (1986). Teachers' Thought Processes. In M. C. Wittrock (Ed.), *Handbook of Research on Teaching* (pp. 255–296). Third Edition. New York: Macmillan.

Clarke, A. (1995). Professional Development in Practicum Settings: Reflective Practice Under Scrunity. *Teaching & Teacher Education, 11*(3), 243–261.

Clarke, S. (1970). General Teaching Theory. *The Journal of Teacher Education, 21*, 403–416.

Connelly, F. M. & Clandinin, D. J. (1985). Personal Practical Knowledge and the Modes of Knowing: Relevance for Teaching and Learning. In E. Eisner (Ed.), *Learning and Teaching the Ways of Knowing* (pp. 174–198). Eighty-fourth Yearbook of the NSSE. Chicago: The University of Chicago Press.

Connelly, F. M. & Clandinin, D. J. (1990). Stories of Experience and Narrative Inquiry. *Educational Researcher, 19*(5), 2–14.

Cortazzi, M. (1993). *Narrative Analysis.* London: Falmer Press.

Damon, W. (1988). *The Moral Child.* New York: The Free Press.

Delamont, S. (1995). Teachers as Artists. In L. W. Anderson (Ed.), *International Encyclopedia of Teaching and Teacher Education* (pp. 6–8). Second Edition. Cambridge, UK.: Pergamon.

Dewey, J. (1926, 1984). *Affective Thought.* Carbondale: Southern Illinois University Press.

Dewey, J. (1929). *The Quest for Certainty.* London: Allen & Unwin.

Dewey, J. (1931). *Art as Experience.* New York: Minton, Balch.

Dewey, J. (1933). *How We Think: A Restatement of the Relation of Reflective Thinking to the Educative Process.* Boston: D.C. Heath and Company.

Dewey, J. (1958). *Experience and Nature.* New York: Dover.

Drerup, H. (1988). Rezeptologien in der Pädagogik. Überlegungen zur neueren schulpädagogischen Ratgeberliteratur. *Bildung und Erziehung, 40*, 101–121.

Dunn, T. G. & Taylor, C. A. (1993). Cooperating Teacher Advice. *Teaching & Teacher Education, 9*(4), 411–423.

Duranti, A. & Goodwin, C. (1992). *Rethinking Context: Language as an Interactive Phenomenon*. Cambridge, MA: Cambridge University Press.

Eisner, E. (1988). The Primacy of Experience and the Politics of Method. *Educational Researcher, 17*(5), 15–20.

Eisner, E. (1991). *The Enlightened Eye: Qualitative Inquiry and the Enhancement of Educational Practice*. New York, MacMillan.

Elbaz, F. (1983). *Teacher Thinking: A Study of Practical Knowledge*. London: Croom Helm.

Elbaz, F. (1990). Knowledge and Discourse: The Evolution of Research on Teaching. In C. Day, M. Pope & P. Denicolo (Eds.), *Insight into Teachers' Thinking and Practice* (pp. 15–42). London: Falmer Press.

Elbaz, F. (1992). Hope, Attentiveness, and Caring for Difference: The Moral Voice In Teaching. *Teaching & Teacher Education, 8*(5/6), 421–432.

Elbaz, F. (1993). Responsive Teaching: A Response from Teachers Perspective. *Journal of Curriculum Studies, 25*(2), 189–199.

Erickson, F. (1986). Qualitative Methods in Research on Teaching. In M. C. Wittrock (Ed.), *Handbook of Research on Teaching* (pp. 119–161).Third Edition. New York: Macmillan.

Fenstermacher, G. D. (1986). Philosophy of Research on Teaching: Three Aspects. In M. C. Wittrock (Ed.), *Handbook of Research on Teaching* (pp. 37–49). Third Edition. New York: Macmillan.

Fenstermacher, G. D. (1990). Some Moral Considerations on Teaching as a Profession. In J. I. Goodlad, R. Soder & K. A. Sirotnik (Ed.), *The Moral Dimensions of Teaching* (pp. 130–151). San Francisco: Jossey-Bass.

Fenstermacher, G. D. (1992). The Concepts of Method and Manner in Teaching. In: F. K Oser, A. Dick & J.-L. Patry (Ed.), *Effective and Responsible Teaching: The New Synthesis* (pp. 95–108). San Francisco: Jossey-Bass.

Fenstermacher, G. D. (1994a). On the Virtues of van Manen's Argument: A Response to Pedagogy, Virtue, and Narrative Identity in Teaching. *Curriculum Inquiry, 24*(2), 215–220.

Fenstermacher, G. D. (1994b). The Knower and the Known: The Nature of Knowledge in Research on Teaching. In L. Darling-Hammond (Ed.), *Review of Research in Education, 20* (pp. 3–56). Washington, DC: AERA.

Fenstermacher, G. & Richardson, V. (1993). The Elicitation and Reconstruction of Practical Arguments in Teaching. *Journal of Curriculum Studies, 25*(2), 101–114.

Fenstermacher, G. D. & Sanger, M. (1998). What is the Significance of John Dewey's Approach to the Problem of the Knowledge? *Elementary School Journal, 98* (5), 467–478.

Fisher, G. (1992). *Mindsets: The Role of Culture and Perception of Internal Relations.* Yarmouth, ME: Intercultural Press.

Fitzgibbons, R. E. (1981). *Making Educational Decisions. An Introduction to Philosophy of Education.* New York: Harcourt Brace Jovanovich.

Fleming, J.S. (1992). Factrel: A General Program For Relating Factors Between Studies via The Kaiser-Hunka -Bianchini Method. *Educational and Psychological Measurement, 52*, 113–115.

Floden, R. & Klinzing, H. (1990). What Can Research on Teacher Thinking Contribute to Teacher Preparation? A Second Opinion. *Educational Researcher, 19*(4), 15–20.

Framework Curriculum for the Comprehensive School 1994. National Board of Education. Helsinki: The State Printing Press.

Frankena, W. K. (1973). *Ethics.* Second Edition. Englewood Cliffs: Prentice Hall.

Freeman, D. (1996). "To Take Them at Their Word": Language Data in the Study of Teachers' Knowledge. *Harvard Educational Review, 66*(4), 732–761.

Fritzell, C. (1996). Pedagogical Split Vision. *Educational Theory, 46*(2), 203–216.

Gage, N. L. (1978). *The Scientific Basis of the Art of Teaching*. New York: Teachers College Press.

Gage, N. L. & Berliner, D. (1984). *Educational Psychology*. Third Edition. Boston: Houghton Mifflin.

Garrison, J. (1996). Dewey, Qualitative Thought, and Context. *Qualitative Studies in Education, 9*(4), 391–410.

Gauthier, D. P. (1963). *Practical Reasoning. The Structure and Foundations of Prudential and Moral Arguments and their Exemplifications in Discourse*. London: Oxford University Press.

Geertz, C. (1973). *The Interpretation of Culture*. New York: Basic Books.

Giangreco, M.F. (1998). What Do I Do Now? In K. Ryan, & J. M. Cooper (Eds.), *Kaleidoscope. Readings in Education* (pp.459–463). Boston: Houghton Mifflin.

Gilligan, C. & Attanucci, J. (1988). Two Moral Orientations. In C. Gilligan et al. (Eds.), *Mapping the Moral Domain* (pp.73–86). Cambridge, Mass: Harvard University Press.

Goffman, E. (1974). *Frame Analysis. An Essay on the Organization of Experience*. Cambridge, MA: Harvard University Press.

Goldman, A. I. (1986*). Epistemology and Cognition*. Cambridge, MA: Harvard University Press.

Goodlad, J., Soder, R. & Sirotnik, K. (Eds.). (1990). *The Moral Dimensions of Teaching*. San Francisco: Jossey Bass.

Goodwin, C. & Duranti, A. (1992). Rethinking Context: An Introduction. In A. Duranti & C. Goodwin (Eds), *Rethinking Context: Language as an Interactive Phenomenon* (pp. 1–42). New York: Cambridge University Press.

Green, T. E. (1971). *The Activities of Teaching*. McGraw-Hill. New York.

Greene, M. (1994). Epistemology and Educational Research: The Influence of Recent Approaches to Knowledge. In L. Darling-Hammond, L. (Ed.), *Review of Research in Education, 20* (pp. 423–464). Washington: AERA.

Greeno, J. (1989). A Perspective on Teaching. *American Psychologist, 44*, 134–141.

Grell, J. & Grell, M. (1979, 1993). *Unterrichts Rezepte*. Weinheim: Beltz.

Grigutscht, S. (1996). *Mathematische Weltbildern von Schülern. Struktur, Entwicklung, Einflußfaktoren*. Gerhard-Mercator-Universität, Duisburg.

Guhl, E. & Ott, E. H. (1985). *Unterrichtsmetodisches Denken und Handeln*. Darmstadt: Wissenschaftliche Buchgesellschaft.

Habermas, J. (1984). *The Theory of Communicative Action. Vol.1: Reason and the Rationalization of Society*. London: Heinemann.

Habermas, J. (1990). *Moral Consciousness and Communicative Action*. Cambridge: The MIT Press.

Habermas, J. (1971). *Knowledge and Human Interests*. Boston: Beacon Press.

Haggarty, L. (1995). The Use of Content Analysis to Explore Conversations Between School Teacher Mentors and Student Teachers. *British Educational Research Journal, 21*(2), 183–197.

Handal, G & Lauvås, P. (1988). *Promoting Reflective Teaching*. Milton Keynes: Open University Press.

Hansen, D. T. (1993). From Role to Person: The Moral Layeredness of Classroom Teaching. *American Educational Research Journal, 30*(4), 651–674.

Hansen, D. T. (1994). Teaching and the Sense of Vocation. *Educational Theory, 44*(3), 259–275.

Hansen, D. T. (1995). *The Call to Teach*. New York. Teachers College Press.

Hargreaves, A. (1991). Foreword. In W. Louden (Ed.), *Understanding Teaching* (pp. vi–viii). New York: Cassell.

Harrison, A. (1978). *Making and Thinking: A Study of Intelligent Activities*. Indianapolis, IN: Hackett Publishing Company.

Hartshorne, J. & May, M. (1930). A Summary of the Work of the Character Inquiry. *Religious Education, 25*, 607–619.

Hatton, N. & Smith, D. (1995). Reflection in Teacher Education: Towards Definition and Implementation. *Teaching & Teacher Education, 11*(1), 33–49.

Hausmann, G. (1959). *Didaktik als Dramaturgie des Unterrichts.* Heidelberg: Quelle & Meyer.

Helkama, K. (1993). Nuoren kehittyvä etiikka. (The Developing Morality of an Adolescent). In T. Airaksinen *et al.* (Eds.), *Hyvän opetus.* (Teaching of the Good). Helsinki: Painatuskeskus.

Herbart, J. F. (1803, 1964). *Pädagogische Schriften.* 3 Bände. Asmus, W. (Hrsg.) Düsseldorf: Kuepper.

Highet, G. (1951). *The Art of Teaching.* London: Methuen.

Hofe, R. vom (1995). *Grundvorstellungen mathematischer Inhalte.* Heidelberg: Akademischer Verlag.

Hollingsworth, S., Dybdalh, M. & Minarik, L. (1993). By Chart, and Chance and Passion. The Importance of Relational Knowing in Learning to Teach. *Curriculum Inquiry, 23,* 5–35.

Howe, K. (1986). A Conceptual Basis for Ethics in Teacher Education. *Journal of Teacher Education, 42*(3), 5–12.

Hoy, W. & Rees, R. (1977). The Bureaucratic Socialisation of Student Teachers. *Journal of Teacher Education, 28*(1), 23–26.

Husu, J. (1996). Distance Education in School Environment: Integrating Remote Classrooms by Video Conferencing. *Journal of Distance Learning, 2*(1), 34–44.

Husu, J. (1997). The Pedagogical Context of Virtual Classroom. In J. Willis, J. D. Price, S. McNeil, B. Robin, & D.A. Willis (Eds.), *Technology and Teacher Education Annual 1997* (pp.534–537). Orlando, FL: AACE.

Hytönen, J. (1995). The Role of School Practice in Teacher Education. In Kansanen (Ed.), *Discussions on some Educational Issues VI.* Research Report 145. Department of Teacher Education, University of Helsinki. (ED394958)

Iisalo, T. (1979). *The Science of Education in Finland 1828–1918.* Helsinki: Societas Scientiarum Fennica.

Jackson, P. W. (1966). *The Way Teaching Is.* Washington, DC: National Education Association.

Jackson, P. W. (1968). *Life in Classrooms.* New York: Holt, Rinehart and Winston.

Jackson, P. W. (1986). *The Practice of Teaching.* New York: Teachers College Press.

Jackson, P. W. (1992). The Enactment of the Moral in What Teachers Do. *Curriculum Inquiry, 22*(4), 401–407.

Jackson, P., Boostrom, R., & Hansen, D. (1993). *The Moral Life of Schools.* San Francisco: Jossey-Bass.

James, W. (1899). *Talks to Teachers on Psychology: And to Students on Some of Life's Ideals.* New York: Henry Holt and Co.

Jank, W. & Meyer, H. (1991). *Didaktische Modelle.* Frankfurt am Main: Cornelsen Scriptor.

Jonsen, A. R. & Toulmin, S. (1988). *The Abuse of Casuistry. A History of Moral Reasoning.* Berkeley, CA: University of California Press.

Kaiser, H.F, Hunka. S. & Bianchini, J.C. (1971). Relating Factors Between Studies Based Upon Different Individuals. *Multivariate Behavioral Research, 6,* 409–422.

Kansanen, P. (1981). The Way Thinking Is: How Do Teachers Think and Decide? In E. Komulainen & P. Kansanen (Eds.), *Classroom Analysis: Concepts, Findings, Applications.* Research Bulletin No. 56. Institute of Education, University of Helsinki. (ED209187)

Kansanen, P. (1991). Pedagogical Thinking: The Basic Problem of Teacher Education. *European Journal of Education, 26*(3), 251–260.

Kansanen, P. (1993). An Outline for a Model of Teachers' Pedagogical Thinking. In P. Kansanen (Ed.), *Discussions on Some Educational Issues IV* (pp. 51–65). Research Report 121. Department of Teacher Education, University of Helsinki. (ED366562)

Kansanen, P. & Uljens, M. (1996). What Is Behind Research on Teacher Education? In D. Kallós & I. Nilsson (Eds.), *Research on Teacher Education in Finland, Germany and Sweden* (pp. 47–65). Monographs on Teacher Education Research Vol 1. Umeå University.

Kelchtermans, G. (1993). Getting the Story, Understanding the Lives: From Career Stories to Teachers' Professional Development. *Teaching & Teacher Education, 9*(5/6), 443–456.

Kelchtermans, G. & Vandenberghe, R. (1994). Teachers' Professional Development: A Biographic Perspective. *Journal of Curriculum Studies*, *26*(1), 45–62.

Kessels, J. P. A. M. & Korthagen, F. A. J. (1996). The Relationship Between Theory and Practice: Back to the Classics. *Educational Researcher*, *25*(3), 17–22.

Kindsvatter, R., Wilen, W. & Ishler, M. (1992). *Dynamics of Effective Teaching*. Second Edition. New York: Longman.

Knecht-von Martial, I. (1986). *Theorie allgemeindidaktischer Modelle*. Bildung und Erziehung, Beiheft 4. Köln: Böhlau.

Kohlberg, L. (1969). Stage and Sequence: The Cognitive-developmental Approach to Socialization. In D. A. Goslin (Ed.), *Handbook of Socialization Theory and Research*. Chicago: Rand McNally.

Kohlberg, L. (1976). Moral Stages and Moralization: The Cognitive-developmental Approach. In T. Lickona (Ed.), *Moral Development and Behavior: Theory, Research and Social Issues*. New York: Holt, Rinehart & Winston.

Kohlberg, L., Wasserman, E. & Richardson, N. (1975). The Just Community School: The Theory and the Cambridge Cluster School Experiment. In Collected Papers on Moral Development and Moral Education, Ch.29. Harvard University, Center for Moral Education.

Kroksmark, T. (1990). *Fenomenografi och lärares didaktik. Konturer till en innehållbeskrivning av lärares undervisningskompetens*. Göteborgs universitet, Institutionen för metodik i lärarutbildningen.

Kuhn, D. (1991). *The Skills of Argument*. New York: Cambridge University Press.

König, E. (1975). *Theorie der Erziehungswissenschaft. Band 1. Wissenschaftstheoretische Richtungen der Pädagogik*. München: Wilhelm Fink.

Lahdes, E. (1986). *Peruskoulun didaktiikka*. (Teaching in the Finnish Comprehensive School). Helsinki: Otava.

Lampert, M. (1984). Teaching About Thinking and Thinking About Teaching. *Journal of Curriculum Studies*, *16*(1), 1–18.

Lampert, M. (1985). How Do Teachers Manage to Teach? Perspectives on Problems in Practice. *Harvard Educational Review, 55*(2), 178–194.

Lampert, M. & Clark, C. (1990). Expert Knowledge and Expert Thinking in Teaching: A Response to Floden and Klinzing. *Educational Researcher, 19*(5), 21–23.

Lather, P. (1996). Situated Pedagogics—Classroom Practices in Postmodern Times. *Theory into Practice, 35*(2), 70–71.

Liston, D. P. & Zeichner, K. M. (1991). *Teacher Education and the Social Conditions of Schooling.* New York: Routledge.

Lortie, D. C. (1975). *Schoolteacher. A Sociological Study.* Chicago, The University of Chicago Press.

Lyons, N. (1990). Dilemmas of Knowing: Ethical and Epistemological Dimensions of Teachers' Work and Development. *Harvard Educational Review, 60*(2), 159–180.

MacIntyre, A. (1985). *After Virtue. A Study in Moral Theory.* Second Edition. London: Duckworth.

Marland, P. & Osborne, B. (1990). Classroom Theory, Thinking, and Action. *Teaching & Teacher Education, 7,* 93–109.

McNamara, D. (1990). Research on Teachers' Thinking: Its Contribution to Educating Student Teachers to Think Critically. *Journal of Education for Teaching, 16*(2), 147–160.

Meri, M. (1992). *Miten piilo-opetussuunnitelma toteutuu.* (The Realization of the Latent Curriculum). Research Report 104. Department of Teacher Education, University of Helsinki.

Meri. M. (1995). Warum auch Rezepte? Einige Leitfäden zur Expertenwissen. In: P. Kansanen (Hrsg.), Diskussionen über einige pädagogische Fragen V (pp 89–100). Research Report 140. Department of Teacher Education, University of Helsinki.

Meri, M. (1998). *Ole oma itsesi. Reseptologinen näkökulma hyvään opetukseen.* (Be Yourself—The Logic of Pedagogical Recipes as a Basis for Good Teaching). Research Report 194. Department of Teacher Education, University of Helsinki.

Meyer, H. (1980, 1991). *Leitfaden zur Unterrichtsvorbereitung*. Frankfurt am Main: Cornelsen Scriptor.

Meyer, H. (1993). Reflexionsebenen unterrichtsmethodischen Handels. Oldenburg: Universität Oldenburg.

Mitchell, D. E. & Spady, W. (1983). Authority, Power and the Legimation of Social Control. *Educational Administration Quarterly, 19*(1), 5–33.

Mitchell, J. (1994). Teachers' Implicit Theories Concerning Questioning. . *British Educational Research Journal, 20*, 69–83.

Mitzschke, M., Rijpkema, J., Wierdsma, T. & Winter, K. (1984). *Rezepte im Schulpraktikum. Rezeptsammlung aus Unterrichtspraktika in den Niederlanden und in der Bundesrepublik Deutschland*. Materialien Universität Oldenburg.

Moss, P. A. (1996). Enlarging the Dialogue in Educational Measurement: Voices from Interpretative Traditions. *Educational Researcher, 25*(1), 20–28, 43.

Nash, R. J. (1996). *"Real World" Ethics. Frameworks for Educators and Human Service Professionals*. New York: Teachers College Press.

Nias, J. (1988). What It Means to "Feel like a Teacher": The Subjective Reality of Primary School Teaching. In J. Ozga (Ed.), *Schoolwork. Approaches to the Labour Process of Teaching* (pp. 195–213). Milton Keynes: Open University Press.

Nias, J. (1989). *Primary Teachers Talking. A Study of Teaching as Work*. London: Routledge.

Nisbett, R. & Ross, L. (1980). *Human Inference: Strategies and Shortcomings of Social Judgment*. Englewood Cliffs, NJ: Prentice-Hall.

Noddings, N. (1992). *The Challenge to Care in Schools*. New York: Teachers College Press.

Nussbaum, M. C. (1986). *The Fragility of Goodness. Luck and Ethics in Greek Tragedy and Philosophy*. New York: Cambridge University Press.

Olson, J. (1988). Making Sense of Teaching: Cognition vs. Culture. *Journal of Curriculum Studies, 20*(2), 167–169.

Olson, J. (1992). *Understanding Teaching. Beyond Expertise.* Milton Keynes: Open University Press.

Olson, M. R. (1995). Conceptualizing Narrative Authority: Implications for Teacher Education. *Teaching & Teacher Education, 11*(2), 119–135.

Oser, F. (1986). Moral Education and Values Education: The Discourse Perspective. In M. C. Wittrock (Ed.), *Handbook of Research on Teaching* (pp. 917–941). New York: Macmillan.

Oser, F. K. (1991). Professional Morality: A Discourse Approach (The Case of the Teaching Profession). In W. M. Kurtines & J. L. Gewirtz (Eds.), *Handbook of Moral Behavior and Development. Volume 2: Research* (pp. 191–228). Hillsdale: Lawrence Erlbaum.

Oser, F. K. (1994a). Moral Perspectives on Teaching. In L. Darling-Hammond (Ed.), *Review of Research in Education, 20* (pp. 57–127). Washington, DC: AERA.

Oser, F. K. (1994b). Morality in Professional Action: A Discourse Approach for Teaching. In F. Oser, A. Dick & J. Patry (Eds.), *Effective and Responsible Teaching: The New Synthesis.* San Francisco: Jossey-Bass.

Oser, F. K. (1996). Kohlberg's Dormant Ghosts: The Case of Education. *Journal of Moral Education, 25*(3), 253–275.

Oser, F. K. & Althof, W. (1993). Trust in Advance: On the Professional Morality of Teachers. *Journal of Moral Education, 22*(3), 253–275.

Packer, M. J. & Winne, P. H. (1995). The Place of Cognition in Explanations of Teaching: A Dialog of Interpretative and Cognitive Approaches. *Teaching & Teacher Education, 11*(1), 1–21.

Pajares, M. F. (1992). Teachers' Beliefs and Educational Research: Cleaning Up a Messy Construct. *Review of Educational Research, 62*(3), 307–332.

Pearson, A. T. (1989). *The Teacher. Theory and Practice in Teacher Education.* New York: Routledge.

Pendlebury, S. (1990). Practical Arguments and Situational Appreciation in Teaching. *Educational Theory, 40*(2), 171–179.

Peterson, P. L. & Clark, C. M. (1978). Teachers' Report of Their Cognitive Processes During Teaching. *American Educational Research Journal, 15*, 555–565.

Pope, M. (1993). Anticipating Teacher Thinking, In: C. Day, J. Calderhead & P. Denicolo (Eds.), *Research on Teacher Thinking. Understanding Professional Development.* Falmer Press: London.

Powell, R. R. (1996). Constructing a Personal Practical Philosophy for Classroom Curriculum: Case Studies of Second-Career Beginning Teachers. *Curriculum Inquiry, 26*(2), 147–173.

Rokeach, M. (1968). *Beliefs, Attitudes and Values.* San Francisco: Jossey-Bass.

Rorty, R. (1979). Philosophy and the Mirror of the Nature. Princeton, NJ: Princeton University Press.

Russell, T. & Munby, T. (1991). Reframing: The Role of Experience in Developing Teachers' Professional Knowledge. In D. Schön (Ed.), *The Reflective Turn: Case Studies In and On Educational Practice* (pp. 164–187). New York: Teachers College Press.

Ryans, D. (1960). *Characteristics of Teachers.* Washington D.C: American Council on Education.

Ryle, G. (1949). *The Concept of Mind.* London: Hutchinson.

Scheffler, I. (1960). *The Language of Education.* Springfield: Charles C. Thomas.

Schutz, A. (1970). *On Phenomenology and Social Relations.* Chigago: University of Chigago Press.

Schön, D. (1983). *The Reflective Practitioner. How Professionals Think in Action.* New York: Basic Books.

Seddon, T. (1994). *Context and Beyond: Reframing the Theory and Practice of Education.* London: The Falmer Press.

Seddon, T. (1995). Defining the Real: Context and Beyond. *Qualitative Studies in Education, 8*(4), 393–405.

Shavelson, R. J. (1973). What is *the* Basic Teaching Skill? *Journal of Teacher Education, 24*, 144–151.

Shulman, L. S. (1986). Those Who Understand: Knowledge Growth in Teaching. *Educational Researcher, 15*(2), 4–14.

Shulman, L. S. (1987). Knowledge and Teaching: Foundations of the New Reform. *Harvard Educational Review, 57*(1), 1–22.

Shulman, L. S. & Carey, N. B. (1984). Psychology and the Limitations of Individual Rationality: Implications for the Study of Reasoning and Civility. *Review of Educational Research, 54*(4), 501–524.

Simon, S., Howe, L., & Kirschenbaum, H. (1972). *Values Clarification*. New York: Hart Publishing Company.

Skinner, B. F. (1954). The Science of Learning and the Art of Teaching. *Harvard Educational Review, 24,* 86–97.

Smith, B. O. (1961). A Concept of Teaching. In B. O. Smith & R. H. Ennis (Eds.), *Language and Concepts in Education* (pp. 86–101). Chicago: Rand McNally.

Smith, B. O. (1987). Definitions of Teaching. In M. J. Dunkin (Ed.), *The International Encyclopedia of Teaching and Teacher Education* (pp. 11–15). Oxford: Pergamon Press.

Sockett, H. (1993). *The Moral Base for Teacher Professionalism*. New York: Teachers College Press.

Statt, D. A. (1990). *The Concise Dictionary of Psychology*. London: Routledge.

Stephens, J. M. (1965). *The Psychology of Classroom Learning*. New York: Holt, Rinehart and Winston.

Strike, K. & Soltis, J. (1985). *The Ethics of Teaching*. New York: Teachers College Press.

Tappan, M. B. & Brown, L. M. (1989). Stories Told and Lessons Learned: Toward a Narrative Approach to Moral Development and Moral Education. *Harvard Educational Review, 59*(2), 182–205.

Thompson, A. G. (1992). Teachers' Beliefs and Conceptions: A Synthesis of the Research. In: D. A. Grows (Ed.), *Handbook of Research on Mathematics Learning and Teaching* (pp. 127–146). New York: Macmillan.

Tiffin, J. & Rajasingham, L. (1995). *In Search of the Virtual Class: Education in an Information Society*. London: Routledge.

Tirri, K. (1996a). Teachers' Professional Morality: How Teacher Education Prepares Teachers to Identify and Solve Moral Dilemmas at School. In H. Niemi & K. Tirri (Eds.), *Effectiveness of Teacher Education. New Challenges and Approaches to Evaluation.* Reports from the Department of Teacher Education A6/1996. Tampere University. (ED425147)

Tirri, K. (1996b). *Themes of Moral Dilemmas Formulated by Preadolescents.* (ED399046)

Tom, A. L. (1984). *Teaching as a Moral Craft.* New York: Longman.

Tom, A. L. (1985). Inquiring into Inquiry-oriented Teacher Education. *Journal of Teacher Education, 36*(5), 35–44.

Toulmin, S. (1958). *The Uses of Argument.* Cambridge: Cambridge University Press.

Törner, G. (1996). *Basic Concepts of Mathematical Contents and Mathematical Worldviews (Mathematical Beliefs) as Didactical Conceptualizations.* Preprint Nr. 340. Gerhard-Mercator-Universität. Duisburg.

Uljens, M. (1992). *What Is Learning a Change of?* Report no 1992:01. Department of Education and Educational Research, University of Göteborg.

Van Manen, M. (1977). Linking Ways of Knowing with Ways of Being Practical. *Curriculum Inquiry, 6,* 205–228.

Van Manen, M. (1990). *Researching Lived Experience. Human Science for an Action Sensitive Pedagogy.* New York: State University of New York Press.

Van Manen, M. (1991a). *The Tact of Teaching: The Meaning of Pedagogical Thoughtfulness.* London: Althouse Press.

Van Manen, M. (1991b). Reflectivity and the Pedagogical Moment: The Normativity of Pedagogical Thinking and Acting. *Journal of Curriculum Studies, 23*(6), 507–536.

Van Manen, M. (1994a). Pedagogy, Virtue, and Narrative Identity in Teaching. *Curriculum Inquiry, 24*(2), 135–170.

Van Manen, M. (1994b). The Pain of Science: Rejoining Fenstermacher's Response. *Curriculum Inquiry, 24*(2), 221–227.

Von Wright, G. H. (1971). *Explanation and Understanding.* London: Routledge and Kegan Paul.

Webb, K. & Blond, J. (1995). Teacher Knowledge: The Relationship Between Caring and Knowing. *Teaching & Teacher Education, 11*(6), 611–625.

Whitehead, J. (1995). Practical, Theoretical, and Epistemological Capacities. *Teaching & Teacher Education, 11*(6), 627–634.

Wittrock, M. C. (1986). Students' Thought Processes. In M. C. Wittrock (Ed.), *Handbook of Research on Teaching* (pp. 297–314). Third Edition. New York: McMillan.

Woods, P. (1996). *Researching the Art of Teaching. Ethnography for Educational Use.* London: Routledge.

Zeichner, K. M. (1983). Alternative Paradigms of Teacher Education. *Journal of Teacher Education, 34*(3), 3–9.

Zeichner, K. M. & Tabachnick, B. R. (1982). The Belief Systems of University Supervisors in an Elementary Student-teaching Program. *Journal of Education for Teaching, 8*(1), 34–54.

Zeichner, K. M. & Liston, D. (1985). Varieties of Discourse in Supervisory Conferences. *Teaching & Teacher Education, 1*(2), 155–174.

Zeuli, J. S. & Buchmann, M. (1988). Implementation of Teacher-Thinking Research as Curriculum Deliberation. *Journal of Curriculum Studies, 20*(2), 141–154.

Znaniecki, F. (1965). *The Social Role of the Man of Knowledge.* New York: Octagon.

Name Index

Abelson, R. 60, 195
Airaksinen, T. 203
Alfs, G. 21, 68, 195
Althof, W. 58, 208
Anderson, L.W. 13, 195, 196, 198
Aristotle 46, 47, 155, 162, 195
Attanucci, J. 55, 201

Bales, R. 129, 195
Barnes, D. 82, 195
Barone, T. 149, 195
Bengtsson, J. 149, 195
Ben-Perez, M. 197
Berlak. A. 38, 195
Berlak. H. 38, 195
Berliner, D.C. 12, 150, 196, 201
Bianchini, J.C. 120, 204
Blond, J. 184, 212
Boostrom, R. 204
Bromme, R. 197
Brown, L.M. 210
Brown, S. 37, 68, 196
Bruffee, K.A. 183, 196
Bruner, J. 38, 45, 82, 183, 196
Buchmann. M. 39, 45, 161, 196, 212
Burbules, N. 176, 196
Burns, R.B. 13, 195

Calderhead, J. 21, 60, 73, 140, 196,
     197, 209
Carey, N.B. 40, 210
Carlgren, I. 43, 197
Carter, K. 22, 48, 53, 82, 182, 197

Clandinin, D.J. 36, 37, 47, 48, 183,
     197, 198
Clark, C.M. 1, 11, 17, 27, 37, 38, 39,
     41, 56, 64, 73, 74, 96, 197,
     198, 206, 209
Clarke, A. 143, 198
Clarke, S. 70, 198
Comenius, A. 148
Connelly, F.M. 36, 37, 43, 48, 183, 197,
     198
Cooper, J.M. 201
Cortazzi, M. 82, 198

Damon, W. 57, 198
Darling-Hammond, L. 200, 201, 208
Day, C. 196, 199, 209
Delamont, S. 148, 198
Denicolo, P. 196, 199, 209
Dewey, J. 45, 97, 182, 185, 198
Dick, A. 199, 208
Doyle, W. 48, 82, 197
Drerup, H. 67, 69, 198
Dunkin, M.J. 210
Dunn, D. 68, 69, 199
Duranti, A. 41, 42, 48, 199, 201
Dybdahl, M. 184, 203

Earlam, C. 196
Eisner, E. 41, 149, 183, 195, 198, 199
Elbaz, F. 37, 39, 48, 72, 161, 165, 167,
     199
Ennis, R.H. 210
Erickson, F. 199

Fenstermacher, G.D. 14, 19, 39, 43, 46, 75, 85, 88, 155, 166, 182, 199, 200
Fisher, G. 48, 200
Fitzgibbons, R.E. 23, 150, 192, 200
Fleming, J.S. 120, 200
Floden, R.E. 74, 161, 196, 200
Frankena, W.K. 27, 200
Freeman, D. 82, 200
Fritzell, C. 44, 200

Gage, N.L 12, 149, 201
Garrison, J. 161, 196, 201
Gautier, D. 130, 201
Geertz. C. 45, 201
Gewirtz, J.L. 208
Giangreco, M.F. 178, 201
Gilligan, C. 55, 201
Goffman, E. 48, 82, 201
Goldman, A.I. 88, 184, 201
Gonzalez, L. 22, 53, 197
Goodlad, J. 39, 51, 199, 201
Goodwin, C. 41, 42, 48, 199, 201
Goslin, D.A. 205
Green, T.E. 61, 201
Greene, M. 45, 181, 182, 201
Greeno, J. 72, 73, 76, 201
Grell, J. 68, 202
Grell, M. 68, 202
Grigutscht, S. 61, 202
Grows, D.A. 210
Guhl, E. 25, 29, 190, 202

Habermas, J. 57, 58, 101, 130, 202
Haggarty, L. 129, 202
Halkes, R. 197
Handal, G. 76, 128, 132, 190, 202
Hansen, D.T. 39, 44, 202, 204
Hargreaves, A. 36, 202
Harrison, A. 45, 69, 202
Hartshorne, J. 56, 202
Hatton, N. 128, 202
Hausmann, G. 149, 203
Heimann, P. 203
Helkama, K. 52, 203
Herbart, J.F. 107, 203
Highet, G. 149, 203

Hollingsworth, S. 184, 203
Houston, W.R. 197
Howe, K. 56, 203
Howe, L. 210
Hoy, W. 61, 203
Hunka, S. 120, 204
Husu, J. 8, 12, 42, 203
Hytönen, J. 63, 118, 203

Iisalo, T. 148, 203
Ishler, M. 203

Jackson, P.W. 8, 37, 39, 41, 52, 87, 186, 197, 203
Jaeger, R.M. 195
James, W. 148, 204
Jank, W. 64, 204
Jonsen, A.R. 46, 204
Jyrhämä, R. 8

Kaiser, H.F. 120, 204
Kallós, D. 204
Kansanen, P. 8, 17, 19, 20, 30, 68, 75, 78, 84, 142, 143, 196, 203, 204
Kelchtermans, G. 82, 84, 158, 204, 205
Kessels, K. 46, 47, 48, 205
Kindsvatter, R. 23, 205
Kirschenbaum, H. 210
Klinzing, H. 74, 200
Knecht-von Martial, I. 29, 205
Kohlberg, L. 55, 57, 205
Komulainen, E. 204
Korthagen, F.A.J. 46, 47, 48, 205
Krokfors, L. 8
Kroksmark, T. 64, 205
Kuhn, D. 7, 150, 151, 152, 153, 162, 166, 167, 170, 171, 172, 174, 205
Kurtines, W.M. 208
König, E. 24, 29, 205

Lahdes, L. 65, 205
Lampert, M. 38, 47, 48, 73, 74, 161, 185, 205, 206
Lather, P. 206

Lauvås, P. 76, 128, 132, 190, 202
Lickona, T. 205
Lindblad, S. 43, 197
Liston, D.P. 76, 128, 129, 130, 131,
    132, 139, 206, 212
Lortie, D.C. 43, 206
Lyons, N. 52, 88, 206

Marland, P. 21, 206
Mattingly 82
May, M. 56, 202
McIntyre, D. 37, 39, 196, 206
McNamara, D. 73, 206
McNeill, S. 203
Meri, M. 8, 104, 105, 113, 114, 117,
    176, 206
Meyer, H. 21, 61, 62, 64, 66, 67, 68,
    69, 103, 119, 175, 176, 204,
    207
Minarik, L. 184, 203
Mitchell, D.E. 176, 207
Mitchell, J. 22, 207
Mitzschke, M. 21, 62, 68, 142, 103,
    104, 207
Moss, P.A. 207
Munby, T. 43, 195, 209

Nash, R.J. 8, 187, 188, 190, 191, 192,
    193, 207
Nias, J. 48, 159, 207
Niemi, H. 211
Nilsson, I. 204
Nisbett, R. 60, 207
Noddings, N. 55, 207
Nussbaum, M.C. 46, 47, 207

Olson, J. 44, 45, 207, 208
Olson, M.R. 183, 208
Osborne, B. 22, 206
Oser, F.K. 19, 20, 39, 51, 52, 53, 54,
    55, 58, 99, 199, 208
Ott, E.H. 25, 29, 190, 202
Ozga, J. 207

Packer, M.J. 42, 89, 208
Pajares, M.F. 60, 208

Patry, J.-L. 199, 208
Pearson, A.T. 14, 28, 208
Pendlebury, S. 155, 156, 208
Peterson, P.L. 1, 11, 14, 28, 64, 198,
    209
Pope, M. 72, 75, 128, 196, 199, 209
Powell, R.R. 48, 209
Price, J.D. 203

Race, P. 196
Rajasingham, L. 42, 210
Rees, R. 61, 203
Richardson, N. 205
Richardson, V. 155, 200
Rijpkema, J. 207
Robin, B. 203
Robson, R. 21, 197
Rokeach, M. 60, 209
Rorty, R. 181, 209
Ross, L. 60, 207
Rud, A.A.Jr. 196
Russell, T. 43, 195, 209
Ryan, K. 201
Ryans, D. 124, 209
Ryle, G. 14, 45, 209

Sanger, M. 46, 200
Scheffler, I. 14, 209
Schutz, A. 182, 209
Schön, D. 24, 28, 76, 128, 209
Seddon, T. 39, 41, 42, 43, 209
Shavelson, R.J. 19, 209
Shulman, L.S. 17, 40, 73, 74, 77, 128,
    210
Simon, S. 56, 210
Sirotnik, K.A. 199, 201
Skinner, B.F. 148, 181, 210
Smith, B.O. 14, 148, 210
Smith, D. 128, 202
Sockett, H. 39, 43, 51, 210
Soder, R. 199, 201
Soltis, J. 51, 210
Spady, W. 176, 207
Statt, D.A. 61, 210
Stephens, J.M. 143, 210
Strike, K. 210

Tabachnick, B.R. 76, 128, 212
Tappan, M.B. 82, 210
Taylor, A. 68, 69, 199
Thompson, A.G. 60, 210
Thorndike, R.L. 181
Tiffin, J. 42, 210
Tirri, K. 8, 55, 57, 211
Tom, A.L. 31, 51, 211
Toulmin, S. 7, 46, 92, 96, 150, 151,
        152, 156, 157, 204, 211
Törner, G. 62, 211

Uljens, M. 15, 30, 204, 211

Vandenberghe, R. 84, 205
van Manen, M. 39, 43, 44, 46, 47, 74,
        75, 76, 128, 130, 211
vom Hofe, R. 62, 203
von Wright, G.H. 26, 212

Wagener, W. 195
Wasserman, E. 205
Webb, K. 184, 212
Whitehead, J. 36, 183, 212
Wierdsma, T. 195, 207
Wilbers, H. 195
Wilen, W. 205
Willis, D.A. 203
Willis, J. 203
Winne, P.H. 42, 89, 208
Winter, K. 207
Wittrock, M.C. 40, 198, 199, 208, 212
Woods, P. 149, 212

Zeichner, K.M. 31, 76, 128, 129, 130,
        131, 132, 139, 140, 142, 206,
        212
Zeuli, J.S. 161, 212
Znaniecki, F. 43, 212